Documents on the Status of Native Americans in the Late Nineteenth Century

Book 2

DOCUMENTS ON THE STATUS OF NATIVE AMERICANS IN THE LATE NINETEENTH CENTURY

Book 2

Compiled and Edited by
Leonard Schlup
and
Mary Ann Blochowiak

With a Foreword by
Troy R. Johnson

The Edwin Mellen Press
Lewiston•Queenston•Lampeter

Library of Congress Cataloging-in-Publication Data

Documents on the status of Native Americans in the late nineteenth century / compiled and edited by Leonard Schlup and Mary Ann Blochowiak ; with a foreword by Troy R. Johnson.
p. cm.
Includes bibliographical references and index.
ISBN-13: 978-0-7734-5089-9
ISBN-10: 0-7734-5089-0
1. Indians of North America--History--19th century--Sources. 2. Indians of North America--Legal status, laws, etc. 3. Indians of North America--Government relations. 4. United States. General Allotment Act (1887) 5. Indian Rights Association--History. 6. United States--History--19th century--Sources. I. Schlup, Leonard C., 1943- II. Blochowiak, Mary Ann.
E77.D63 2008
323.1197--dc22

2008021261

hors série.

A CIP catalog record for this book is available from the British Library.

Front cover: "Chasing Evil Spirits" by Jack Hokeah (1902-1969), one of a group of Oklahoma artists known as the Kiowa Five.
Courtesy Western History Collections, University of Oklahoma Libraries

The Edwin Mellen Press
Box 450
Lewiston, New York
USA 14092-0450

The Edwin Mellen Press
Box 67
Queenston, Ontario
CANADA L0S 1L0

The Edwin Mellen Press, Ltd.
Lampeter, Ceredigion, Wales
UNITED KINGDOM SA48 8LT

Printed in the United States of America

Contents

Book 1

Book 2

Chapter 4

Documents 1890-99

4-1. Thomas J. Morgan to Henry L. Dawes

January 4, 1890

On January 4, 1890, Commissioner of Indian Affairs Thomas J. Morgan wrote a highly defensive and revealing letter regarding his administration of matters related to Native Americans. Even a religious question entered the controversy. Morgan sent this lengthy message to Henry L. Dawes (1816-1903), U.S. senator from Massachusetts from 1875 to 1893. A Republican, Dawes sponsored the Dawes (General Allotment) Act of 1887 and chaired the Senate Committee on Indian Affairs in the Forty-seventh through the Fifty-second Congresses.

. . . I am in receipt of your communication of December 20th, enclosing a statement of reasons against my confirmation as Commissioner of Indian Affairs, filed with your Committee by a correspondent whose name is not transmitted.

I am very happy to comply with your request to make a reply thereto. I have now been in office six months and my administration of the difficult duties assigned to me is a matter of record and open to inspection. I shall be very glad to lay before your Committee any part of the records of the Office that you may desire to have.

So far as I am aware, no complaint has been made against my administration of the Office in relation to any other of the great interests involved in it, except that of education.

The present policy of the Government of educating Indians in government schools, has been in operation many years, has been endorsed by both political parties, and has already accomplished good results.

On the passage of the Dawes bill in 1887, giving to the Indians their land in severalty, it became evident to all thoughtful observers that the work of educating the Indians to prepare them for the duties and privileges of American citizenship, had received new emphasis.

The policy of the present administration is to improve the educational system as rapidly and as fully as possible.

President Harrison in his first annual message to Congress, says:

> The report of the Secretary of the Interior exhibits the transactions of the Government with the Indian tribes. Substantial progress has been made in the education of the children of school age and in the allotment of lands to the adult Indians. It is to be regretted that the policy of breaking up the tribal relation and of dealing with the Indian as an individual did not appear earlier in our legislation. Large reservations, held in common, and the maintenance of the authority of the chiefs and head men, have deprived the individual of every incentive to the exercise of thrift, and the annuity has contributed an affirmative impulse towards a state of confirmed pauperism.
>
> Our treaty stipulations should be observed with fidelity and our legislation should be highly considerate of the best interests of an ignorant and helpless people. The reservations are now generally surrounded by white settlements. We can no longer push the Indian back into the wilderness, and it remains only, by every suitable agency to push him upward into the estate of a self-supporting and responsible citizen. For the adult, the first step is to locate him upon a farm, and for the child, to place him in a school.
>
> School attendance should be promoted by every moral agency, and those failing, should be compelled. The national schools for Indians have been very successful, and should be multiplied, and, as far as possible, should be so organized and conducted as to facilitate the transfer of the schools to the States or Territories in which they are located, when the Indians in a neighborhood have accepted citizenship, and have become otherwise fitted for such a transfer. This condition of things will be attained slowly, but it will be hastened by keeping it in mind. And in the meantime, that cooperation between the Government and the mission schools, which has wrought so much good, should be cordially and impartially maintained.

The views of the Honorable the Secretary of the Interior are shown by these extracts from his first annual report:

> Among his first official acts the present Secretary framed a letter of advice addressed to each Indian Agent, to be transmitted with his

commission. This was by direction of the President. Each Agent was informed that the office to which he was appointed was to be deemed of great interest to the Government and to the Indians who would be brought under his charge and direction; that sobriety and integrity must mark the conduct of every one concerned or associated directly or indirectly with the Agency; that an improved condition in its affairs would be expected within a reasonable time, both as to the method of doing business and as to the condition of the Indian children and the agricultural and other industrial pursuits of the adult Indians must receive the Agent's constant and careful attention, to the end that they might be advanced in the ways of civilization and made independent through self-support; and that the commission transmitted could be held only upon the express understanding that the Agent receiving it would use his utmost efforts to further these objects and purposes. . . .

Beside this general treatment, individual education of the Indians in the schools has received from the beginning of the administration, and will continue to receive, increased attention. The subject has been much discussed both in preceding reports and in Congress; but it will never be exhausted until the Indian has become self-supporting. . . .

But it would be unjust to previous Secretaries and many able legislators to claim that all of the work is yet to be done. A great deal has already been accomplished, the results of which have been most beneficial, and by the broader and more systematic application of these results alone, it is deemed that the problem of making the Indian self-supporting may be solved. . . .

Through many trials and long experiences, as well as through the exercise of signal ability by the superintendents and their assistants, these schools have reached a high development, and strike with astonishment any one who have never beheld them, and thus had demonstrated to him both the Indian's adaptability to school life and industrial training, and the wisdom of the Government in its organization and support of these excellent institutions. . . . This school system, with its attendant practices, is worthy of adoption and expansion until it may be made to embrace all Indian youth. It is a model produced by the Government's own generosity and by the ability of those selected by it for superintendents and teachers. It is not something newly discovered or to be advocated as a recent invention. It has been in full operation for years. In the department of letters it gives a good common school education. In the department of labor it inculcates both a love for labor and a habit of working. It may be easily systematized so as to have its form adopted in schools of different grades, and so that its pupils may be gradually, when fitted and entitled, transferred to the white common schools.

> It therefore seems but a step to extend this system so as to have it embrace and affect, with the cooperation of the church mission schools, the whole youth of the Indian tribes. This cooperation has long existed; the missions have placed much reliance upon it, and its sudden withdrawal would be neither generous nor fair. The national system may grow very rapidly and yet others be most welcome as co-workers in the benevolent cause; but the national system should have precedence, and in case of conflict, it should be preserved and advanced.

In my annual report to the Honorable Secretary of the Interior (pages 3, 11 and 93 to 114) a copy of which accompanies this, I have outlined a plan of non-sectarian, non-partisan government Indian schools, designed to put into practical operation the policy of the Government.

I submit also, a copy of a letter of transmittal to the Honorable Secretary of the Interior, of my supplemental report on education, in which I have more fully explained the spirit and method of the Indian Office.

We did not find all the schools in a satisfactory condition, and for six months have been earnestly engaged in making such changes as seemed necessary to improve the service.

How much some reform was needed may be seen from statements made in the pamphlet marked "A", laid before you. As these statements are supposed to have been written by the late chief of the Educational Division of the Indian Bureau, they may be regarded perhaps, as semi-official, although I think the picture is overdrawn.

According to this testimony (see pages 3 and 4, pamphlet "A"), the government schools with few exceptions, were not only failures, but many of them had a disgraceful and scandalous history.

According to the same authority (see page 18, "Exhibit A,"):

> He (the Commissioner) knows that in the government schools the superintendents and teachers, and the other employes, are not always either learned or good people, but that they are sometimes bad in every sense of the word. He knows that good and efficient employes are obtained for the Indian school service only by accident. He knows that he can apply no test of merit to the men and women he appoints to the school service upon the recommendation of politicians and other persons who believe that anybody is good enough for that ser-

> vice. And he knows, too, that this deplorable condition will continue to exist in this service until, in the pat language of the Civil Service reformers, it has been taken out of politics.

It is not surprising that we have found it necessary to made a good many changes and that others will be necessary before the difficult work of reform is completed.

The most important change was the dismissal of the chief of the Education Division, who had little power of organization and apparently little appreciation of the real work of his office. I felt that very little could by done to improve the service while the details of administration were left to him. The greatly improved condition of the government Indian school service, especially in the organization of the Education Division, is due to that change.

Soon after his removal, he published (it is believed) in an opposition newspaper, a sensational article entitled "MAKE ROME HOWL", which is reprinted in pamphlet "B". Both these pamphlets were presumably prepared by him. A committee of Bishops appointed at the Catholic Congress in Baltimore, accepting these ex parte statements as true, laid them before the President, and they are now laid before you by (I suppose) the director of the Bureau of Catholic Indian Missions.

The great burden of the charge is, that I removed from government schools, eleven Catholic employes.

Regarding this I wish to say that,

(1) During the six months of my administration I have removed a very much larger number of Protestants than Catholics, so far, at least, as I have any knowledge of the religious beliefs of those who have been removed.

(2) That almost all of these Catholics were removed on the recommendation of the Superintendent of Indian Schools, after a personal visit. My responsibility in the matter consisted almost wholly in approving the recommendations of the Superintendent of Indian Schools, who is specifically charged by law with the duty of recommending changes to me, and who made these recommendations on his personal knowledge, after visiting the schools. My knowledge was almost wholly confined to that derived from his written reports. While I do not wish to shirk any responsi-

bility in this matter, my reply to these accusations against me would be sufficient if I simply said that I acted upon his recommendations. I will add, however, that his recommendations seemed to me to fully warrant my action.

(3) I submit, however, a statement prepared three months ago for the Honorable Secretary of the Interior, explaining the removals.

(4) I ask attention also to the report of the Superintendent on Indian Schools, to be presented to you, in which he explains in detail the removals complained of.

(5) I respectfully submit that my motives for my action in the premises can be known only to myself. I wish to put myself on record here with the utmost possible clearness, definiteness, and emphasis, in declaring that from the first day of July, when I took charge of the Indian Office, to the present time, while I have been compelled to make many changes, in order to rescue the Indian school service from the condition which my accuser pronounces "deplorable and scandalous", and to place it on the same high plane of efficiency and respectability on which the public schools of the country generally rest, I have been actuated but by one single motive, and this is to render these government Indian schools the best possible agencies for the preparation of the Indians wards of the Nation for American citizenship. I have removed no one because he was a Catholic or because he was a Democrat, but have sought honestly, fearlessly and intelligently to administer the trust confided to me in such manner as to command the respect of every intelligent, unprejudiced American citizen. In most instances I did not know at the time of the removal, the religious belief of the person removed.

But it is said I am "conducting the Office of Indian Affairs in a sectarian manner, in prejudice to the Catholic Church." The word "sectarian" conveys, unfortunately, different meanings to different minds, so that it is necessary to attempt some definition of the word before I can intelligently plead to the charge. The "Church News," a Catholic newspaper, in its issue of Sunday, October 20th, in an article entitled "A BIGOTED POLICY," makes this statement:

> If Commissioner Morgan is sincere in his desire to make the Indian schools non-sectarian, he will have one of two things to do—turn them over to the Catholics who are not sectarians, or put in control

> idiots who are without sufficient intelligence to have any religious convictions. No one, however, believes for a moment that he knows what a sectarian school is.

Accepting this definition of sectarianism, I presume I ought humbly to confess myself guilty of "conducting the Office of Indian Affairs in a sectarian manner," since I have neither turned the schools over to the Catholics, nor put them in the control of idiots. I had innocently supposed that schools might be conducted by intelligent men outside of the Roman Catholic Church and still be non-sectarian. I trust, however, that I may be excused on the charitable ground suggested by the writer of the above,—that I do not know what a sectarian school is.

Before leaving this part of the subject, I desire to ask the attention of your honorable Committee to these two facts:

First. Although I have been Commissioner of Indian Affairs for more than six months, and have had most important relations with the Bureau of Catholic Indian Missions, located in this city, I have never been honored with a call from Father Stephan, the head of the Bureau. I have never met him, nor, so far as I know, have I even seen him. He has never sought from me any explanation of my action, has never made to me any complaints against my policy, and almost the only knowledge which I have of him is derived from the reports of his earnest attempts to defeat my confirmation.

Second. I received from my wife's cousin, a well known Catholic writer whose friendship we greatly enjoy, a letter of introduction to His Eminence [James] Cardinal Gibbons, which I transmitted to him by post. I submit herewith the correspondence between myself and the highest dignitary of the Catholic Church in America. Your Committee will observe that I called his attention to the fact that the newspaper criticisms on me were "false and slanderous," and respectfully informed him that if the Bishops would lay before me any complaints against my official actions, I would make them an explanatory reply. To this letter I received no response.

I do not see how I could have gone further than I did go to secure harmony and agreement with my Catholic brethren without a loss of self respect.

My reputation for veracity is probably sufficiently established to warrant me in declining to vindicate it from suspicions based upon discrepancies in reported newspaper interviews.

If there is any point in those specifications or in any other part of the charges that seem to your Committee to call for explanation, I shall be very glad to give it. Everything admits of easy explanation if you care to have it.

As to military record, I join heartily in the request of your correspondent, that you will "make inquiry concerning my military record," if you deem it important.

I hand you herewith a copy of the record of the proceedings of the court martial that I have obtained from the War Department. The evidence adduced against me is the best evidence of my integrity.

My record as a soldier for forty months in the service of my country is very dear to me, and I shall be glad to facilitate your Committee in any inquiry you should desire to make.

I served under General Benjamin Harrison, and on the staff of Major General O. O. Howard, and they, with scores of other officers, with whom I served, can give you valuable information.

With a clear consciousness of my own integrity, I submit my case to your honorable body with the full assurance that I shall receive from you that treatment which is due to a public officer who is honestly endeavoring to the best of his ability to discharge his difficult duties with "malice toward none, with charity for all, and with love for the right as God gives him to see the right."

Source: Thomas J. Morgan to Henry L. Dawes, January 4, 1890, Benjamin Harrison Papers, Manuscripts Division, Library of Congress, Washington, D.C.

4-2. Preston B. Plumb to Herbert Welsh

January 26, 1890

In an 1890 letter to Herbert Welsh, corresponding secretary of the Indian Rights Association, U.S. Senator Preston B. Plumb of Kansas addressed the matter of Thomas J. Morgan's fitness to serve as commissioner of Indian affairs and the larger question of Native American education, pointing out the differences he and Welsh maintained on this subject.

. . . I have yours of the 31st. ult. covering various documents relating to Mr. Morgan, Commissioner of Indian Affairs. Mr. Morgan's army record does not, in my judgment, in any proper way relate to the question of his confirmation as Commissioner of Indian Affairs. He may have done improper things while in the military service of the United States and have repented of them in such a way as to make it improper that they should be brought up against him. On this subject I am satisfied to take the judgment of the President, who appointed him, and who having been an excellent soldier himself would not have appointed any one whom he believed had a stained military record. As yet I have not given any serious consideration as to what my action would be concerning the confirmation of Mr. Morgan. I can say to you very frankly, however, that I do not regard him as a man wholly fit for the place. No doubt he is honest; in fact honesty is not so rare a quality that it calls for special commendation, but I believe that he is lacking in a knowledge of the Indian and his needs, and that his proposed plan of educating the Indian is calculated to destroy rather than build up. Any scheme or plan which proceeds upon the assumption that the Indian is as well calculated to receive what is now known as high school education as the white man, is bound to do much more harm than good if applied. There has been too much of this already, and as I understand Mr. Morgan, he proposes to still further aggravate it. I do not consider the Indian under my special charge. There are enough people looking after him who take an interest in him because he is a long way off, and because they find in him a subject on whom they can practice their peculiar notions without any personal risk. Philanthropy at long range has, also, very obvious advantages over that at close range. I have heretofore been quite willing that these people should take charge of the Indian, at the same time I have not been unobservant of the fact that that charge was very helpful to him, provided always it was expected that he would ever become a self supporting member of the community. I will not say that every Indian educated according to the present plan has been educated to his hurt, but I do personally know that large number of them have been so educated. I know of one agency at which two Indian employes who were educated at Carlisle are living in polygamous relations and at which agency every educated Indian, as well as every one who has been married, has taken to himself a wife after the blanket fashion, paying no attention to the marriage sacrament as understood among white people. It is also the testimony of the agent and every employe at that agency, as well as of the army officers at the adjoining military Post, that the Indians who have been educated and returned to the reservation have done less manual labor and have sunk lower socially and otherwise, than the Indians who had not been to school. In other words it seems to me that we have taken away the stay of barbarism and put nothing in its place. I do not speak of this to complain of it. My protest was uttered in the beginning, since which time I have been consenting practically to every thing proposed by those who have taken charge of this important subject. I am not now protesting against the continuation of this system. Some things have got to be demonstrated by experience, rather than by argument, and this matter of Indian education is one of them. I do not therefore know that I shall feel called upon to oppose the confirmation of Mr. Morgan, although at the present moment I do not think of any person of whom I have any thing like personal knowledge, who in my judgment is more unfit for the position of Indian Commissioner than he. I recall the fact that I was in favor of the removal of Mr. [John H.] Oberly, with a somewhat rueful face. He was a good man, but I believed that a better man from among the Republicans could be found. I know the President conscientiously desired to get a better man and very probably he thinks he did, but I think he is very greatly mistaken.

I am both willing and anxious that every Indian child of proper age shall be educated according to the full extent of his merit and needs, and at the public expense. I think he ought to be educated for the practical things of life. I believe that under the present plan he is not being so educated, and I believe, and in fact I think I know, that a very large majority of those who are sent back to the reservation from Indian schools, go back to become bad, and not good examples, and to do evil and not good for themselves. The difference between you and me about this matter is a fundamental one. You are undoubtedly sincere. Are you willing to concede as much to one who differs with you? . . .

Source: Preston B. Plumb to Herbert Welsh, January 26, 1890, Benjamin Harrison Papers, Manuscripts Division, Library of Congress, Washington, D.C.

4-3. Sermon to Ghost Dancers

Short Bull

October 31, 1890

A Brule Lakota (Sioux), Short Bull (ca. 1845-1924), also known as Tatanka Petcela, was a Ghost Dancer, shaman, and Kicking Bear's brother-in-law. He participated in the 1876 Battle of Little Bighorn, met Wovoka in 1890, and later that year led Ghost Dancers from the Rosebud Reservation to the Pine Ridge Reservation, where on October 31, he delivered a powerful sermon. Short Bull eventually joined the Congregational Church as well as William F. Cody's Wild West Show.

My friends and relations: I will soon start this thing in running order. I have told you that this would come to pass in two seasons, but since the whites are interfering so much, I will advance the time from what my father above told me to do, so the time will be shorter. Therefore you must not be afraid of anything. Some of my relations have no ears, so I will have them blown away.

Now, there will be a tree sprout up, and there all the members of our religion and the tribe must gather together. That will be the place where we will see our dead relations. But before this time we must dance the balance of this moon, at the end of which time the earth will shiver very hard. Whenever this thing occurs, I will start the wind to blow. We are the ones who will then see our fathers, mothers, and everybody. We, the tribe of Indians, are the ones who are living a sacred life. God, our father himself, has told and commanded and shown me to do these things.

Our father in heaven has placed a mark at each point of the four winds. First, a clay pipe, which lies at the setting of the sun and represents the Sioux tribe. Second, there is a holy arrow lying at the north, which represents the Cheyenne tribe.

Third, at the rising of the sun there lies hail, representing the Arapaho tribe. Fourth, there lies a pipe and nice feather at the south, which represents the Crow tribe. My father has shown me these things, therefore we must continue this dance. If the soldiers surround you four deep, three of you, on whom I have put holy shirts, will sing a song, which I have taught you, around them, when some of them will drop dead. Then the rest will start to run, but their horses will sink into the earth. The riders will jump from their horses, but they will sink into the earth also. Then you can do as you desire with them. Now, you must know this, that all the soldiers and that race will be dead. There will be only five thousand of them left living on the earth. My friends and relations, this is straight and true.

Source: Short Bull, Sermon, October 31, 1890, Red Leaf Camp, Pine Ridge Reservation, in Thomas E. Sanders and Walter W. Peek, eds., *Literature of the American Indian* (Beverly Hills, Calif.: Glencoe Press, 1973), 343.

4-4. The Messiah Letter

1890

Wovoka (ca 1858-1932), also known as Jack Wilson, was a Paiute mystic considered a messiah by his followers. He delivered a number of prophecies that foretold that the white race would vanish, leaving the red man with an abundance of buffalo, a return to the old ways of life, and eternal salvation. His Messiah Letter came at the time of the Ghost Dance and provided much food for thought.

When you get home you must make a dance to continue five days. Dance four successive nights, and the last night keep up the dance until the morning of the fifth day, when all must bathe in the river and then disperse to their homes. You must all do in the same way.

I, Jack Wilson, love you all, and my heart is full of gladness for the gifts you have brought me. When you get home I shall give you a good cloud which will make you feel good. I give you a good spirit and give you all good paint. I want you to come again in three months, some from each tribe there.

There will be a good deal of snow this year and some rain. In the fall there will be such a rain as I have never given you before.

Grandfather (the messiah) says, when your friends die you must not cry. You must not hurt anybody or do harm to anyone. You must not fight. Do right always. It will give you satisfaction in life. This young man has a good father and mother.

Do not tell the white people about this. Jesus is now upon the earth. He appears like a cloud. The dead are all alive again. I do not know when they will be here; maybe this fall or in the spring. When the time comes there will be no more sickness and everyone will be young again.

Do not refuse to work for the whites and do not make any trouble with them until you leave them. When the earth shakes do not be afraid. It will not hurt you.

I want you to dance every six weeks. Make a feast at the dance and have food that everybody may eat. Then bathe in the water. That is all. You will receive good words again from me some time. Do not tell lies.

Source: The Messiah Letter, in Thomas E. Sanders and Walter W. Peek, eds., *Literature of the American Indian* (Beverly Hills, Calif.: Glencoe Press, 1973), 337.

4-5. Letter to Editor of *Chicago Tribune*

A Sioux Indian

1890

A Sioux Indian submitted a concise but highly perceptive and thought-provoking letter to the editor of the Chicago Tribune *during the Ghost Dance period in 1890 in response to an unsympathetic editorial. These sincere and revealing statements should have generated more attention at the time.*

You say, "If the United States army would kill a thousand or so of the dancing Indians there would be no trouble." I judge by [your] language you are a "Christian" and are disposed to do all in your power to advance the cause of Christ. You are doubtless a worshiper of the white man's Saviour, but are unwilling that the Indians should have a "Messiah" of their own.

The Indians have never taken kindly to the Christian religion as preached and practiced by the whites. Do you know why this is the case? Because the Good Father of all has given us a better religion—a religion that is all good and no bad, a religion that is adapted to our wants. You say if we are good, obey the Ten Commandments and never sin any more, we may be permitted eventually to sit upon a white rock and sing praises to God forevermore, and look down upon our heathen fathers, mothers, brothers and sisters who are howling in hell.

It won't do. The code of morals as practiced by the white race will not compare with the morals of the Indians. We pay no lawyers or preachers, but we have not one-tenth part of the crime that you do. If our Messiah does come we shall not try to force you into our belief. We will never burn innocent women at the stake or pull men to pieces with horses because they refuse to join in our ghost dances. You white people had a Messiah, and if history is to be believed nearly every nation has had one. You had twelve Apostles; we have only eleven, and some of those are already in the military guard-house. We also had a Virgin Mary and she is in the guard-house. You are anxious to get hold of our Messiah, so you can put him in irons. This you may do—in fact, you may crucify him as you did that other one, but you cannot convert the Indians to the Christian religion until you contaminate them with the blood of the white man. The white man's heaven is repulsive to the Indian nature, and if the white man's hell suits you, why, you keep it. I think there will be white rogues enough to fill it.

Source: A Sioux Indian to Editor, *Chicago Tribune*, 1890, in Thomas E. Sanders and Walter W. Peek, eds., *Literature of the American Indian* (Beverly Hills, Calif.: Glencoe Press, 1973), 357-58.

4-6. The Butchering at Wounded Knee

Black Elk

1890

A Lakota holy man, (Nicholas) Black Elk (1863-1950) was born a member of the Oglala tribe in present-day Wyoming. Converted to Roman Catholicism, he performed for Buffalo Bill's Wild West Show during the late 1880s. In the early part of the twentieth century, he served as a Christian missionary, visiting Lakota communities. Throughout his long life Black Elk witnessed many events, tragedies, successes, reconciliations, and transformations for Native Americans. Nobody better served as a bridge between Native Americans of the Gilded Age and those of modern America than Black Elk. In 1932 John Neihardt, a Nebraska poet, compiled and published an autobiographical story of the famous Native American whose influence was enormous. In Black Elk Speaks, *Black Elk recounted the horrors at Wounded Knee in 1890, among other memories.*

That evening before it happened, I went in to Pine Ridge and heard these things, and while I was there, soldiers started for where the Big Foots were. These made about five hundred soldiers that were there next morning. When I saw them starting I felt that something terrible was going to happen. That night I could hardly sleep at all. I walked around most of the night.

In the morning I went out after my horses, and while I was out I heard shooting off toward the east, and I knew from the sound that it must be wagon-guns (cannon) going off. The sounds went right through my body, and I felt that something terrible would happen.

When I reached camp with the horses, a man rode up to me and said: "Hey-hey-hey! The people that are coming are fired on! I know it!"

I saddled up my buckskin and put on my sacred shirt. It was one I had made to be worn by no one but myself. It had a spotted eagle outstretched on the back of it, and the daybreak star was on the left shoulder, because when facing south that shoulder is toward the east. Across the breast, from the left shoulder to the right hip, was the flaming rainbow, and there was another rainbow around the neck, like a necklace, with a star at the bottom. At each shoulder, elbow, and wrist was an eagle feather; and over the whole shirt were red streaks of lightning. You will see that this was from my great vision, and you will know how it protected me that day.

I painted my face all red, and in my hair I put one eagle feather for the One Above. It did not take me long to get ready, for I could still hear the shooting over there.

I started out alone on the old road that ran across the hills to Wounded Knee. I had no gun. I carried only the sacred bow of the west that I had seen in my great vision. I had gone only a little way when a band of young men came galloping after me. The first two who came up were Loves War and Iron Wasichu. I asked what they were going to do, and they said they were just going to see where the shooting was. Then others were coming up, and some older men.

We rode fast, and there were about twenty of us now. The shooting was getting louder. A horseback from over there came galloping very fast toward us, and he said: "Hey-hey-hey! They have murdered them!" Then he whipped his horse and rode away faster toward Pine Ridge.

In a little while we had come to the top of the ridge where, looking to the east, you can see for the first time the monument and the burying ground on the little hill where the church is. That is where the terrible thing started. Just south of the burying ground on the little hill a deep dry gulch runs about east and west, very crooked, and it rises westward to nearly the top of the ridge where we were. It had no name, but the Wasichus sometimes call it Battle Creek now. We stopped on the ridge not far from the head of the dry gulch. Wagon guns were still going off over there on the little hill, and they were going off again where they hit along the gulch. There was much shooting down yonder, and there were many cries, and we could see cavalrymen scattered over the hills ahead of us. Cavalrymen were riding along the gulch and shooting into it, where the women and children were running away and trying to hide in the gullies and the stunted pines.

A little way ahead of us, just below the head of the dry gulch, there were some women and children who were huddled under a clay bank, and some cavalrymen were there pointing guns at them.

We stopped back behind the ridge, and I said to the others: "Take courage. These are our relatives. We will try to get them back." Then we all sang a song which went like this:

A thunder being nation I am, I have said.
A thunder being nation I am, I have said.
You shall live.

You shall live.
You shall live.
You shall live.

Then I rode over the ridge and the others after me, and we were crying: "Take courage! It is time to fight!" The soldiers who were guarding our relatives shot at us and then ran away fast, and some more cavalrymen on the other side of the gulch did too. We got our relatives and sent them across the ridge to the northwest where they would be safe.

I had no gun, and when we were charging, I just held the sacred bow out in front of me with my right hand. The bullets did not hit us at all.

We found a little baby lying all alone near the head of the gulch. I could not pick her up just then, but I got her later and some of my people adopted her. I just wrapped her up tighter in a shawl that was around her and left her there. It was a safe place, and I had other work to do.

The soldiers had run eastward over the hills where there were some more soldiers, and they were off their horses and lying down. I told the others to stay back, and I charged upon them holding the sacred bow out toward them with my right hand. They all shot at me, and I could hear bullets all around me, but I ran my horse right close to them, and then swung around. Some soldiers across the gulch began shooting at me too, but I got back to the others and was not hurt at all.

By now many other Lakotas, who had heard the shooting, were coming up from Pine Ridge, and we all charged on the soldiers. They ran eastward toward where the trouble began. We followed down along the dry gulch, and what we saw was terrible. Dead and wounded women and children and little babies were scattered all along there where they had been trying to run away. The soldiers had followed along the gulch, as they ran, and murdered them in there. Sometimes they were in heaps because they had huddled together, and some were scattered all along. Sometimes bunches of them had been killed and torn to pieces where the wagon guns hit them. I saw a little baby trying to suck its mother, but she was bloody and dead.

There were two little boys at one place in this gulch. They had guns and they had been killing soldiers all by themselves. We could see the soldiers they had killed.

The boys were all alone there, and they were not hurt. These were very brave little boys.

When we drove the soldiers back, they dug themselves in, and we were not enough people to drive them out from there. In the evening they marched off up Wounded Knee Creek, and then we saw all that they had done there.

Men and women and children were heaped and scattered all over the flat at the bottom of the little hill where the soldiers had their wagon-guns, and westward up the dry gulch all the way to the high ridge, the dead women and children and babies were scattered.

When I saw this I wished that I had died too, but I was not sorry for the women and children. It was better for them to be happy in the other world, and I wanted to be there too. But before I went there I wanted to have revenge. I thought there might be a day, and we should have revenge. After the soldiers marched away, I heard from my friend, Dog Chief, how the trouble started, and he was right there by Yellow Bird when it happened. This is the way it was:

In the morning the soldiers began to take all the guns away from the Big Foots, who were camped in the flat below the little hill where the monument and burying ground are now. The people had stacked most of their guns, and even their knives, by the tepee where Big Foot was lying sick. Soldiers were on the little hill and all around, and there were soldiers across the dry gulch to the south and over east along Wounded Knee Creek too. The people were nearly surrounded, and the wagon-guns were pointing at them.

Some had not yet given up their guns, and so the soldiers were searching all the tepees, throwing things around and poking into everything. There was a man called Yellow Bird, and he and another man were standing in front of the tepee where Big Foot was lying sick. They had white sheets around and over them, with eyeholes to look through, and they had guns under these. An officer came to search them. He took the other man's gun, and then started to take Yellow Bird's. But Yellow Bird would not let go. He wrestled with the officer, and while they were wrestling, the gun went off and killed the officer. Wasichus and some others have said he meant to do this, but Dog Chief was standing right there, and he told me it was not so. As soon as the gun went off, Dog Chief told me, an officer shot and killed Big Foot who was lying sick inside the tepee.

Then suddenly nobody knew what was happening, except that the soldiers were all shooting and the wagon-guns began going off right in among the people.

Many were shot down right there. The women and children ran into the gulch and up west, dropping all the time, for the soldiers shot them as they ran. There were only about a hundred warriors and there were nearly five hundred soldiers. The warriors rushed to where they had piled their guns and knives. They fought soldiers with only their hands until they got their guns.

Dog Chief saw Yellow Bird run into a tepee with his gun, and from there he killed soldiers until the tepee caught fire. Then he died full of bullets.

It was a good winter day when all this happened. The sun was shining. But after the soldiers marched away from their dirty work, a heavy snow began to fall. The wind came up in the night. There was a big blizzard, and it grew very cold. The snow drifted deep in the crooked gulch, and it was one long grave of butchered women and children and babies, who had never done any harm and were only trying to run away.

Source: Black Elk, "The Butchering at Wounded Knee," in *Black Elk Speaks: Being the Life Story of a Holy Man of the Oglala Sioux* (New York: William Morrow Company, 1932), 255-62.

4-7. Dissemination of Tales among the Natives of North America

Franz Boas

January 1891

A native of Germany who earned a doctorate in physics from the University of Kiel in 1881, Franz Boas (1858-1942), professor of anthropology at Columbia University for forty years, was an editor, educator, social activist, scholarly writer, and cultural relativist. Rejecting racial theories of intelligence, Boas pioneered in modern folklore research and earned the sobriquet "father of modern anthropology." His essay,

"The Decorative Art of the Indians of the North Pacific Coast," published in Bulletin of the American Museum of Natural History *(1897), became a classic work in the field. Reprinted below is the article by Boas entitled "Dissemination of Tales Among the Natives of North America," published in the fourth volume of* Journal of American Folk-lore.

The study of the folk-lore of the Old World has proved the fact that dissemination of tales was almost unlimited. They were carried from east to west, and from south to north, from books to the folk, and from the folk to books. Since this fact has become understood, the explanation of tales does not seem so simple and easy a matter as it formerly appeared to be.

We will apply this experience to the folk-lore and mythologies of the New World, and we shall find that certain well-defined features are common to the folk-lore of many tribes. This will lead us to the conclusion that diffusion of tales was just as frequent and just as widespread in America as it has been in the Old World.

But in attempting a study of the diffusion of tales in America we are deprived of the valuable literary means which are at our disposal in carrying on similar researches on the folk-lore of the Old World. With few exceptions, only the present folk-lore of each tribe is known to us. We are not acquainted with its growth and development. Therefore the only method open to us is that of comparison. This method, however, is beset with many difficulties. There exist certain features of tales and myths that are well-nigh universal. The ideas underlying them seem to suggest themselves easily to the mind of primitive man, and it is considered probable that they originated independently in regions widely apart. To exemplify: The tale of the man swallowed by the fish, or by some other animal, which has been treated by Dr. E. B. Tylor ("Early History of Mankind," p. 345; "Primitive Culture," vol I, p. 328), is so simple that we may doubt whether it is due to dissemination. The German child tells of Tom Thumb swallowed by the cow; the Ojibway, of Nanabozhoo swallowed by the fish; the negro of the Bahamas, according to Dr. Edwards, of the rabbit swallowed by the cow; the Hindoo, of the prince swallowed by the whale; the Bible, of the prophet Jonah; the Micronesian, of two men inclosed in a bamboo and sent adrift." Are these stories of independent origin, or have they been derived from one source? This vexed question will embarrass us in all our studies on the folk-lore of primitive people.

Then, we may ask, is there no criterion which we may use for deciding the question whether a tale is of independent origin, or whether its occurrence at a certain place is due to diffusion? I believe we may safely assume that, wherever a story which consists of the same combination of several elements is found in two regions, we must conclude that its occurrence in both is due to diffusion. The more complex the story is, which the countries under consideration have in common, the more this conclusion will be justified. I will give an example which will make this clearer. [Emile] Petitot ("Traditions Indiennes du Canada Nord-ouest," p. 311) tells a story of the Dog-Rib Indians of Great Slave Lake: A woman was married to a dog and bore six pups. She was deserted by her tribe, and went out daily procuring food for her family. When she returned she found tracks of children around her lodge, but did not see anyone besides her pups. Finally she discovered from a hiding-place that the dogs threw off their skins as soon as she left them. She surprised them, took away the skins, and the dogs became children,—a number of boys and one girl. These became the ancestors of the Dog-Rib Indians. We may analyze this story as follows: 1. A woman mated with a dog. 2. Bears pups. 3. Deserted by her tribe. 4. Sees tracks of children. 5. Surprises them. 6. Takes their skins. 7. They become a number of boys and one girl. 8. They become the ancestors of a tribe of Indians. These eight elements have been combined into a story in the same way on Vancouver Island, where a tribe of Indians derives its origin from dogs. The single "elements" of this tale occur in other combinations in other tales. The elements may have arisen independently in various places, but the sameness of their combination proves most conclusively that the whole combination, that is, the story, has been carried from Arctic America to Vancouver Island, or *vice versa*.

It is, however, necessary to apply this method judiciously, and the logical connection of what I have called "elements" must be taken into account. A single element may consist of a number of incidents which are very closely connected and still form one idea. There is, for instance, an Aino tale of a rascal who, on account of his numerous misdeeds, was put into a mat to be thrown into a river. He induced the carriers to go to look for a treasure which he claimed to possess, and meanwhile induced an old blind man to take his place by promising him that his eyes would be opened. Then the old man was thrown into the river. and the rascal took possession of his property. We find this identical tale in Anderson's fairy tales, and are also reminded of Sir John Falstaff. While it is quite probable that these tales have a common root, still they are so consistent in themselves that the same idea might have arisen independently on several occasions. In cases like this we have to look for corroborating evidence.

This may be found either in an increase of the number of analogous tales, or in their geographical distribution. Whenever we find a tale spread over a continuous area, we must assume that it spread over this territory from a single centre. If, besides this, we should know that it does not occur outside the limits of this territory, our conclusion will be considerably strengthened. This argument will be justified even should our tale be a very simple one. Should it be complex, both our first and second methods may be applied, and our conclusion will be the more firmly established.

I will give an example of this kind. Around the Great Lakes we find a deluge legend: A number of animals escaped in a canoe or on a raft, and several of them dived to the bottom of the water in order to bring up the land. The first attempts were in vain, but finally the muskrat succeeded in bringing up a little mud, which was expanded by magic and formed the earth. Petitot recorded several versions of this tale from the Mackenzie Basin. It is known to the various branches of the Ojibway and to the Ottawa. Mr. [James Owen] Dorsey recorded it among tribes of the Siouan stock, and kindly sent me an Iowa myth, related by the Rev. W. Hamilton, which belongs to the same group. On the Atlantic coast the legend has been recorded by [David] Zeisberger, who obtained it from the Delawares, and Mr. Mooney heard it told by the Cherokees in a slightly varied form.

They say that in the beginning all animals were up above, and that there was nothing below but a wide expanse of water. Finally, a small water-beetle and the water-spider came down from above, and, diving to the bottom of the water, brought up some mud, from which the earth was made. The buzzard flew down while the land was still soft, and by the flapping of its wings made the mountains. The Iroquois have a closely related myth, according to which a woman fell down from heaven into the boundless waters. A turtle arose from the flood, and she rested on her back until an animal brought up some mud, from which the earth was formed. I have not found any version of this legend from New England or the Atlantic Provinces of Canada, although the incident of the turtle forming the earth occurs. We do not find any trace of this legend in the South, but on turning to the Pacific coast we find it recorded in three different places. The Yocut in California say that at a time when the earth was covered with water there existed a hawk, a crow, and a duck. The latter, after diving to the bottom and bringing up a beakful of mud, died. Whereupon the crow and the hawk took each one half of the mud, and set to work to make the mountains. This tale resembles in some respects the Cherokee tale. Farther north I found the tale of the muskrat bringing up the mud among the Molalla, the Chinook, and the Bilqula, while all around these places it is unknown. As, besides, these are the places where intercourse with the interior takes place, we must conclude that the tale has been carried to the coast from the interior. Thus we obtain the result that the tale of the bringing up of the earth from the bottom of the water is told all over an enormous area, embracing the Mackenzie Basin, the watershed of the Great Lakes, the Middle and South Atlantic coasts, and a few isolated spots on the Pacific coast which it reached overflowing over the mountain passes.

We will now once more take up the legend of the woman and her pups. I mentioned that two almost identical versions are known to exist, one from Great Slave Lake, the other from Vancouver's Island. The legend is found in many other places. On the Pacific coast it extends from southern Oregon to southern Alaska, but in the north and south slight variations are found. Petitot recorded a somewhat similar tale among the Hare Indians of Great Bear Lake, so that we find it to occupy a continuous area from the Mackenzie to the Pacific coast, with the exception of the interior of Alaska. Among the Eskimo of Greenland and of Hudson Bay we find a legend which closely resembles the one we are considering here. A woman married a dog and had ten pups. She was deserted by her father, who killed the dog. Five of her children she sent inland, where they became the ancestors of a tribe who are half dog, half man. The other five she sent across the ocean, where they became the ancestors of the Europeans. The Greenland version varies slightly from the one given here, but is identical with it in all its main features. Fragments of the same story have been recorded by Mr. James Murdoch at Point Barrow. We may analyze this tale as follows: 1. A woman married a dog. 2. She had pups. 3. Was deserted by her father. 4. The pups became ancestors of a tribe. Here we have four of the elements of our first story combined in the same way and forming a new story. Besides this, the geographical distribution of the two tales is such that they are told in a continuous area. From these two facts we conclude that they must have been derived from the same source. The legend of the half-human beings with dog legs forms an important element in Eskimo lore, and according to Petitot is also found among the Loucheux and Hare Indians. This increases the sweep of our story to that part of North America lying northwest of a line drawn from southern Oregon to Cape Farewell, the southernmost point of Greenland. It is worth remarking that in Baffinland the mother of the dogs is at the same time, the most important deity of the Eskimo. These arguments hardly need being strengthened.

We may find, however, additional reasons for our opinion in the fact that there are other stories common to Greenland and Oregon. One of the most remarkable among these is the story of the man who recovered his eyesight. The tale runs about as follows: A boy lost his eyesight, and ever since that time his mother let him starve. His sister, who loved him dearly, fed him whenever she was able to do so. One day a bear attacked their hut, and the mother gave the boy his bow and arrow, levelled it, and the boy shot the bear. His flesh served the mother and sister for food all through the winter, while she had told the boy that he had missed the bear and that it had made its escape. In spring a wild goose flew over the hut and asked the boy to follow it. The bird took the boy to a pond, dived with him several times, and thus restored his eyesight. The boy then took revenge on his mother. I recorded this story once on the shores of Baffin Bay, once in Rivers Inlet in British Columbia.. Rink tells the same story from Greenland. Here we have an excellent example of a very complex story in two widely separated regions. We cannot doubt for a moment that it is actually the same story which is told by the Eskimo and by the Indian. Besides this story there are quite a number of others which are common to the Eskimo and to tribes of the North Pacific coast.

From these facts we conclude that diffusion of tales between the Eskimo and the Indian tribes of the western half of our continent has been quite extensive. On the other hand, notwithstanding many assertions to the contrary, there are hardly any close relations between the tales of the Algonquin and the Eskimo. In [Charles G.] Leland's collection of New England tales, for instance, I found only one or possibly two elements that belong to Eskimo lore,—the capture of a bathing girl by taking away her clothing, and the killing of birds; which were enticed to come into a lodge. Both of these appear, however, in combinations which differ entirely from those in which they occur in the Eskimo tales.

There are, however, very close relations between the tales of the Algonquin and those of the Pacific coast. I will select one of the most striking examples. Leland, in his collection of Algonquin legends (p. 145), tells of two sisters who slept in a forest, and, on seeing stars, wished them to become their husbands. On the following morning they found themselves in heaven, one the wife of a man with beautiful eyes, the other the wife of a man with red twinkling eyes,—both the stars whom they had desired for their husbands. Then they peeped down through a hole in the ground and perceived the earth, to which they eventually returned. This abstract may stand for another story which I collected at Victoria, B. C. There are quite a number of other Algonquin tales which are found also on the Pacific coast. I select some more examples from Leland's book because the distance between the tribes he studied and those of the Pacific coast is the greatest. He tells of the rabbit which tried to rival in a variety of ways a number of animals. The same tales are told of Hiawatha and Nanabozhoo; in Alaska they are told of the raven. In a Passamaquoddy legend it is stated (Leland, op. cit., p. 38) that a witch asked a man to free her from vermin which consisted of toads and porcupines. When she asked the man to crush the poisonous vermin he deceived hcr by crushing cranberries, which he had brought along instead. I collected the same tale in a number of places on the North Pacific coast.

This series of complex stories from the extreme east and the extreme west of our continent leaves no doubt that each originated at one point.

The end of the story of the women who were married to stars differs somewhat in New England and on the Pacific coast. In the East the stars permit the women to return, while in the West they find the possibility of return by digging roots contrary to the commands of their husbands. In doing so they make a hole through the sky and see the earth. They then make a rope, which they fasten to their spades and let themselves down.

We find the same incident in a story which Mr. A. S. Gatschet collected among the Kiowa. In the creation legend of this tribe, it is told that a woman was taken up to the sky. The analysis of the two legends reveals the following series of identical incidents: 1. A woman taken up to the sky. 2. Is forbidden to dig certain roots. 3. She disobeys her husband, and discovers a hole through which she can see the world. 4. She secretly makes a rope and lets herself down. In this case we may apply our first principle, and conclude that the tale in this form must have sprung from one centre. This conclusion is strengthened by the fact that the rest of the Kiowa legend coincides with another tale from the Northwest coast, which is also a creation legend. The Kiowa tale continues telling how the son of the sun fed upon his mother's body. Then an old woman captured him by making arrows and a ball (which is used as a target) for him and inducing him to steal them. I have recorded this tale among the Tsimshian at the northern boundary of British Columbia.

The comparisons which we have made show that each group of legends has its peculiar province, and covers a certain portion of our continent. We found a number of tales common to the North Pacific and the Arctic coasts. Another series we found common to the territory between the North Atlantic and Middle Pacific coasts.

The Kiowa tale and the Northwestern tale indicate a third group which seems to extend along the Rocky Mountains. I will not lay too much stress upon the last fact, as the province of these tales needs to be better defined. It appears however, clearly, that tales, and connected with it, we may add, other cultural elements, have spread from one centre over the Arctic and North Pacific coasts, while there is hardly anything in common to the Eskimo and Algonquin. These facts strengthen our view that the Eskimo, before descending to the Arctic coast, inhabited the Mackenzie Basin, and were driven northward by the Athapaskans. We must also assume that a certain cultural centre corresponds to our second province of legends.

We will finally compare some American myths with such of the Old World, but we shall confine ourselves to those to which our first principle may be applied. I have found a series of complicated tales which are common to both. One of the most remarkable is the story of the cannibal witch who pursued children. [M. A.] Castrèn ("Ethnologische Vorlesungen," p. 165) has recorded the following Samoyede fairy tale: Two sisters escaped a cannibal witch who pursued them. One of the girls threw a whetstone over her shoulder. It was transformed into a cañon, and stopped the pursuit of the witch. Eventually the latter crossed it, and when she almost reached the sisters, the elder threw a flint over her shoulder, which was transformed into a mountain and stopped her. Finally the girl threw a comb behind her, which was transformed into a thicket. On the North Pacific coast we find the identical story, the child throwing three objects over its shoulders,—a whetstone which became a mountain, a bottle of oil which became a lake, and a comb which became a thicket.

Among a series of Aino tales published by Basil Hall Chamberlain I find four or five ("Folk-Lore Journal," 1888, p. 1 ff. Nos. 6, 21, 27, 33, 36) which have very close analoga on the North Pacific coast.

Another very curious coincidence is found between a myth from the Pelew Islands and several from the North Pacific coast. J. Kubary (in "A. Bastian, Allerlei aus Volks-und Menschenkunde," I. p. 59 ff.) tells the following: A young man had lost his fish-hook, the line having been broken by a fish. He dived after him, and, on reaching the bottom of the sea, reached a pond, at which he sat down. A girl came out of a house to fetch some water for a sick woman. He was called in and cured her, while all her friends did not know what ailed her. In British Columbia we find the same story, an arrow being substituted for the hook, a land animal for the fish. There are a number of other remarkable coincidences in this tale with American tales from the Pacific coast. It is said, for instance, that a man owned a wonderful ramp, consisting of two mother-of-pearl shells, which they kept hidden, and which was finally taken away by a boy, exactly as the sun was stolen by the raven in Alaska.

It is true that comparisons ought to be restricted to two well-defined groups of people; coincidences among the tales of one people and a great variety of others have little value. Still, diffusion has taken place all along the east and north sides of Asia. Setting aside the similarity of the Northwest American tales with those from Micronesia, I believe the facts justify the conclusion that transmission of tales between Asia and America has actually taken place, and, what is more remarkable, that the main points of coincidence are not found around Behring Strait, but farther south; so that it would appear that diffusion of tales, if it took place along the coast line, was previous to the arrival of the Eskimo in Alaska. I admit, however, that these conclusions are largely conjectural, and need corroboration from collections from eastern Asia and from Alaska, which, however, unfortunately do not exist.

I hope these brief notes will show that our method promises good results in the study of the history of folk-lore.

It is particularly important to emphasize the fact that our comparison proves many creation myths to be of complex growth, in so far as their elements occur variously combined in various regions. This makes it probable that many elements have been embodied ready-made in the myths, and that they have never had any meaning, at least not among the tribes in whose possession we find them. Therefore they cannot be explained as symbolizing or anthropomorphizing natural phenomena; neither can we assume that the etymologies of the names of the heroes or deities give a clue to their actual meaning, because there never was such a meaning. We understand that for an explanation of myths we need, first of all, a careful study of their component parts, and of their mode of dissemination, which must be followed by a study of the psychology of dissemination and amalgamation. Only after these have been done we shall be able to attack the problem of an explanation of myths with the hope of success.

Source: Franz Boas, "Dissemination of Tales among the Natives of North America," *Journal of American Folk-lore* 4 (January 1891):13-20.

➳ ● ➳

4-8. Thomas J. Morgan to John W. Noble

January 5, 1891

Shortly after the Wounded Knee tragedy, Commissioner of Indian Affairs Thomas J. Morgan updated Secretary of the Interior John W. Noble, a Missouri Republican, on various matters relative to Native Americans. Morgan hoped for patience and understanding, contending that it was better to save lives than destroy them.

. . . I have the honor to submit the following statement regarding the matter of supplies for the Sioux Indians of Dakota.

In order that the purpose of my communication may be very specific, let me say that the statement has been repeated in the public press that the Sioux are slowly starving to death and that the present unhappy troubles among them are due to the cutting down of their rations and to the blunders of the Indian Office.

In order to meet these criticisms in such a way that the public may have an intelligent appreciation of the matters involved it will be necessary for me to make an extended reply.

I will make as brief a statement of the main points involved as is possible, consistent with clearness, and will subjoin to my statement a fuller discussion of the points involved.

It will be seen at once that the criticism is an arraignment, first, of the entire policy of the Government in dealing with the Indians. What this policy is I have set forth in an appendix marked "A."

In the next place, the criticisms are a reflection upon the persons engaged and who are directly responsible for the present administration of Indian affairs. Who these persons are and the relations they sustain severally to this matter, I have discussed in a paper marked "B."

The specific question presents itself for answer, "Are the Indians starving, and if so, who is to blame for it?"

In answering this question it seems to be pertinent to set forth somewhat in detail the reasons for furnishing subsistence to the Sioux, and the amount actually furnished.

In 1877, the United States entered into an agreement with the Sioux Nation (Articles 4 and 5 of which are herewith in appendix marked C), promising to furnish them certain subsistence and other supplies. This agreement is still in force and the questions now raised are questions as to how far the Government has kept its obligations.

It is worthy of special note that the end aimed at, in the agreement, was the civilization of the Indians. They were to settle down permanently; their children were to be educated; they were to live like white men; and the rations issued to them or so much as might be necessary, were to be continued until "the Indians are able to support themselves." It is clearly evident that the Government never intended that the Indians should look to it for continuous support; that no promises of this kind were ever made; and that the Indians themselves did not expect it and apparently did not desire it. The object of the rations was not that the Indians might be fed by the Government, but simply that they might be assisted and kept from want during the period of their probation while they were learning the art of self support.

No one will question the wisdom of this policy. No intelligent man will doubt that the welfare of the Indian demands that just as soon as possible he shall be rendered self-supporting, and that any help in the way of food or other supplies furnished him by the Government, in excess of his absolute needs, so as to remove from him the spur and stimulus to labor, is not a kindness but an injury.

The only serious question which can be raised in this connection is, how long a time are these rations to be continued, and under what circumstances the Government shall reduce or discontinue them.

It should be noted that the agreement expressly stipulates that

> whenever the said Indians shall be located upon lands which are suitable for cultivation, rations shall be issued only to the persons and families of those persons who labor (the aged, sick and infirm excepted); and as an incentive to industrious habits the Commissioner of Indian Affairs may provide that such persons be furnished in payment for their labor, such other necessary articles as are requisite for civilized life.

It certainly will be accepted as a truism that the Government had a right to demand of the Indians that they put forth for self support, whatever efforts might reasonably be demanded of them considering their nature and surroundings. It will also be admitted that, considering the end in view, it would be a humane act on the part of the Government to decrease the rations even though such decrease should bring temporary hardship, provided such hardship should serve as a stimulus to labor and self help. Of course no one would urge that the Indians should be starved. In fact all that can be demanded, either in fulfilment of treaty obligation, or as an act of justice or humanity, is this, that the Indians shall put forth all proper exertion in the way of gaining a livelihood by their own labor, as other men are forced to do, and that in connection with such effort on their part food supplies shall be issued to them in such quantities (not exceeding the amounts named in the agreement), and for such length of time as a sincere regard for the highest welfare of the Indians shall dictate.

It will be observed that this agreement went into effect nearly 14 years ago. Since that time, almost without exception, the full amount of rations named in the agreement have been issued to the Indians, and the sums expended therefor each year are shown in appendix D. The exceptions have been caused by delayed or reduced appropriations by Congress. These rations the Indians have supplemented to a small extent, by their own earnings in freighting, and by the raising of small and uncertain crops, and as the Indians have sometimes been over-counted, they have sometimes received over-issues of rations.

In 1889, however, Congress reduced appropriations for the subsistence and civilization of the Sioux to the lowest point reached since the agreement of 1877, viz: to $900,000, $100,000 less than the amount estimated and appropriated for the two preceding years. This caused a reduction of 2,600,000 pounds in the amount of beef purchased for the Sioux for the fiscal year ending June 30, 1890. Up to that time I find no complaint of short rations to the Sioux, except that sometimes the full weight of cattle delivered in the fall was considerably reduced before the time came to issue them to the Indians. In the fall of 1889, the Sioux Commission, with considerable difficulty, and many promises, negotiated with the Sioux for a cession of their land to which the majority assented, but to which a large and influential minority were bitterly opposed. It was immediately after these negotiations that the reduced appropriations above referred to necessitated a reduced beef ration. At the same time the drought and the neglect of their gardens, caused by their prolonged absences from home to council with the Commission, made an entire failure of the crops which otherwise might have supplemented the Government rations.

To this matter the Sioux Commission called special attention in their report dated December 24, 1889, as follows:

> During our conference at the different agencies we were repeatedly asked whether the acceptance or rejection of the act of Congress would influence the action of the Government with reference to their rations, and in every instance the Indians were assured that subsistence was furnished in accordance withe former treaties, and that signing would not affect their rations, and that they would continue to receive them as provided in former treaties. Without our assurances to this effect it would have been impossible to have secured their consent to the cession of their lands. Since our visit to the agencies it appears that large reductions have been made in the amounts of beef furnished for issues, amounting at Rosebud to 2,000,000 pounds, and at Pine Ridge to 1,000,000 pounds, and lesser amounts at the other agencies. This action of the Department, following immediately after the successful issue of our negotiations cannot fail to have an injurious effect. It will be impossible to convince the Indians that the reduction is not due to the fact that the Government, having obtained their lands, has less concern in looking after their material interests than before. It will be looked upon as a breach of faith, and especially as a violation of the express statements of the Commissioners.
>
> Already this action is being used by the Indians opposed to the bill, notably at Pine Ridge, as an argument in support of the wisdom of their opposition.

In forwarding this report to Congress, the Department called special attention to the above-quoted statements of the Commission, and said:

> The Commission further remarks that as to the quality of rations furnished there seems to be no just cause for complaint, but that it was particularly to be avoided that there should be any diminution of the rations promised under the former treaties *at this time*, as the Indians would attribute it to their assent to the bill. Such diminution certainly should not be allowed, as the Government is bound in good faith to carry into effect the former treaties where not directly and positively affected by the act, and if under the provisions of the treaty itself the ration is at any time reduced, the Commissioners recommend that the Indian should be notified before spring opens, so that crops may be cultivated. It is desirable that the recent reduction made should be restored, as it is now impossible to convince the Indians that it was not due to the fact that the Government, having obtained their lands, had less concern in looking after their material interests.

Notwithstanding this plea of the Commission and of the Department, the appropriations made for the subsistence and civilization of the Sioux during the current fiscal year was only $950,000, or $50,000 less than the amount estimated and appropriated for 1888 and 1889, and the appropriation, not having been made until August 19th last, rations to be supplied had to be temporarily purchased and issued in limited quantities pending arrival of new supplies to be secured from this appropriation.

In this connection, I ask attention to appendix “E” containing an extract from the report of the Pine Ridge Agent, dated August 26, 1890.

It should here be stated that in the draught of a bill prepared by the Department and submitted to the President, January 30, 1890, to accompany the report of the Sioux Commission, and intended to carry out in part the provisions of the Sioux Act of March 2, 1889, was a clause appropriating the sum of $100,000 for additional beef to supply the deficiency in the subsistence supplies for the year ending June 30, 1890, and in fulfilment of pledges made to the Indians by the Commission.

A bill containing said item of appropriation passed the Senate April 26, 1890; the House Committee on Indian Affairs reported it favorably, with the statement that the provision was in pursuance of provisions made by the Commissioners to the

Indians, outside of the agreement entered into, but in good faith, and that they were reasonable and should be faithfully kept. The bill did not become a law, and the appropriation was not made.

I will also state, parenthetically, that while some of the other items included in that draught of a bill for carrying out the provisions of the Sioux Agreement, were covered by provisions in other legislation, yet Congress not only failed to give the $100,000 to restore the beef rations, but also failed to redeem other pledges made by the Commission and the agreement, among them the following:

The support of schools, for which $150,000 was asked;

The payment of $200,000 in compensation for ponies taken from the Sioux in 1876 and 1877;

The reimbursement of the Crow Creek Indians for a reduction made in their per capita allowance of land below that allowed the other Sioux, which would require $187,000, and

The purchase of lands for the Santee Sioux which would require $32,000.

The unwisdom, the expensive economy, and from the Indian standpoint breach of faith in the cutting down of rations, as above set forth, being admitted, it now remains to be seen to just what extent rations were reduced below the amounts stipulated in the agreement of 1877, how much was actually provided for the Indians, and how near the limit of supplies would bring them to the point of starvation.

For the fiscal year ending June 30, 1890, there were purchased for the Sioux 18,131,611 pounds of beef (gross) and 2,899,583 pounds of flour. Shrinkage in the beef purchased in the fall and held during the winter would probably reduce the amount about 2,800,000 pounds. These 18,131,611 pounds of beef and 2,879,583 pounds of flour divided among 22,324 Sioux, the number given in the report of this office for 1889, would allow for each man, woman and child, about 1 9/10 pounds of beef, gross, and 36/100 of a pound of flour per day, (not counting some additional supplies of bacon, coffee, sugar, corn and beans), while the ration stipulated in the agreement was to be 3 pounds of beef, gross, and one-half pound of flour per day, plus coffee, sugar, corn and beans.

For the current fiscal year as shown in the report of this office, dated December 4, 1890, (House Ex. Doc. No. 52, of the present session of Congress), the beef purchased and contracted for the Sioux amounts to 17,683,282 pounds. Add to this 522,847 pounds of bacon purchased and 261,519 pounds of bacon on hand (counting one pound of bacon as equivalent to 6 pounds of gross beef), and subtract about 2,000,000 pounds for shrinkage of cattle delivered in the fall, and held during the winter, and we have a total of 20,389,478 pounds of beef. The flour purchased and contracted for amounts to 2,792,200 pounds. This divided among 20,058 Indians enumerated in the census of 1890, gives to each man, woman and child 75/100 pounds of beef and 38/100 of a pound of flour per day, to which may be added small quantities of the additional supplies names above.

With these rations Indians may be improvident enough to become hungry, but they cannot be considered as reduced to starvation.

With reference to the purchase and distribution of beef for the Sioux and northern Indians, it is due to the present Commissioner of Indian Affairs to say that unusual precautions have been exercised by him during the current fiscal year to secure cattle that would stand the rigors of a northern winter. To accomplish this it was required that none be received except those that had been kept at least twelve consecutive months north of the southern boundary of the State of Kansas,—a restriction more severe than was formerly imposed. In addition to this, bids were asked for cattle "double Montana wintered," and pains were taken to secure that class where practicable, and still further, an increased price was paid to have cattle delivered at such times as would be most to the advantage of the Indians, and in addition to all this, by the special direction of the Secretary of the Interior, preparations were in progress and being pushed as fast and as far as the means at the control of the Bureau would warrant for the establishment of sub-issue stations in order that the beef might be delivered to the Indians at points nearer their homes, so that they might be spared the loss of time heretofore required in going long distances to and from the agencies in order to secure their supplies.

A somewhat detailed statement of the methods used by the Government which insure the delivery to the Indians of the supplies purchased for them will be found herewith in appendix "F."

After the late cession of land by the Sioux, Congress authorized the appointment of a Special Agent who should be charged with the duty of taking an accurate census of these people with a view of determining both as to their numbers, their present condition and the outlook for their future self-support. Mr. A. T. Lea was appointed to perform this service. There seems to have been more or less of opposition to the work on the part of the Indians. When he had completed his task at the Rosebud Agency he reported that the number of Indians whom he had enrolled was 5,245 as compared with the number 7,586 reported by the Agent to whom rations were being issued. The attention of the Agent was called to this discrepancy whereupon he took a special census which differed from that of Agent Lea by about 100. Having no reason to doubt the substantial accuracy of this census, orders were given by the Department for the reduction of rations to correspond with the actual number of Indians at the Rosebud Agency. This seems to have created dissatisfaction, but unless the census as taken by the Special Agent and corroborated by the regular agent is inaccurate, there is not only no reason for dissatisfaction on the part of the Indians, but there is grave reason for dissatisfaction on the part of the Government that they have been drawing rations for about 2,100 people more than they actually possessed.

From the above statement it will be seen that so far as the furnishing of subsistence to the Sioux is concerned the Government has strictly fulfilled its obligations to them, as set forth in the agreement of 1877; that where there has been a reduction of the amount of rations it has been made by Congress in the exercise of that discretion which was clearly reserved to them by the terms of the agreement; that this reduction, whether wise or unwise, was not brought about by the Interior Department but rather against its expressed wishes; that the reduction was not brought down to a starving point and that if there has been suffering among the Indians for want of food, it has been due partially to drought and other causes for which the Government is not in any wise responsible.

In this connection attention is specially invited to the fact that the discontent at the Pine Ridge Agency began in midsummer when as yet there were no complaints and no likelihood of actual suffering for food. See extract from report of Agent [H.D.] Gallagher in the appendix, marked E.

Having answered the question so far as information in my possession enables me to do so, as to whether the Sioux Indians are starving, and if so, who is responsible for it, let me say a word as to the proposed remedy for this supposed state of things.

Admitting, which is not admitted, that they are starving or that they are suffering for want of food, would there be any gain to them by placing the military in charge rather than leaving them under the control of the Department of the Interior?

Whoever is responsible for the distribution of supplies can distribute only such as are provided for by act of Congress. A civil agent can do this as well as a military officer. In the absence of any and all proof whatever to the contrary, it is a very serious and cruel assumption that men chosen from the walks of civil life; recommended by responsible men; appointed to their places by the Chief Executive and confirmed by the Senate; supervised in their work by honest inspectors, are necessarily incapable or dishonest, and that the only remedy for this is to displace them en masse and substitute for them army officers. The question seems to me hardly to admit of argument. First, let it be shown in any particular case that any given Agent is dishonest or incapable, give him an opportunity to vindicate his honor, reputation and standing as a man before he is summarily displaced from his position of trust and responsibility.

The system of accounting for disbursement and distribution of supplies in the Indian Department is probably as exact and searching and difficult as in any other branch of the Government. All papers after having been examined in the Indian Bureau are transmitted to the Treasury Department for final settlement, and must pass the rigid scrutiny which that Department bestows upon all such documents.

In conclusion let me say a word in regard to the cause or causes of the present unhappy state of the Indians. Of course, owing to the fact that the Indians made no declaration of war, and that there is great difficulty in getting at their state of mind by reason of the differences of language and the almost insurmountable difficulty of procuring accurate interpretation of their statements, it is impossible to give any more than a conjectural statement as to the true causes of their present attitude toward the Government. I think, however, from what information I have been able to gather, that the following brief resumé may be taken as an approximate statement of the causes:

(1) The wide-spread feeling of unrest and apprehension in the minds of the Indian tribes, originally growing out of the rapid advance of civilization and the great change which this advance has necessitated in their habits and mode of life.

(2) The very large reduction of the great Sioux reservation brought about by the Sioux Commission through the consent of the large majority of the adult males, as already stated, was bitterly opposed by a large, influential minority. For various reason they regarded the cession as unwise, and did all in their power to prevent its consummation, and since that time have been constant in their expressions of dissatisfaction, and in their endeavors to awaken a like feeling in the minds of those who signed the agreement.

(3) The failure to fulfill speedily all the promises made to them by the Sioux Commission, especially the restoration of the rations diminished by act of Congress, as a condition of securing the signatures of the majority, discouraged those who signed and gave some reason to the taunts and reproaches heaped upon them by the non-progressive party.

(4) The wording of the agreement which changed the boundary line between the Rosebud and Pine Ridge diminished reservations, necessitated a removal of a portion of the Rosebud Indians from lands which by the agreement were included in the Pine Ridge reservation to lands offered them in lieu thereof upon the diminished Rosebud reserve. This, although involving no great hardship to any considerable number, added to the discontent.

(5) The diminution and partial failure of the crops for 1889, by reason of their neglect by the Indians who were congregated in large numbers at the council with the Sioux Commission, and the further diminution of their ordinary crops by the drought of 1890.

(6) It seems also that some of the Indians were greatly opposed to the census which Congress ordered should be taken. The census at Rosebud, as reported by Special Agent Lea, and confirmed by a special census taken by Agent [James G.] Wright, revealed the somewhat startling fact that rations had been issued to Indians very largely in excess of the numbers actually present, and this diminution of numbers as shown by the census necessitated a diminution of the rations which was based of course upon the census.

These, so far as I can gather, are the primary causes of the original manifestation of a turbulent spirit.

(7) The fright occasioned by the sudden appearance of the military among them, and other influences connected with and inseparable from military movements, have had their influence to increase largely the numbers of the hostiles and to intensify their spirit of opposition to the Government.

(8) It is also undoubtedly true that the so called "Messiah craze," now so familiar to every body, by which many Indians were led to expect the speedy destruction of the white race, the return of the buffalo and the restoration of the old conditions had its influence in leading many of them to assume an attitude of hostility to the Government.

In conclusion let me express the wish that the Indians now in seeming rebellion may be dealt with patiently and that they be brought back if possible to submission to the Government without further shedding of blood. It is better to save life than to destroy it. . . .

Source: Thomas J. Morgan to John W. Noble, January 5, 1891, Benjamin Harrison Papers, Manuscripts Division, Library of Congress, Washington, D.C.

➳ • ➳

4-9. Account of the Death of Sitting Bull and Attending Circumstances

James McLaughlin

January 19, 1891

Born a Roman Catholic in Canada, James McLaughlin (1842-1923) entered the U.S. Indian Service of the Interior Department on July 1, 1871, and thereafter held various appointments in North Dakota and South Dakota. He procured authentic accounts of the Battle of the Little Bighorn (1876) from Sioux participants, suppressed the Ghost Dance movement on the Standing Rock Reservation (1890), concluded more than forty agreements between the United States government and Native Americans, developed friendships and acquaintances with Chief Joseph and numerous others, and in 1895 secured an appointment as U.S. Indian inspector. In 1910 he wrote My Friend the Indian. *From his headquarters at the Standing Rock Agency in North Dakota, McLaughlin dispatched a lengthy letter to Herbert Welsh, at the office of the Indian Rights Association, on January 12, 1891, explaining in detail recent happenings and the circumstances surrounding Sitting Bull's death.*

. . . The newspaper reports regarding the arrest and death of Sitting Bull have nearly all been ridiculously absurd, and the following is a statement of the facts:—

I was advised by a telegram from the Indian Office, dated Nov. 14th, 1890, that the President had directed the Secretary of War to assume a military responsibility for the suppression of any threatened outbreak among the Sioux Indians, and on December 1st, 1890, another telegram instructed me that as to all operations intended to suppress any outbreak by force, to "co-operate with and obey the orders of the military officers commanding on the reservation." This order made me subject to the military authorities, and to whom I regularly reported the nature of the "Messiah Craze" and the temper of the Indians of the reservation.

As stated in my letter to you, dated November 25th last, the Messiah doctrine had taken a firm hold upon Sitting Bull and his followers, and that faction strove in every way to engraft it in the other settlements; but by close watching and activity of the police we prevented it from getting a start in any of the settlements outside of the upper Grand River, which districts were largely composed of Sitting Bull's old followers, over whom he always exerted a baneful influence, and in this craze they fell easy victims to his subtlety, and believed blindly in the absurdities he preached of the Indian millennium. He promised them the return of their dead ancestors and restoration of their old Indian life, together with the removal of the white race; that the white man's gunpowder could not throw a bullet with sufficient force in future to injure true believers; and even if Indians should be killed while obeying this call of the Messiah, they would only be the sooner united with their dead relatives, who were now all upon the earth (having returned from the clouds), as the living and dead would be reunited in the flesh next spring. You will readily understand what a dangerous doctrine this was to get hold of a superstitious and semi-civilized people, and how the more cunning "medicine men" could impose upon the credulity of the average uncivilized Indian.

This was the status of the Messiah craze here on November 16th, when I made a trip to Sitting Bull's camp, which is forty miles south-west of Agency, to try and get Sitting Bull to see the evils that a continuation of the Ghost dance would lead to, and the misery that it would bring to his people. I remained over night in the settlement and visited him early next morning before they commenced the dance, and had a long and apparently satisfactory talk with him, and made some impression upon a number of his followers who were listeners, but I failed in getting him to come into the Agency, where I hoped to convince him by long argument. Through chiefs Gall, Flying-By and Gray Eagle, I succeeded in getting a few to quit the dance, but the more we got to leave it the more aggressive Sitting Bull became so that the peaceable and well-disposed Indians were obliged to leave the settlement and could not pass through it without being subjected to insult and threats. The "Ghost Dancers" had given up industrial pursuits and abandoned their houses, and all moved into camp in the immediate neighborhood of Sitting Bull's house, where they consumed their whole time in the dance and the purification vapor baths preparing for same, except on every second Saturday, when they came to the Agency for their bi-weekly rations.

Sitting Bull did not come into the Agency for rations after October 25th, but sent members of his family, and kept a bodyguard when he remained behind while the greater portion of his people were away from the camp; this he did to guard against surprise in case an attempt to arrest him was made. He frequently boasted to Indians, who reported the same to me, that he was not afraid to die and wanted to fight, but I considered that mere idle talk and always believed that when the time for his arrest came and the police appeared in force in his camp, with men at their head whom he knew to be determined, that he would quietly accept the arrest and accompany them to the Agency, but the result of the arrest proved the contrary. Since the Sioux Commission of 1889 (the Foster, Crook and Warner Commission) Sitting Bull has behaved very badly, growing more aggressive steadily, and the Messiah doctrine, which united so many Indians in common cause, was just what he needed to assert himself as "high priest," and thus regain prestige and former popularity among the Sioux by posing as the leader of disaffection.

He being in open rebellion against constituted authority, was defying the Government, and encouraging disaffection, made it necessary that he be arrested and removed from the reservation, and arrangements were perfected for his arrest on December 6th, and everything seemed favorable for its accomplishment without trouble or bloodshed at that time; but the question arose as to whether I had authority to make the arrest or not, being subject to the military, to settle which I telegraphed to the Commissioner of Indian Affairs on December 4th, and on the 5th received a reply which directed me to make no arrests whatever, except under orders of the military, or upon an order from the Secretary of the Interior. My reason for desiring to make the arrest on December 6th, was that it could be done then with the greater assurance of success and without alarming the Indians to any great extent, as the major portion of them would have been in for rations at the Agency, forty miles distant from where the arrest would have been made, and I also foresaw, from the movements of the military, that the order for his arrest would soon be issued, and that another ration day (two weeks more) would have to elapse before it could be so easily accomplished.

On December 12th the following telegram was received by the Post Commander of Fort Yates, who furnished me with a copy:—

> The Division commander has directed that you make it your especial duty to secure the person of Sitting Bull. Call on Indian Agent to co-operate and render such assistance as will best promote the purpose in view. . . .

Upon receipt of the foregoing telegram the Post Commander sent for me, and held a consultation as to the best means to effect the desired arrest. It was contrary to my judgment to attempt the arrest at any time other than upon one of the bi-weekly ration days when there would be but a few Indians in Sitting Bull's neighborhood, thus lessening the chances of opposition or excitement of his followers. The Post Commander saw the wisdom of my reasoning, and consented to defer the arrest until Saturday morning, December 20th, with the distinct understanding, however, that the Indian police keep Sitting Bull and his followers under strict surveillance to prevent their leaving the reservation, and report promptly any suspicious movements among them.

Everything was arranged for the arrest to be made on December 20th; but on December 14th, at 4 P.M., a policeman arrived at the Agency from Grand River, who brought me a letter from Lieutenant of Police Henry Bull Head, the officer in charge of the force on Grand River, stating that Sitting Bull was making preparations to leave the reservation; that he had fitted his horses for a long and hard ride, and that if he got the start of them, he being well mounted, the police would be unable to overtake him, and he, therefore, wanted permission to make the arrest at once. I had just finished reading Lieut. Bull Head's letter, and commenced questioning the courier who brought it, when Col. [William F.] Drum, the Post Commander, came into my office to ascertain if I had received any news from Grand River. I handed him the letter which I had just received, and after reading it, he said that the arrest could not be deferred longer, but must be made without further delay; and immediate action was then decided upon, the plan being for the police to make the arrest at break of day the following morning, and two troops of the 8th Cavalry to leave the post at midnight, with orders to proceed on the road to Grand River until they met the police with their prisoner, whom they were to escort back to the post; they would thus be within supporting distance of the police, if necessary, and prevent any attempted rescue of Sitting Bull by his followers. I desired to have the police make the arrest, fully believing that they could do so without bloodshed, while, in the crazed condition of the Ghost Dancers, the military could not; furthermore, the police accomplishing the arrest would have a salutary effect upon all the Indians, and allay much of the then existing uneasiness among the whites. I, therefore, sent a courier to Lieut. Bull Head, advising him of the disposition to be made of the cavalry command which was to cooperate with him, and directed him to make the arrest at daylight the following morning.

Acting under these orders, a force of thirty-nine policemen and four volunteers (one of whom was Sitting Bull's brother-in-law, "Gray Eagle") entered the camp at daybreak on December 16th, proceeding direct to Sitting Bull's house, which ten of them entered, and Lieut. Bull Head announced to him the object of their mission. Sitting Bull accepted his arrest quietly at first, and commenced dressing for the journey to the Agency, during which ceremony (which consumed considerable time) his son, "Crow Foot," who was in the house, commenced berating his father for accepting the arrest and consenting to go with the police; whereupon he (Sitting Bull) got stubborn and refused to accompany them.

By this time he was fully dressed, and the policemen took him out of the house; but, upon getting outside, they found themselves completely surrounded by Sitting Bull's followers, all armed and excited. The policemen reasoned with the crowd, gradually forcing them back, thus increasing the open circle considerably; but Sitting Bull kept calling upon his followers to rescue him from the police; that if the two principal men, "Bull Head" and "Shave Head," were killed the others would run away, and he finally called out for them to commence the attack, whereupon "Catch the Bear" and "Strike the Kettle," two of Sitting Bull's men, dashed through the crowd and fired. Lieut. "Bull Head" was standing on one side of Sitting Bull and 1st Sergt. "Shave Head" on the other, with 2d Sergt. "Red Tomahawk" behind, to prevent his escaping; "Catch the Bear's" shot struck Bull Head in the right side, and he instantly wheeled and shot Sitting Bull, hitting him in the left side, between the tenth and eleventh ribs, and "Strike the Kettle's" shot having passed through Shave Head's abdomen, all three fell together. "Catch the Bear," who fired the first shot, was immediately shot down by private of police "Lone Man," and the fight then became general—in fact, a hand-to-hand conflict—forty-three policemen and volunteers against about one hundred and fifty crazed Ghost Dancers.

The fight lasted about half an hour, but all the casualties, except that of Special Policeman John Armstrong, occurred in the first few minutes. The police soon drove the Indians from around the adjacent buildings, and then charged and drove them into the adjoining woods, about forty rods distant, and it was in this charge that John Armstrong was killed by an Indian secreted in a clump of brush. During the fight women attacked the police with knives and clubs, but in every instance they simply disarmed them and placed them under guard in the houses near by until the troops arrived, after which they were given their freedom. Had the women and children been brought into the Agency there would have been no stampede of the Grand River people; but the men, realizing the enormity of the offence they had committed by attacking the police, as soon as their families joined them, fled up Grand River, and then turned south to the Morian and Cheyenne Rivers.

The conduct of the Indian police upon that occasion cannot be too highly commended. The following is an extract of the official report of E. G. Fechet, Captain 8th Cavalry, who commanded the detachment of troops sent to Grand River:—

> I cannot too strongly commend the splendid courage and ability which characterised the conduct of the Indian police commanded by Bull Head and Shave Head throughout the encounter. The attempt to arrest Sitting Bull was so managed as to place the responsibility for the fight that ensued upon Sitting Bull's band, which began the firing. Red Tomahawk assumed command of the police after both Bull Head and Shave Head had been wounded, and it was he who, under circumstances requiring personal courage to the highest degree, assisted Hawk Man to escape with a message to the troops. After the fight, no demoralization seemed to exist among them, and they were ready and willing to cooperate with the troops to any extent desired.

The following is a list of the killed and wounded casualties of the fight:—

Henry Bull Head, First Lieutenant of Police, died 82 hours after the fight.
Charles Shave Head, First Sergeant of Police, died 25 hours after the fight.
James Little Eagle, Fourth Sergeant of Police, killed in the fight.
Paul Afraid-of-Soldiers, Private of Police, killed in the fight.
John Armstrong, Special Police, killed in the fight.
David Hawkman, Special Police, killed in the fight.
Alexander Middle, Private of Police, wounded, recovering.
Sitting Bull, killed, 56 years of age.
Crow Foot (Sitting Bull's son), killed, 17 years of age.
Black Bird, killed, 43 years of age.
Catch the Bear, killed, 44 years of age.
Spotted Horn Bull, killed, 56 years of age.
Brave Thunder, No.1, killed, 46 years of age.
Little Assiniboine, killed, 44 years of age.
Chase Wounded, killed, 24 years of age.
Bull Ghost, wounded, entirely recovered.
Brave Thunder, No. 2, wounded, recovering rapidly.
Strike the Kettle, wounded, now at Fort Sully, a prisoner.

This conflict, which cost so many lives, is much to be regretted, yet the good resulting therefrom can scarcely be overestimated, as it has effectually eradicated all seeds of disaffection sown by the Messiah Craze among the Indians of this Agency, and has also demonstrated to the people of the country the fidelity and loyalty of the Indian police in maintaining law and order on the reservation. Everything is now quiet at this Agency, and good feeling prevails among the Indians, newspaper reports to the contrary notwithstanding. No Indians have left this Agency since the stampede of December 15th, following the conflict with the police, and no others will. There were three hundred and seventy-two men, women and children left at that time, of whom about one hundred and twenty are males over sixteen years of age, and of whom two hundred and twenty-seven are now prisoners at Fort Sully, and seventy-two are reported to have been captured at Pine Ridge Agency some time ago. . . .

Source: James McLaughlin, "Account of the Death of Sitting Bull and the Circumstances Attending It," (Philadelphia: Indian Rights Association, 1891).

»→ • ←«

4-10. Amendment to the Dawes Act

February 28, 1891

Congress amended the Dawes Act on February 28, 1891, to provide for equal allotments and for the leasing of allotments in certain situations.

Be it enacted. . . , That section one of the act entitled "An act to provide for the allotment of lands in severalty to Indians on the various reservations, and to extend the protection of the laws of the United States and the Territories over the Indians, and for other purposes," approved February eighth, eighteen hundred and eighty-seven, be, and, the same is hereby, amended so as to read follows:

SEC. 1. That in all cases where any tribe or band of Indians have been, or shall hereafter be, located upon any reservation created for their use, either by treaty stipulation or by virtue of an Act of Congress or Executive order setting apart the same for their use, the President of the United States be, and he, hereby is, authorized, whenever in his opinion any reservation, or any part thereof, of such Indians is advantageous for agricultural or grazing purposes, to cause said reservation, or any part thereof, to be surveyed, or resurveyed, if necessary, and to allot to each Indian located thereon one-eighth of a section of land: *Provided*, That in case there is not sufficient land in any of said reservations to allot lands to each individual in quantity as above provided the land in such reservation or reservations shall be allotted to each individual pro rata, as near as may be, according to legal subdivisions: *Provided further*, That where the treaty or act of Congress setting apart such reservation provides for the allotment of lands in severalty to certain classes in quantity in excess of that herein provided the President, in making allotments upon such reservation, shall allot the land to each individual Indian of said classes belonging thereon in quantity as specified in such treaty or act, and to other Indians belonging thereon in quantity as herein provided: *Provided further*, That where existing agreements or laws provide for allotments in accordance with the provisions of said act of February eighth, eighteen hundred and eighty-seven, or in quantities substantially as therein provided, allotments may be made in quantity as specified in this act, with the consent of the Indians, expressed in such manner as the President, in his discretion, may require: *And provided further*, That when the lands allotted, or any legal subdivision thereof, are only valuable for grazing purposes, such lands shall be allotted in double quantities.

SEC. 2. That where allotments have been made in whole or in part upon any reservation under the provisions of said act of February eighth, eighteen hundred and eighty-seven, and the quantity of land in such reservation is sufficient to give each member of the tribe eighty acres, such allotments shall be revised, and equalized under the provisions of this act: *Provided*, That no allotment heretofore approved by the Secretary of the Interior shall be reduced in quantity.

SEC. 3. That whenever it shall be made to appear to the Secretary of the Interior that, by reason of age or other disability, any allottee under the provisions of said act, or of any other act or treaty can not personally and with benefit to himself occupy or improve his allotment or any part thereof the same may be leased upon such terms, regulations and conditions as shall be prescribed by such Secretary, for a term not exceeding three years for farming or grazing, or ten years for mining purposes: *Provided*, That where lands are occupied by Indians who have bought and paid for the same, and which lands are not needed for farming or agricultural purposes, and are not desired for individual allotments the same may be leased by authority of the Council speaking for such Indians, for a period not to exceed five years for grazing, or ten years for mining purposes in such quantities and upon such terms and conditions as the agent in charge of such reservation may recommend, subject to the approval of the Secretary of the Interior.

SEC. 4. That where any Indian entitled to allotment under existing laws shall make settlement upon any surveyed or unsurveyed lands of the United States not otherwise appropriated, he or she shall be entitled, upon application to the local land office for the district in which the lands are located, to have the same allotted to him or her and to his or her children, in quantities and manner as provided in the foregoing section of this amending act for Indians residing upon reservations; and when such settlement is made upon unsurveyed lands the grant to such Indians shall be adjusted upon the survey of the lands so as to conform thereto; and patents shall be issued to them for such lands in the manner and with the restrictions provided in the act to which this is an amendment. And the fees to which the officers of such local land office would have been entitled had such lands been entered upon the general laws for the disposition of the public lands shall be paid to them from any moneys in the Treasury of the United States not otherwise appropriated, upon a statement of an account in their behalf for such fees by the Commissioner of the General Land Office, and a certification of such account to the Secretary of the Treasury by the Secretary of the Interior.

SEC. 5. That for the purpose of determining the descent of land to the heirs of any deceased Indian under the provisions of the fifth section of said act, whenever any male and female Indian shall have co-habited together as husband and wife, according to the custom and manner of Indian life the issue of such co-habitation shall be, for the purpose aforesaid, taken and deemed to be the legitimate issue of the Indians so living together, and every Indian child, otherwise illegitimate, shall for such purpose be . . . deemed to be the legitimate issue of father of such child. . . .

Source: *U.S. Statutes at Large*, 26:794-96.

4-11. Thomas J. Morgan to Benjamin Harrison

July 21, 1891

Thomas J. Morgan, commissioner of Indian affairs from 1889 to 1893, dispatched a personal letter to President Benjamin Harrison on July 21, 1891, pertaining to Native American matters.

. . . I am in receipt of your very kind note of July 20th, for which I thank you. I would have been most glad to have gone to you myself about this action, but it seemed to me so largely a matter of Bureau administration, that I hardly felt at liberty to trouble you with the details, unless called upon to do so. Before taking any action at all, I laid the case before Mr. Halford [Elijah W. Halford was Harrison's private secretary], asking him to speak to you about it, which I supposed he did at once.

The step was taken after full consultation with the Secretary, and I did not know but that he, too, might have mentioned it to you. It was, in fact, he who suggested it, but in order that I might feel perfectly sure that we fully understood each other, I went to him a second time, and received from him his deliberate, emphatic, and repeated assurance that he would "back" me in it, to use his own words.

In a separate envelop I enclose for your information a complete copy of the correspondence, and would also be glad to have you read my letters to Mr. Halford.

I have given a great deal of attention and thought to this question and do not see, as yet, that I have made any mistake. I think my position is not only justifiable, but strong and wise, that the circumstances not only warranted, but demanded it, if the Commissioner had any self respect or the Office any dignity. I enclose a clipping from the New York Tribune, showing how a great conservative paper views the situation, and also a copy of a letter from the Assistant Commissioner, Mr. [R. V.] Belt, who is thoroughly familiar with all the circumstances, and who is not only conservative, but timid. The truth is that this crisis and change had to come sooner or later, the Catholic Bureau could not forever run the Indian Office, and *any* man whom you would have been willing to place in charge of these great interests, would have rebelled against such a form of slavery, to say nothing of the particular attacks on me.

You will not fail to notice that this is not a blow at the Catholics, but at an insolent, dictatorial Bureau, whose usefulness, if it ever had any, it has outgrown. During both these years I have awarded larger sums to the Catholic contract schools than they have ever had before, and the Indian Office can just as well look after them and the money it disburses to them, as to have the Catholic Bureau do it. The other denominations have no great organization here. The money awarded to their contract schools has been given through their Boards, but I have notified them that it will now be paid by the Office directly to the schools, thus putting all denominations on the same footing.

I am in touch, as you doubtless know, with the best elements of thought in the country and I think I am safe in predicting that this action will be almost universally approved; indeed, I have already received many communications . . . to this effect, and am especially glad to say that it has the commendation of many Catholics, who acknowledge no necessity for such a Bureau.

I am free to confess, My Dear General, that I am not a politician and my judgment of the political effect of this action may not be worth much, but from what I have heard and seen, I believe it will win many friends for the administration. I beg to enclose copy of a letter from Judge Perkins, just received, showing the views of one politician, and I have others and many verbal expressions of the same character. Senator [Richard F.] Pettigrew [South Dakota] is outspoken in his commendation. I think we have every thing to gain and nothing to lose—although of course a protest against the action was to be expected—by maintaining the ground that has been taken.

You will bear in mind that the educational feature is but one department of the immense work done by this Office, this unfortunate Catholic controversy but a mere point in the multitudinous interests committed to its care, all of which pass through my hand or under my eye, and it is almost the only point where my administration has been criticised. The Office and Indian service have never been in so good a condition as now, there has been steady advance all along the line, I have tried to the best of my ability to carry out your instructions when tendering me the place, and have the strongest support of the public at large. I quote a few lines received this morning from Judge [James Bradley] Thayer, of Harvard University:—

> I have been very greatly interested in your report. Indeed, I have never read one which seemed to me its equal for the fulness of its information and its intelligent discussion. . . . If we could keep you and let you have your way [for] twenty years, one would be content with things as they are.

All through these passing months large numbers of just such letters have come to me, which have been some reward for the work to which I have given by best energies, and the unjust abuse which has been heaped upon me by the mistaken attaches of this Catholic Bureau.

I shall regret it more than any one else if my action embarrasses you or seems to you in any way unwise for I have the love and loyalty of an old soldier for the Colonel he admired and obeyed. I considered the step in all its bearings, with all its "far-reaching consequences" as the Bureau puts it, and with the assurances of the Secretary and the conscientious belief that it was the only wise and honorable course open to the Office, was prepared to take the results. As no great question was involved, as the Secretary approved and suggested the action, and as it was chiefly one of administration, it seemed, to the best of my judgement that it came directly within the province of the Office to make the change. Of course I am fully committed to it, and while the administration of the Office is committed to me will have to stand by my colors, with the pluck of an old soldier who has passed through many a hotter fire, and fully believe in victory. . . .

Source: Thomas J. Morgan to Benjamin Harrison, July 21, 1891, Benjamin Harrison Papers, Manuscripts Division, Library of Congress, Washington, D.C.

4-12. A People Without Law

James Bradley Thayer

November 1891

Born in Haverhill, Massachusetts, James Bradley Thayer (1831-1901) graduated from the Harvard Law School in 1856. He practiced law in Boston until 1874, when he became professor of law at Harvard University, remaining in that capacity until his death. Thayer wrote several books, including Cases on Constitutional Law *(1895) and* The Development of Trial by Jury *(1896). His erudite and timely two-part article, "A People Without Law," appeared in the October and November, 1891, numbers of* Atlantic Monthly. *An earlier essay by Thayer on the Dawes Bill and Native Americans was published in the same periodical in 1888.*

In saying “A People without Law” I mean our Indians. He who tries to fix and express their legal status finds very soon that he is dealing chiefly with the political condition, so little of any legal status at all have Indians. But we must at once discriminate and remind ourselves that there are different sorts of Indians. What makes any of them peculiar, in a legal point of view, is the fact that they belong to a separate political body, and that our government mainly deals with them, not as individuals, as it does with you and me, but in a lump, as a people or tribe.

When an Indian has detached himself from his own people, and adopted civilized ways of life, and resides among us, he at once becomes, by our present law, a citizen like the rest of us. There are many Indians in the country who have done this. We may set them one side. There are even many Indians in tribes who are our fellow-citizens. In the language of Judge [Benjamin R.] Curtis in the Dred Scott case, “By solemn treaties large bodies of Mexican and North American Indians have been admitted to citizenship of the United States.” The Pueblo Indians, for instance, have been judicially declared by the courts of New Mexico to be, in this way, citizens of the United States, although, oddly enough, we keep agents among them. In such cases, the tribal relation, while it is of course a matter of much social importance, is of no legal significance at all; it is like being a Presbyterian, or a member of the Phi Beta Kappa, or a Freemason; and each Indian, however little he knows it, holds a direct relation of allegiance to the United States. Again, there are Indians in the separate States, as in Massachusetts, Maine, and New York, who, although in tribes, have never held any direct relations with the United States, but have been governed as subjects by these States. The problem of this class of people has been slowly and quietly working out under the control of the separate States, without any interference from the general government, until, in some cases, politically and legally speaking, they are not Indians. In Massachusetts, in 1869, every Indian in the State was made a citizen of the State, and it is supposed, I rather think correctly, that they have thus become citizens of the United States. It would not have been so if the general government had entered into relations with them before this declaration. Then the assent of the United States would have been required to make them citizens of that government. But whether citizens of the United States or not, they are citizens and voters in Massachusetts, and might determine the election of a President of the United States by their votes. In the States of Maine and New York the courts still call them the "wards of the State," and as such the States govern them as they think proper, as being subjects, and not citizens.

Leaving these exceptional classes of Indians, what I propose to speak of is the legal status of that less than a quarter of a million people with whom the United States government holds relations under the clause of the Constitution which gives to Congress the right to "regulate commerce . . . with the Indian tribes,"—the people with whom we carry on war, and who live mainly on reservations secured to them by treaties or otherwise. There are, to be sure, some thousands of tribal Indians who wander about loosely over the plains, but in the main the class that I am to deal with, the class that is intimated when we talk of the "Indian question," may be shortly designated as the Reservation Indians. And yet here I must again discriminate. Out of these Reservation Indians we may conveniently set aside the seventy thousand or so who belong among the "civilized tribes" in the Indian Territory,—the Choctaws, Cherokees, and the rest. These are, to be sure, in strictness, Reservation Indians, and their legal status is highly interesting; a time is coming when it will require the close attention of statesmen, but it does not so much press upon public attention just now. These people govern themselves with a good degree of success; they have constitutions and laws closely modeled upon ours, and have made much progress in the ways of civilized life. As regards their political relation to us, they rest, so far, in a good deal of security on the peculiarly solemn guarantees with which our government accompanied its settlement of them on their lands. But, as I have intimated, the time will probably come when, with or without their consent, there must be a readjustment of our relations with them. In looking ahead, we must contemplate an ultimate absorption of that region into the Union. Already, lately, there has taken place, in some measure, and extension over it of federal courts and federal law. If, then, we deduct these "civilized Indians," there remain somewhere between 130,000 and 180,000 others, whom I am calling Reservation Indians, either living on reservations or candidates for that sort of life; and it is these whose case I wish to consider. In this statement the Alaska Indians are not included. They are too little known, and their relations to the other inhabitants of that country and to our government too little ascertained, to make it practicable to consider them.

I am speaking of "Reservation Indians," but what are Indian reservations? They are tracts of land belonging to the United States which are set apart for the residence of Indians. This is done in various ways,—by treaty, by a law, by an executive order. Often the reservation is a region given to the Indians in exchange for their ancestral home and hunting-ground; sometimes it is a diminished part of this ancestral ground. The Indians, in most cases, are recognized as having a legal right to the occupation of this land. They do not generally own the fee of it; that is in the government. If the tribe should become extinct or abandon the land, the title would rest wholly in the United States. Their title is the same that they were recognized as having in the soil which they originally occupied and ranged over when the Europeans came here,—a right of occupancy merely, yet a right recognized by the courts so long, at any rate, as it is recognized by the political department. This right is merely tribal; the individual does not own land or have any legal right in it. On these reservations the Indians keep up, in point of theory and in the main, their separate national housekeeping, make their own laws, govern themselves. They owe no allegiance to us; each Indian owes allegiance to his tribe and its chiefs. With these separated people, as I said, we carry on war, and until lately we have concluded treaties. Such was the way, also, of our English ancestors.

It has turned out, however, for one reason and another, that they succeeded very poorly at making their own laws and governing themselves; and we did not quite let them alone. We found, for instance, that it would not do to let in outsiders to trade freely with them, and that we must keep ourselves advised as to what they were doing, and whether they were standing to their promises; and so we sent agents among them to represent us in delivering to them the goods and money we owed them, and to protect them against intrusion. We could not allow intoxicating liquors to be sold among them, or firearms. We must, in short, fully "regulate commerce" with them. In this way it came about that we really interfered a great deal with the theory of their separate national housekeeping. Yet, further, when wars came, and with them the upsetting of everything and the rearranging by new treaties, of course we interfered still more. As time went by it was perceived that the Indian self-government amounted to little, and we occasionally stepped in with laws to fill the gap. But it is only occasionally and in scraps that we have done this; for the most part, we still stand by and see them languishing under the decay of their own government, and give them nothing in its place,—no courts to appeal to, and no resort when they are wronged excepting to fight. We keep them in a state of dependence upon the arbitrary pleasure of executive and administrative officials, without the steady security of any system of law.

In such a state of things as this, with a wretched system in existence, and with the need of a change, two courses are open to a good citizen, not exclusive of each other, but yet quite different. One is to endeavor to procure an honest, righteous administration of the existing system while it lasts, the punishment of offenders, the securing of good officials, the dismissal of bad ones, redress for outrages, and the creation of a public sentiment that will help to these ends. The other course is to displace that radically bad element of the existing system, the "lawlessness" of it, which poisons everything that is done, and disheartens the reformer by supplying new outrages as fast as he can correct the old ones. These two courses, as I said, are not exclusive of each other. He who would, first of all, abolish certain evil features of our present method of dealing with the Indians may well join in the endeavor to mitigate and mend the administration of the present system while it lasts. And yet a persuasion of the need and the possibility of a radical change will surely affect the judgment in determining the relative importance of things; it will settle the question of *emphasis*, that more important thing in thought and conduct. I desire at the outset to express a conviction that the chief thing to be done, the thing imperative now, the thing that must not wait, whatever else is postponed, is a radical change in the particular of giving to the Indians courts and a system of law upon their reservations; and also to express the conviction that this is not only a thing so much to be desired, but that it is practicable, if those who are interested in this subject will only insist upon it in this spirit.

(1.) Let us now, in coming to close quarters with this matter, run over certain facts of the legal and political history of our relations with the Indians. Of the more familiar matters I shall say little, but we will try to observe some of the leading points,—enough of them to come to a fair understanding of the situation.

When the Europeans came hither, in the fifteenth century and later, it was unavoidable that there should be conflicts between them and the people whom they found here. Not only the nature of the situation, but the European ideas of the relation to each other of white men and men of other colors, made it certain that there would be trouble. Had the new-comers all been saints and sages, this would still have happened, for they and the savages did not and could not understand each other. Their purposes crossed. Necessity drove each to his acts that seemed hostile to the other. How could the savages fail to regard as enemies the strange people who seized and carried away to an unknown fate their neighbors and friends; who carried off their stores of food, and stripped the graves of their families? How could they know what the Europeans were at? And if they did know, how could they help fearing for themselves and their household gods? The Europeans, however, were not saints and sages, but average men of their time; and the natives were savages. In war both were ferocious and brutal; and the savages were ferocious and brutal to the last degree. In that famous first letter of Columbus,—lately reprinted in the Latin version of 1493 by Professor [Henry W.] Haynes, of Boston, with a scholarly translation,—telling of his earliest discoveries, we read these ominous words: "As soon as I had come into this sea I took by force some Indians from the first island." How did the Indians who remained like that? Somehow or other Columbus carried away nine of them to Spain. Was it likely to be any relief to their families to know that they were destined to be duly baptized at Barcelona? Columbus's plans contemplated the regular deportation of them as slaves. In the next century, the Spaniards, in their dealings with the Indians, did not at all improve upon Columbus. Of De Soto, in the fourth decade of the sixteenth century, we are told in Miss [Alice] Fletcher's Report on Indian Education and Civilization, "De Soto's wanderings across the country might be traced by the groans of Indian captives, male and female, reduced to slavery and compelled to bear the burdens of the soldiers by the flames of dwellings, the desolation of fields, and the heaps of slain, young and old."

The English were not so bad, yet the adventurers who sailed along these coasts continued the same work of spreading terror and hatred among the natives. The Englishman [Geroge] Waymouth, sailing up a river of the State of Maine in 1605, "kidnapped and carried away five of the natives." "We used little delay," he says, "but suddenly laid hands upon them; and it was as much as five or six of us could do to get them into the (boat), for they were strong, and so naked as our best hold was by their long hair on their heads." Nine years later, Thomas Hunt, a ship-master, carried away seven and twenty Indians from the coast of Massachusetts, and sold them in Spain as slaves. Six years later, in November, 1620, the Mayflower company began its dealing with Indian affairs (while exploring Cape Cod before landing at Plymouth) by repeatedly taking the Indian stores of corn and beans which they had laid away for their own supply; proposing to themselves, indeed, what the Indians must be pardoned for not appreciating, "so soon as they could meet with any of the inhabitants of that place, to make them large satisfaction." They seem also to have opened Indian graves, for we are told of the bowls, trays, dishes, knife, pack needle, the "little bow," and strings and bracelets of fine white beads that they found in one of them. They were now among the people whose neighbors had been kid-napped by Thomas Hunt. It is not strange, therefore, to read that when they saw some Indians a week later and tried to approach them, these ran away; and to find that the first actual intercourse between our New England ancestors and the natives was as follows,—I quote from Dr. [John G.] Palfrey's History of New England: "The following morning (December 8), at daylight, they had just ended their prayers, and were preparing breakfast at their camp on the beach, when they heard a yell, and a flight of arrows fell among them. The assailants turned out to be thirty or forty Indians, who, being fired upon, retired."

Observe, I am not just now concerned in blaming either the Pilgrims or the natives. I am drawing attention to facts, and beg my reader to remember that, all things considered, such events were sure to happen. They help us to guess and forecast the relation of separation that was to take place between the new-comers and their neighbors. As time went on, and new Europeans swarmed in settlements along the coast and on the rivers and meadows of the interior,—drawn often to the same points, to well-watered spots on the sea-coast, the fording-places of a river, the lower falls of a tidal stream, or some fine inland river bottom, by the same attraction which had gathered the natives there,—as these things happened, all men know how collisions came and frightful wars and devastation, how the savages were beaten and crowded back. The necessity of self-preservation was held to justify any atrocities. "The awful conditions of the case," says our grave historian, Dr. Palfrey, in speaking of the performances of [John] Mason and [John] Underhill in the Pequot war of 1637, "forbid being dainty about the means of winning a victory, or about using it in such a manner that the chance shall not have to be tried again."

Complications arose. Not only English, but French and Dutch had set foot on this continent, and they were rivals here. At home, also, these Europeans fought; this induced sympathetic fighting here; and this, again, drew in the savages, whose quarrels, as among themselves and with the colonists, were fomented for the advantage of the fighting Europeans. Whittier in his beautiful early poem of Pentucket (the Indian name of Haverhill) gives a picture of one of the incidents of these wars, when the allied French and Indians attacked that border town, his birthplace. . . . Haverhill was my own birthplace, and I well recall the dreadful fear of Indians which the children of that town continued to cherish so late as fifty odd years ago,—a century and a quarter after these events. I can remember coming home from school in mortal terror lest my family had all been carried away by the Indians during my absence.

As time went on, in some colonies the Indians were driven to the west, out further into the vast unknown wilderness, and were forbidden to cross the line of demarcation between them and the whites; and state reservations were established along the border, on which friendly Indians were induced to settle, acting at once as a precaution and buffer against the shock of hostile attack. During this process other things had happened. Individual Indians had settled among the whites, and had sunk into the mass of the people, and were governed like the rest. To some extent, also, tribes of Indians had been caught and surrounded by the flood of the new civilization, and remained islanded permanently as a separate people in the midst of it, yet governed more or less under the laws of the colonies. It was such cases as these, probably, that were referred to in the first permanent statute of our present national government, passed in 1802, to regulate "commerce with the Indian tribes." The sixteenth section of that act begins, "Nothing in this act shall be construed to prevent any trade or intercourse with Indians living on lands surrounded by settlements of the citizens of the United States, and being within the ordinary jurisdiction of any of the individual States." It was owing, very likely, to this relegation to the States of the affairs of such Indians as are here described that we may trace the circumstance, often not understood, that some States, like New York, Massachusetts, and Maine, have continued to deal freely with Indian tribes within their borders. These tribes, in the language of the statute of 1802, had come to be "surrounded by settlements of the citizens of the United States, and . . . within the ordinary jurisdiction of the . . . States." As a dry question of power, Congress might at any time have taken control of them. But while Congress was staying its hand, it might happen, and has happened in Massachusetts, that the tribal relation had been dissolved. It has happened in the case of individual Indians, whose separation from their tribe has been recognized by the States, and in the case of whole tribes. In such instances, the "Indian tribe," in the sense of the Constitution of the United States, that is in the sense of a separate political community, has ceased to exist before it was ever recognized by the general government; and therewith the power of Congress has gone, because, as regards these persons, there exists no longer the opportunity to exercise it.

(2.) It will be observed that I have now brought the United States upon the scene. New problems have thus emerged. What are the relations between this new government and the Indians? How has their relation to the separate local governments been affected?

The new government had its immediate origin in a sense of danger from England, and in the need of protection from that peril, and the like. One of the first things that presented itself was the possibility of harm from the savages; for the colonies had had a direful experience of what an enemy might do who chose to ally himself with these people. Accordingly, in July, 1775, the Continental Congress resolved "that the securing and preserving the friendship of the Indian nations appears to be a subject of the utmost moment to these colonies," and proceeded to adopt the first of our national arrangements for managing Indian affairs. Commissioners were appointed for each of the three departments (North, Middle, and South) into which all the Indians were divided. These commissioners were to have power to make treaties with the Indians, and to watch the operations of the British superintendents. "The commissioners," it was resolved, ". . . (are to) have power to take to their assistance gentlemen of influence among the Indians in whom they can confide, and to appoint agents residing near or among the Indians to watch the conduct of the (British) superintendents or their emissaries." There are many signs of the anxious care of Congress in this matter. Treaties with the Indians were immediately made. Congress, in January, 1776, directed the importation of $200,000 worth of goods on public account, to be sold by the Indian commissioners to persons licensed to trade with the Indians, at cost and expenses and a commission of two and a half per cent. These traders were to sell only at fixed points and fixed prices. In the same year it was resolved that disputes between the whites and Indians should be determined (if the Indians would agree) by arbitrators chosen one by each party, and one by the commissioners. Many of the Indians took part against us. The anxiety that was felt and the magnitude of the "Indian question" of that day are shown by the way in which this figures in the Declaration of Independence in 1776, and in the Articles of Confederation in 1778-81. "He has endeavored," is the charge of the Declaration against the British king, "to bring on the inhabitants of our frontier the merciless Indian savages, whose known rule of warfare is an undistinguished destruction of all ages, sexes, and conditions." In the ninth of the Articles of Confederation, the separate States, which are forbidden to carry on war, may do this where a State "shall have received certain advice of a resolution being formed by some nation of Indians to invade" it; and these Articles entrust to the Union "the sole and exclusive right and power of regulating the trade and managing all affairs with the Indians not members of any of the States; *provided*, that the legislative right of any State within its own limits be not infringed or violated."

The Confederation proceeded, of course, like its predecessor the Continental Congress, to make treaties with the Indians as separate people; for example, the treaty with the Cherokees in 1785, at Hopewell, in which it was provided that if an outsider settled on Indian land he should forfeit the protection of the United States, and be subject to punishment by the Indians. In 1786 a formal ordinance was adopted for the regulation of Indian affairs in the territory on the west, lately ceded by the States of the Atlantic margin. This region, divided into two departments, was assigned to superintendents acting under the Secretary of War, who were to attend to the regulation of trade with the Indians and the distribution of presents among them, and to report upon any signs of disaffection. Only licensed citizens of the United States could trade with the Indians; but any such citizen who brought a recommendation from the governor of his State, paid fifty dollars, and gave a bond had a right to be licensed.

Now came the organization of the new government, our present United States, in 1787-89. This, while preserving the old *names* of the "United States" and the "Union," was in reality, as we all know, a very different thing indeed. For certain great purposes it was a nation, gathering into one, for the accomplishment of these purposes, the combined power of all the colonies, and standing, as regards these ends, as a single state covering the entire country; to which, as being in these particulars the supreme state, every citizen had a direct relation and owed sole allegiance. This was not so before. Accordingly, now we not only find the general government endowed, as before, with the power of representing all the country in its relation to the Indian tribes, but we also find a dropping out of the old ambiguous and troublesome clauses about saving the legislative right of the separate colonies. The Constitution of the new government provided that Congress should have power "to regulate commerce with foreign nations, and among the several States and with the Indian tribes." Here, again, as in the two great documents before named, the Declaration of Independence thirteen years before, and the Articles of Confederation eight years before, we remark the importance of the "Indian question" of the period by the express and conspicuous mention of it, and by the circumstance that the handling of it is deemed matter of general concern. It was dealing with separate nations; if not with a foreign people, yet a separate one.

(3.) In starting now to take a brief survey of the legal position of the Indians under the new Constitution, and of the scope of the power which the nation has over them, let us stop a moment on the threshold and allow ourselves to conjecture what questions might present themselves and what answers would be given. Will the Indian tribes, our ancestors might have asked, remain permanently as separate political bodies? Or will they become broken up and absorbed into our own population? As regards the other anomalous element in our body politic, slave, the word "slave" had been left out of the Constitution; it was expected that slavery would disappear, and there was an objection in some minds to having any permanent trace of it in the document. As to Indians it was not so; the insertion among the provisions for the basis of representation of the phrase "Indians not taxed" indicated perhaps not merely the recognition of the fact that there were then some Indians who had become embodied among our people, but also an expectation that such a process would go on. Assuming that it would, how long would it last? And meantime supposing there were war with Indians and a conquest, what would happen? Was it thought that the Indians might be driven wholly out of our borders,—north, or south, or into the unfathomed west beyond the Mississippi? If they were subdued, how would they be governed? Would the United States have free and full power of governing them as it thought wise, as a subject people; or would it be restrained by the Constitution and its amendments, which secured trial by jury and other rights? Apart from war and conquest, would the Indians become enfeebled and lose their power of self-government: Would they ask, or, if they did not ask, would they need to be governed by us? Would they continue to occupy the great tracts which were then recognized as "Indian country," or would new States grow up, and the white people spread over into the Indian land?

Some of these questions undoubtedly presented themselves. Certainly the makers of the Constitution counted upon the growth of new States at the west. Was not the Ordinance of 1787, adopted while the Constitution was making, an express provision for that? Unquestionably they expected, except for the exigencies of war, that the Indians would long continue a separate people, and that so long as they did the right to occupy their lands would remain to them until it was parted with by their own consent. That the Indians were expected to be gradually more or less absorbed into our population we may believe, for that process had long gone on in the colonies. That our ancestors supposed that in one way or another the Indians would ultimately disappear as a separate element we may also believe, for they recognized them as capable of civilization, and laid plans for their education, training, and Christianizing. In July, 1775, Congress had voted money toward the education of certain Indians at "Dr. Wheelock's school," now Dartmouth College, and in the next year they had made provision for the residence of "ministers and schoolmasters" among the Indians, in order to promote "the propagation of the gospel and the cultivation of the civil arts" among them. And although the experience of the colonies was not calculated to encourage any confident expectation of working out a high form of civilization among the native tribes as a separate population yet it might well lead to an expectation of a gradual fading out of the peculiarities of tribal life and tribal government, and a gradual subjection of them to the whites; for, as I said, it had been so in the colonies. We may believe, then, that the chance was not wholly overlooked that the general government might, for one reason or another, and for a longer or a short time, have to govern the Indians as subjects. If it conquered them in war, it could hardly be doubted that the power to govern them would be the same as if a foreign people were conquered; and if, in the gradual course of events, they should come to be surrounded by our people, and the tribal bond should be enfeebled and tribal government ineffective and the people a source of danger to us, it may well have been expected that our government would take full control of them and govern them.

Our ancestors had themselves been witnesses to things that would suggest these possibilities. They, as well as we, had had experience of the shoving back of Indians as the whites crowded in, of the gradual surrounding of Indian settlements by whites and their submission to white legislation. They had witnessed in the separate colonies, for example in Virginia and Massachusetts, the same process which we in our day are witnessing on the continental scale. What happened in those colonies is happening now between the Mississippi and the Pacific. How had this matter been dealt with at the periods of which the framers of the Constitution had knowledge? In Massachusetts, as early as 1693-94, the legislature introduced law among the Indians. "To the intent that the Indians may be forwarded in civility and Christianity," they provided for the appointment of "one or more discreet persons within several parts of the Province to have the inspection and more particular care and government of the Indians in the respective plantations, . . . to have . . . the power of a justice of the peace over them" in civil and criminal cases "according to the . . . laws of the Province," etc. And in January, 1789, just before the United States Constitution went into operation, a statute of Massachusetts established a board of five overseers of the Marshpee Indians, "with full power . . . to regulate the police of the said plantation, to establish rules . . . for the well ordering and managing the affairs . . . of the said Indians, . . . appoint . . . a guardian or guardians to the said Indian and other proprietors to carry into execution their said regulations and orders." These overseers or guardians were authorized to pass upon all contracts, leases, and the like made with the Indians, and to bring actions in their behalf and adjust controversies between them and the whites. They were also to render legal accounts regularly to the governor and council. Under these and like statutes the Indians of Massachusetts were governed entirely, governed not as citizens, but as a subject population; being, in the language of the Supreme Court of Massachusetts, speaking through Mr. Justice [Horace] Gray in 1871, "Not subject to taxation, *nor endowed with the ordinary civil and political rights of citizens*, but . . . treated as wards of the commonwealth." In

Virginia, also, before and after the making of the Constitution of the United States, where Indian tribes had become reduced to very small numbers, trustees were appointed to sell their land and apply the proceeds for their benefit, while the survivors appear to have sunk into the mass of the free population of the colony.

There is a hint in these things, for, as the reader will observe, I have been speaking of the purposes and expectations of those who framed the Constitution of the United States; of what they meant when they spoke of "Indians not taxed," and of regulating commerce "with the Indian tribes;" and of what they meant by their silence when they said nothing more. In view of the historical facts now mentioned, of the nature of the government which was then created and the powers conferred upon it, we must conclude, I think, that while the United States, might, if it saw fit, keep on in the old method of dealing with the Indians as a separate people, it also might, in various contingencies easily possible to foresee, change the plan, and govern the Indians as a subject population in methods suited to their stage of development.

(4.) Let us now turn from the attitude of conjecture and forecast, and trace what has happened in point of fact. In the first place, very many treaties were made, mainly for the purpose of getting and exchanging land. The number, down to 1871, when the making of Indian treaties was abandoned, was little under four hundred. One tenth of these were made before this century. Passing by these, the details of which are very numerous, I confine myself to the general laws. Our present United States took its first permanent step in general legislation about the Indians in the statute of March 30, 1801: "An Act to regulate trade and intercourse with the Indian tribes, and to preserve peace on the frontiers." Its provisions are largely continued in all later laws. I will give a brief abstract of it, and the reader will notice how closely this statute follows the theory of regarding the Indians as a separate and self-governing people. After providing for marking certain extensive boundary lines previously fixed by treaty between "the United States and various Indian tribes," it forbids our citizens and others from going into this Indian country without a passport, and committing any act against the person or property of Indians in their own country which would be a crime if committed against a citizen of the United States within any State. The offender, if property was taken, was to restore to the Indians twofold. If he could not pay at least the full value, it should be paid out of the treasury of the United States, but only on condition that the Indians abstained from violence in righting themselves. Settlement on Indian lands, and trading without a license from the superintendent appointed by the United States for the particular Indian department, were forbidden; but anybody (limited, by a later statue, to citizens of the United States) giving bond with sureties was to be licensed. The sale of the Indian title to land, except under a treaty or agreement with the United States, was forbidden. In order to promote civilization among friendly tribes, and to secure their continued friendship, the President was authorized to supply them, to a specified amount, with useful domestic animals and implements of husbandry, and goods or money, and to appoint "persons from time to time as temporary agents to reside among the Indians." If Indians should cross the line into any State or Territory of the United Stats and commit crime or outrage, the injured party or his representatives were to apply to the Indian superintendent or other designated officer and furnish proofs, and this officer was to make demand upon the Indian's nation or tribe for satisfaction. If this satisfaction were neglected or refused for a year, the President was to be informed, and was to take further steps to secure it. The individual injured was ultimately to be paid by the United States, unless otherwise indemnified; but if he should take the remedy into his own hands by violence, he forfeited this right. Outside territorial courts and United States courts were to have jurisdiction of offenses, under this act. The military might turn out anybody who was unlawfully in the Indian country.

So far no attempt was made to govern the Indians, or to administer justice on their land. Of course the theory was that of a people who did all this for themselves. But in a statute of March, 1817, we see something new. The doing in the Indian country of any act which would be punishable if committed in any place under the exclusive jurisdiction of the United States is made punishable as it would be if committed there, and jurisdiction is given to the superior court of the Territory, or the United States court of the district, into which the offender should first be brought. But offenses of Indians upon Indians are excepted. Here is a beginning of governing the Indian country, for this covers offenses between whites and between Indians and whites. And then comes another recognition of the Indian weakness. By a statute of 1819, "For the purpose of providing against the further decline and final extinction of the Indian tribes adjoining to the frontier settlements of the United States, and for introducing among them the habit and arts of civilization," the President, with the Indians' consent, may employ among them persons to teach them in the mode of agriculture suited to their situation, and their children in reading, writing, and arithmetic. Soon afterwards we find in the statutes a reflection of that terrible pressure of the whites upon the Indians of certain Southern States which led to driving them across the Mississippi. By a statute of 1830 the sum of $500,000 was appropriated to carry out the plan for removing all Indians, with their consent, from the existing States or organized Territories to the unorganized region west of the Mississippi, with authority solemnly to assure the Indians making the exchange that the United States will forever secure and guarantee to them the country thus given, and, if preferred, will give them a patent for it, the land to revert to the United States if the tribes become extinct or abandon the land.

On June 30, 1834, a revision was passed of the important statute of 1802, already summarized, superseding the chief of the laws above named. It first gave a definition of what was meant by "Indian country," in clumsy phrases which were interpreted by the Supreme Court of the United States in 1877 to mean all the land west of the Mississippi outside of the States of Louisiana and Missouri and the Territory of Arkansas and the lands east of the Mississippi which now constitute the States of Michigan and Wisconsin. The definition was dropped in the Revised Statutes of 1874, and no other was substituted. The definition of "Indian country" now accepted by the Supreme Court of the United States is "all the country to which the Indian title has not been extinguished, anywhere within the limits of the United States." This includes the country acquired by the United States since 1834, and does not except what is within the boundary of the States unless, as in Colorado, it may have been otherwise provided when they were admitted into the Union. The statute of 1834, after defining the Indian country, reenacted, with modifications, the previous provisions regulating trade and intercourse. There is the same clear theory of recognizing the Indians as a separate people, but we find one or two more of those striking changes which mark the inroads upon this theory. Instead of trusting wholly to the Indians to extradite an offending member, we find now that the superintendents, agents, and sub-agents are to endeavor, by such means as the President may authorize, to arrest and bring to trial (before the outside courts) any Indians committing crimes on the reservation. That is a large discretion. The reader will remember that some crimes on the reservations were forbidden by the statute of 1817. The President may also employ the military in seizing such Indians. The superintendents, agents, and sub-agents are empowered to search for and destroy spiritous liquors, by whomsoever introduced, and to destroy any distillery, though set up by an Indian. The provision of 1817 for extending to the Indian country the criminal code of the United States for places under the exclusive jurisdiction of the United States is continued, but excludes, as before, the act of one Indian against another.

In 1849 the progress of ideas about the Indians was further marked by transferring the management of Indian affairs from the War Department, where hitherto it had lain, to the newly created Department of the Interior. The care of the Indians was ceasing to be thought of as a matter incidental to foreign affairs or to war. Vast tracts of country and great numbers of Indians had been added to our country by the ending of the Mexican war, and many of these Indians were made citizens by the treaty. People had been flocking to California and the Western plains, and complicating Indian administration still further. After the war of secession, in 1866, provision was made for the enlistment of Indians in our armies as scouts,—an excellent step lately followed up by the present administration. Other changes were caused by the Pacific Railroad; for as General [Francis A.] Walker says, "In 1867-69 the great plough of industrial civilization drew its deep furrow across the continent, from the Missouri to the Pacific, . . . (bringing changes) which without it would have been delayed for half a century." The Revised Statutes of the United States, compiled in

1874, reveal the still increasing complexity of Indian affairs. The "peace policy" had been adopted, and we find now not merely the regular Indian commissioner authorized in 1832, but an additional board of commissioners, not exceeding ten (serving without pay), to supervise contracts and purchases for Indians, and for other purposes; also five salaried inspectors to visit, examine, and report on the different superintendencies and agencies, and see to enforcing the due performance of their duty by the superintendents, agents, and other employees. The old provisions for authority to the President to employ teachers among the Indians, "with their own consent," are retained. In general we mark an increase of interference with the Indians and of discretionary power over them in the executive department, as in allowing the President to distribute the money or goods due to a tribe to the heads of families (instead of the tribal authorities), and directly to the individuals who are entitled to participate. Agents are required to protect in the enjoyment of their lands those Indians who have received lands in severalty, and are desirous to adopt the habits of civilized life. This draws attention to a process which had been going on by treaty, of dividing up tribal lands to the individual Indians. If any other Indian molest a landowner, the tribal annuities are to be cut down; and if the trespasser be a chief, the local superintendent of Indian affairs *may depose him from his office* of chief for three months. Think of that,—the deposing of the sacred ruler of a separate "nation" by a small United States official! This is indeed a bold inroad on the theory of Indian self-government. The sale of ardent spirits to any Indian under the charge of a superintendent, *anywhere in the country*, is forbidden—a restraint upon Indians which does not apply to any other class of human beings. The general laws of the United States defining and punishing forgery and depredations on the mails are also extended to the Indian country, by a statute of 1855.

Meantime, the practices of the agents and of the Indian Department generally had more than kept pace in this direction with the course of legislation. "Under the traditional policy of the United States," says General Walker, "the Indian agent was a minister resident to a domestic dependent nation." But in actual fact he had grown long ago to be a ruler over them. "All offenses," wrote an Indian agent to the commissioner in September, 1890, "are punished *as I deem expedient*, and the Indians offer no resistance."

It remains to speak more particularly of three recent statutes, and then to consider the duty of our government.

Three important statutes about the Indians remain to be mentioned, one of which was incorporated in the Revised Statues.

(*a.*) A statute of March 3, 1871, reads: "No Indian nation or tribe within the territory of the United States shall be acknowledged or recognized as an independent nation, tribe, or power with whom the United States may contract by treaty,"—saving, however, the obligation of previous treaties. This was enacted twenty years ago. Did it abolish the existence of these separate political powers, nations, or tribes? No, we all know that they have continued and been recognized just as before. Did it abolish the carrying on of war with the Indians? No, we remember the horrible events of last winter, and a recent judicial decision in South Dakota, that the Indian known as "Plenty Horses" was not guilty of homicide in killing a white man during those troubles, because it was not an act of war. Do we then carry on war with Indians and not make treaties with them? Yes. A strange and absurd situation, is it not? Yet we do make "agreements" with them as with a separate people; and the chief result of this law is, and was intended to be, that it is no longer the President and Senate (the treaty-making power) that conclude these measure, but the legislative body, Congress. This statute was the result of a struggle on the part of the House of Representatives to share in these proceedings, and was forced upon the Senate on the last day of a session by putting it into an appropriation bill. It was thought at the time by so competent an observer as General Walker, formerly Commissioner of Indian Affairs, to be "a deadly blow at the tribal autonomy;" and so it was, in the logic of it. But the step was not then followed up, for it did not represent any clear determination of Congress to end the old methods; and this strange notion of refusing to make treaties with a people with whom we continue to go to war has remained on our statute book as another of the many anomalies that mark our Indian policy. Is it not plain, however, that if we abandon the policy of treaties with Indians we should give up the practice of war with them? Our arrangements with them are now called agreements; but this gives them no added sanction; they are still to be dealt with on the analogy of treaties.

(*b.*) The second statute to which I refer is that of March 3, 1885. It followed up timidly the logic of the law of 1871, though for only a step or two; but it marked the greatest advance yet reached in the process of assuming the direct government of the Indians. The law provides that thereafter Indians should be punished for committing upon Indians or others any one of seven leading crimes (murder, manslaughter, assault with intent to kill, rape, arson, burglary, or larceny); if in a Territory (whether on or off a reservation), under the territorial laws and in the territorial courts; and if in a State and on a reservation, then under the same laws and in the same courts as if the act were done in a place within the exclusive jurisdiction of the United States. This is a very important statute. In principle it claims for the United States full jurisdiction over the Indians upon their reservations, whether in a State or Territory. Heretofore, the laws, for example the statute of 1817 and the renewals of it, had excepted the acts of Indians committed upon their fellows within the Indian country. The acts of Indians against white persons or of whites against Indians had been dealt with, but the internal economy of Indian government was not invaded in its dealing or refusing to deal with the relations of members of the tribe to one another. The constitutionality, even, of such legislation as this of 1885 had been denied. Judges had been careful to avoid asserting this full power in cases where the reservation was in a State. Thus the Supreme Court of the United States, in 1845, in holding good the law of 1817, which punished (in this particular case) the act of a white man against a white man in the Indian country, among the Cherokees, said: "Where the country occupied by them is not within the limits of one of the States, Congress may by law punish any offense committed there, no matter whether the offender be a white man or an Indian." In 1834 Mr. Justice [John] McLean had denied the power of Congress to legislate in this way for an Indian reservation in a State, while admitting it in a Territory; and in December, 1870, the judiciary committee of the Senate of the United States even went so far as to say, "An act of Congress which should assume to treat the members of a tribe as subject to the municipal jurisdiction of the United States would be unconstitutional and void." But the air was at last cleared in 1886, when the Supreme Court of the United States had to deal with the indictment, under this statute, of one Indian for the murder of another Indian on a reservation in the State of California. It was laid down in this case, one of the landmarks of our Indian law, that the government of the United States has full power, under the Constitution, to govern the Indians as its own subjects, if it sees fit to do so, and to such partial or full extent as it sees fit; that nothing in the tribal relation or in any previous recognition of it by the United States cuts down this legislative power; that this is so not merely in the Territories, but on reservations within the States. The case, as I said, arose on a reservation in the State of California. "This proposition itself," said the court, with no dissent, speaking through Mr. Justice [Samuel F.] Miller (that is, the proposition to punish under the laws of a Territory and by its courts a tribal Indian who commits a crime upon another tribal Indian on a reservation in a Territory),

> is new in legislation of Congress. . . . The second, which applies solely to offenses . . . committed within the limits of a State and . . . of a reservation, . . . is a still further advance as asserting this jurisdiction over the Indians within the limits of the States of the Union. . . . After an experience of a hundred years of the treaty-making system of government, Congress has determined upon a new departure,—to govern them by acts of Congress. . . . It seems to us that this is within the competency of Congress.

Not less important than the decision itself is the principle on which it is put. In supporting the statute the government counsel had relied on the clause in the Constitution which gives Congress power "to regulate commerce with . . . the Indian tribes." But the court boldly rejected this as "a very strained construction of this clause," and rested its decision upon no specific provision of the Constitution, but upon the just inferences to be drawn from the nature of the situation, namely, that the Indians are a decayed power, residing upon our soil and under the protection of the general government,—a people who must be governed by somebody, and whom, so long as their separate political existence is recognized by the United States, nobody but the United States has any right to govern. "The Constitution," says the court,

> is almost silent in regard to the relations of the government . . . to the numerous tribes of Indians within its borders. . . . While we are not able to see in wither of these clauses of the Constitution" (namely, the one relating to the basis of representation, "excluding Indians not taxed," or the clause giving Congress power to regulate commerce with the Indian tribes) "any delegation of power to enact a code of criminal law, . . . (yet) these Indians are within the geographical limits of the United States. The soil and the people within those limits are under the political control (either) of the government of the United States or of the States of the Union. There exist . . . but these two. The territorial governments owe all their power to the statutes of the United States. . . . (But) Congress has defined a crime committed within the State and made it punishable in the courts of the United States. . . . Congress has done it. It can do it with regard to all offenses to which the federal authority extends. . . . This is within the competency of Congress. These Indian tribes *are* the wards of the nation. They are . . . *dependent* on the United States, dependent largely for their daily good, dependent for their political rights. They owe no allegiance to the States and receive from them no protection. Because of the local ill feeling, the people of the States where they are found are often their deadliest enemies. From their very weakness and helplessness, so largely due to the course of dealing of the federal government with them and the treaties in which it has been promised them, arises the duty of protection, and with it the power . . . . The power of the general government . . . is necessary to their protection as well as to the safety of those among whom they dwell. It must exist in that government because it never has existed anywhere else, because the theatre of its exercise is within the geographical limits of the United States, because it never has been denied, and because it alone can enforce its laws on all the tribes.

Here, it will be noticed, is a comprehensive and statesmanlike declaration. It covers the entire ground; the government, if it pleases, can go on to extend its law fully over the Indians while they are still a separate people. Observe, now, one thing. The existence of this right and power, and the clear and authoritative declaration of it by the Supreme Court of the Untied States for the first time in 1886, have brought home to the Congress of the United States and to us all, now within these recent years, a great weight of responsibility. It may have been thought possible before to deny the legal power fully to govern the Indians, It cannot be denied now. Under such circumstances, the mere neglect or refusal to act is itself action, and action of the worst kind.

(*c.*) The third and last of these statutes—and the last upon which I shall comment—is the General Land in Severalty Law (often known as the Dawes Bill). This was passed in February, 1887, within nine months of the great decision upon which I have just been remarking: the dates are May 10, 1886, and February 8, 1887. But it was pending in Congress at the time of that decision, and had long been pending there under bitter opposition. This great enactment opens the way, within a generation or two, to settle the whole Indian question. Whether it is to be regarded as a good law or a bad one, however, depends on the moderation with which it is administered. The peculiarity of it is not that its methods are news, for similar arrangements had repeatedly been made, for a score of years before, in the case of particular tribes, as the Winnebagoes in 1863, the Stockbridge Munsee Indians in 1871, the Utes in 1880, and the Omahas in 1882. But now, by a general law applicable to all reservations, the President is given power to make almost every Reservation Indian outside the civilized tribes a landowner in severalty and a citizen of the United States *against his will*. The right of citizenship is made to follow the ownership of land.

The scheme of the act is this: Whenever the President thinks that any Indian reservation, or any part of one, is advantageous for agricultural or grazing purposes, he may cause the whole or any part of the reservation to be surveyed and allotted in severalty, in specified amounts, among all the heads of families, single persons and orphan children of the tribe or band. The Indian heads of families may select for their children, and the Indian agents for the orphans. If in four years from the ordering of an allotment, no selection is made in any given case, it may be made by an agent on the order of the Secretary of the Interior. Patents (that is, deeds) are to be issued by the Secretary of the Interior on his approval of the allotments, setting forth that the United States will hold the land in trust for the allottee for twenty-five years, and then convey in fee to him or his heirs, free of all incumbrances. Meantime the allottee cannot convey or incumber the land, and, as it seems, it is not taxable. When these allotments and patents are all made (and perhaps sooner) the Indians are said by the terms of the statute to pass at once from the jurisdiction of the United States to that of the Territory or State in which the reservation is situated, and to become at once citizens of the United States. The construction of the law is doubtful, but it is the view, I believe, of the Indian Bureau at Washington that these results happen not merely when all is done, but man by man, as each has his allotment and patent. I venture to question the soundness of that view. This statute also provides for allotments, with like results, to tribal Indians not on reservations who may settle upon the public lands. It makes citizens at once of all Indians who leave their tribe and voluntarily live apart from it, adopting the habits of civilized life. This last class of persons had been declared by the Supreme Court of the United States, in November, 1884, not to be citizens of the United States, in the absence of such legislation. It is important, also, to notice that Indians are stimulated to take their allotments by a clause that this shall be a ground of preference in appointments on the Indian police and other public offices.

But the allotment may leave a surplus of land still belonging to the Indians. The Severalty Act provides that after the lands have been allotted to all the tribe, or sooner if the President thinks it for the interest of the tribe, such portions as they will consent to sell may be purchased by the United States, for the sole purpose of selling it again (in tracts of not over one hundred and sixty acres to any one person) to actual settlers, who are not to have a deed until after five years of occupancy. The money is to be held by the United States for the benefit of the Indians. One observes that this last provision for obtaining the surplus land requires the consent of the tribe; the allotment does not. What happens, then, if this consent is not given? Evidently the tribe and tribal ownership of land may continue for some purposes after all the allotments are made. There are other difficulties in the construction of the act; but these need not detain us.

Now this statute puts it in the power of the President to forward rapidly the absorption of the Indians into our body politic. It does not compel him to do it. How fast he will move we cannot tell; but it is manifestly possible for him to move a great deal faster than is wise. It cannot be well to incorporate into our Western Territories and States the bulk of the Reservation Indians as citizens within any short time. Observe what Senator Dawes said at the Mohonk Conference in October, 1887, soon after the passing of this law:

> President Cleveland said that he did not intend, when he signed this bill, to apply it to more than one reservation at first, and so on, which I thought was very wise. But you see he has been led to apply it to half a dozen. The bill provides for capitalizing the remainder of the land for the benefit of the Indian, but the greed of the land-grabber is such as to press the application of this bill to the utmost. There is no danger but this will come most rapidly,—too rapidly, I think. The greed and hunger and thirst of the white man for the Indian's land are almost equal to his "hunger and thirst for righteousness." That is going to be the difficulty in the application of this bill. He is going to press it forward too fast.

And the Senator added this advice: "Say that no Indian shall be put upon a homestead, under this act, until he realizes what is meant by it, and until he has such material round about him as will enable him to maintain himself there, and then let him work out his own destiny." That was wisely said.

In order to guard against this danger, there ought to be an amendment to the Severalty Law, requiring for many years to come the sort of evidence of fitness which has heretofore been demanded in several case of allotments authorized by treaty or special law, as in that of certain Wisconsin Indians in 1865, and certain Kansas Indians in 1873. In the last-named case the provision was this:

> If any adult member of said tribe shall desire to become a citizen of the United States, shall prove by at least two competent witnesses, to the satisfaction of the Circuit Court of the United States for the State of Kansas, that he or she is sufficiently intelligent and prudent to manage his or her own affairs, and has for the period of five years been able to maintain himself or herself and family, and has adopted the habits of civilized life, and shall take an oath of allegiance to the United States, as provided by law for the naturalization of aliens, he or she shall be declared by said court to be a citizen of the United States, which shall be entered of record, and a certificate thereof given to said party.

This sort of provision, in the case of an adult, is a reasonable and fit one. Without it there is no sufficient assurance that the Indians will not be crowded out into the world much too fast. I notice that our excellent Indian commissioner, General [Thomas J.] Morgan, who will remain in his present office, I trust, until he is promoted to a higher one, expresses the very sensible opinion, in his last report, that the surplus land ought not to be negotiated for until the allotments are all made. Now consider what the pressure to get hold of these lands is going to be. "The greed of the land-grabber," like a strong mainspring, will be forever operating to secure the surplus land. If, as seems wise, the allotments must first be made, then it will be forever operating to secure allotments; and if, as the law is now interpreted, the Indians cannot have their allotments and patents without being thereby made citizens and subject to state and territorial law, the pressure of this dangerous and constant mainspring will be transferred to that point, and will be felt in a most serious way in hurrying them out from under the protection of the general government long before they should go. Consider what the condition of a vast proportion of them still is. "I wish," said the agent at the Santee Agency in Nebraska, in his report to the commissioner in August last, "To impress upon the department that these Indians are yet as overgrown children. But very few of the adults are able to speak English, and during this generation will need more or less encouragement and training." Remember the Messiah craze, and the state of advancement in civilization that it indicated. An agent of the Sac and Fox Reservation in Iowa reported to the commissioner last August: "I have lived near these people twenty years, and I can see but little improvement among them during that time as a whole. . . . (Their) general appearance . . . to-day is one of filth, ignorance, laziness, and poverty."

Again, if it be true, as it is thought to be in some quarters (although I do not believe it), that the Indians, as fast as they get their allotments, are taken by this law wholly out from the possibility of control by such courts as may be constitutionally provided on the reservations for the tribal Indians who have not yet had allotments, then in that respect the law should be changed. They should not be so taken out. They should be held under the protection of the United States, as regulated through courts of its own upon the reservations, for a considerable period.

Still further, since the Indian land cannot be taxed for twenty-five years, the United States government should pay the local taxes; otherwise these poor people, when enlarged, cannot get any proper help from the authorities of their counties or States. What an undesirable neighbor will he be who pays no taxes, and expects other people to tax themselves to support him in the matter of roads, schools, and courts? This mischief has already been bitterly felt among the Omahas and others. Read, for instance, what the agent at the Sisseton Reservation in South Dakota says, in his report of September 29, 1890, to Commissioner Morgan. He is speaking of Indians who have lately been made citizens.

> In this connection I will state that although the law of Congress and the department authorities direct these Indians to the county courts of the settlement of all minor crimes and civil cases, still it is apparent that this course at present is impracticable. The authorities of the counties decline to audit any expenses of prisoners, paupers, or litigants who hold lands under the allotment act. All the information I have upon this subject convinces me that Indians and mixed bloods who hold lands under the allotment act will not have the same privileges as the white man in the county courts. Nor will prisoners', paupers', and litigants' expenses be paid.

Under the law as it now stands this result is almost unavoidable. Of course, also, education must be provided for, and we may well second and applaud the far-seeing plans of General Morgan to that end. I only wish that he would insist more upon one point, namely, that no education can be better for these Indians, as a preparation for the condition of citizenship, than practice in political usages and duties,—a chance, for instance, to vote in town meeting and serve on a jury, a chance to spend their own money and earn their own living, with the ordinary security and restraints of legal obligation and legal right, the ordinary stimulus of competition, and the ordinary hope of gain. There is no education, there is no civilizing agency, so important as this for the present generation of Indians who are beyond childhood, and so for all of them as they pass that line.

While, then, this great measure, the Severalty Law, in course of time is going to put an end to the strange anomaly of the Indian situation, in that form of it which now presses upon our attention,—that is, as touching the bulk of the tribal Indians outside the so-called civilized tribes,—the process must inevitably take many years. How many? The Commissioner of Indian Affairs informed me recently that in the four years and a half (nearly) since the Severalty Law was passed about 12,752 allotments have been made under its provisions, and about 1437 patents have been issued,—say at the average of 2800 allotments a years, and 600 patents. Patents, it will be remembered, are issued upon the approval of allotments by the Secretary of the Interior. That leaves about thirteen times as many more allotments to be made, and the time required for winding up the reservations, at that rate, would be nearly sixty years. Suppose it to be half that time,—this is quite too long to allow us to yield to the arguments of those who say: "Let the matter alone; it is a vanishing state of things; all will have passed away before you can mend matters." During this process of "vanishing," such bloody fruits of our present system are showing themselves, and will continue to show themselves, as the dreadful outbreak and slaughter of last winter. How soon we can mend matters depends on ourselves and our representatives at Washington. Matters can be mended at the next session of Congress if the people sternly demand it.

What then shall we do?

(1.) We must not leave things alone for one or two generations, to be worked out by the Severalty Law unaided. We cannot do that. See what General Morgan says of the existing system, in his last report:

> The entire system of dealing with them (the Indians) is vicious, involving as it does the installing of agents with semi-despotic power over ignorant, superstitious, and helpless subjects; the keeping of thousands of them on reservations practically as prisoners, isolated from civilized life, and dominated by fear and force; the issue of rations and annuities, which inevitably tends to breed pauperism; the disbursement of millions of dollars' worth of supplies by contract, which invites fraud; the maintenance of a system of licensed trade, which stimulates cupidity and extortion.

If it be thought that a wise and steady administration of the present system will answer well enough, I reply that we cannot have, under such a government as ours, a steady, firm, uniform administration of the merely political sort, in the case of so complicated a matter as our Indian affairs. Good administration is the weak point in our form of government; for the proof of that it is enough to appeal to the record of a hundred years. We may mend and patch, but the result will be bad oftener than good.

(2.) If it be said, "Very well, let us hurry through the allotments; let us do as was done with the slaves after the war, remove all civil disabilities at once and set up the Indians forthwith as citizens," I have already dealt with that sort of suggestion. But let me say a word or two more. This is, indeed, the kind of short cut which suits a democratic people when it is once aroused to the necessity of have a change; then the tendency is to go straight to the mark. One reason for this is the instinctive apprehension, in such a community, of its own weakness in administering any complicated system or adhering long and steadily to a purpose. The slow method (it says to itself), the method of gradual approach, is not safe. Accordingly, we all know that this sort of swift dispatch has been urged. It is the way which preoccupied and impatient minds are apt to recommend; and some others also. It was the one preferred by that excellent soldier and friend of the Indians, General [George] Crook. Undoubtedly it has its advantages. To give the Indians the ballot at once would do for them what was done for the slaves; it would put into their hands a weapon which would powerfully help them in working out their political salvation among their neighbors. Whatever temporary disturbances may take place, the ultimate result is certain, that he who has the ballot is one who will be protected from abuse. Such was General Crook's reasoning about it.

But this course, as I have said, has insuperable objections. The great body of the tribal Indians are totally unfit for the ballot, and it would be inexcusable to force such a body of voters suddenly upon the States where they live. It was bad enough, although politically necessary, to do this sort of thing at the end of the war, in communities which had revolted, staked all upon war, and lost. It would be inexcusable to do it in the midst of a loyal population, who are entitled to have their wishes consulted by the government. And above all, it would be an abandonment by the government of its highest present duty to the red men, that of governing and sheltering them. In view of what has happened at the South with the negroes, and of the well-known local hostility to the Indians at the West, it cannot be doubted that they would suffer much. Remember that with the giving of full citizenship there would take place a loss of all power in the federal government to legislate specially for them. Nothing is clearer than that they need, and will need for a good while, the very careful and exceptional protection of the nation. The power to give this special and exceptional protection exists, now, growing out of the strange political situation which I have expounded; and it is the one best thing there is about the present state of things. We must seize upon this and use it.

(3.) How shall we use it? That is the question that still recurs. We use our power now in dealing with the Indians by this vile process which pretends to leave them to govern themselves, and yet, in its actual application, denies them liberty and shuts them up on reservations; pauperizes them; insults and breaks down all of law, custom, and religion that they have inherited from their fathers and have been taught to venerate; excludes civilization, trade, law; and subjects them to the unsteady tyranny of the politicians. This way of using our power should be at once abandoned. But there is a wise way to use it, and I am glad to say that while Congress has lagged the Indian commissioners have made, since 1882, a slight but useful beginning in the right direction. Upon some agencies the agent is directed to appoint Indians to hear and judge the complaints of their fellows against one another, subject to the revision of the agent himself, and ultimately of the commissioner. The testimony is uniform, I think, as to the salutary and steadying effect of these "courts." Of course they are not courts in our ordinary sense, for they do not administer law, but merely certain rules of the Indian Department. They bear about the same relation to courts, in the proper sense of the term, that courts-martial do; they are really a branch of the executive department. But their effect in educating the Indians and assisting the department in its heavy burden of government has been such as to point clearly to the wisdom of following up this good beginning (the suggestion of Commissioner Hiram Price, I believe) and giving the Indians real courts and real law. This is what we must do,—extend law and courts of justice to the reservations.

A simple thing, indeed, is it not? Does this seem to my reader, I wonder, as it does to me, obviously just, obviously wise, obviously expedient? Yet our legislators at Washington let it linger year after year, and we cannot get it done. We must demand of them that they no longer neglect it,—that they abandon any attitude of obstruction upon this subject, any mistaken fancy that the Severalty Law has actually done all that have been made possible by it. I express the conviction not merely of one person, but of a vast number of the friends of the Indians, in declaring that the one most pressing and vital necessity to-day, in this matter, is that of bringing the Indians and all their affairs under the steady operation of law and courts. This is saying no new thing. Many of us who had the honor of advocating the Severalty Law before it was passed always coupled it with the demand for extending law to the Indians. This necessity has long been obvious; indeed, it sickens one to look back and see how uniform and how pressing has been the cry for this, during many years, as the thing most needful.

Let me repeat some of these utterances. Nearly twenty years ago, in 1873, the Indian commissioner urged this matter in his report, and again, in 1874, pressed it, with careful specific recommendations for establishing a system of law among the Indians. In 1876 the Indian commissioner (J. Q. Smith) said in his annual report:

> My predecessors have frequently called attention to the startling fact that we have within our midst 275,000 people, the least intelligent portion of our population, for whom we provide no law, either for their protection or for the punishment of crime committed among themselves. . . . Our Indians are remitted by a great civilized government to the control, if control it can be called, of the rude regulations of petty ignorant tribes. Year after year we expend millions of dollars for these people, in the faint hope that, without law, we can civilize them. That hope has been to a great degree a long disappointment, and year after year we repeat the folly of the past. That the benevolent efforts and purposes of the government have proved so largely fruitless is, in my judgment, due more to its failure to make these people amenable to our laws than to any other cause, or to all other causes combined. I believe it to be the duty of Congress at once to extend over Indian reservations the jurisdiction of the United States courts, and to declare that each Indian in the United States shall occupy the same relation to law that a white man does. . . . I regard this

suggestion as by far the most important which I have to make in this report.

In 1877 the wise and devoted Bishop [William Hobart] Hare said, in a passage which was quoted at length by the Indian commissioner in his report of 1883 with renewed recommendations:

> Civilization has loosened, in some places broken, the bonds which regulate and hold together Indian society in its wild state, and has failed to give the people law and officers of justice in their place. This evil still continues unabated. Women are brutally beaten and outraged; men are murdered in cold blood; the Indians who are friendly to schools and churches are intimidated and preyed upon by the evil-disposed; children are molested on their way to school, and schools are dispersed by bands of vagabonds: but there is no redress. This accursed condition of things is an outrage upon the one Lawgiver. It is a disgrace to our land. It should make every man who sits in the national halls of legislation blush. And, wish well to the Indians as we may, and do for them what we will, the efforts of civil agents, teachers, and missionaries are like the struggles of drowning men weighted with lead as long as, by the absence of law, Indian society is left without a base.

In that same year (1877) Indian agents declared over and over again that a system of law on the reservations was the great need. "By far the greatest need of this agency," said one of them, "is civil law. Give us civil law and power to execute it." In 1878 the Indian commissioner in his report quoted Joseph, the famous and very able Nez Percé chief, as saying that

> the greatest want of the Indians is a system of law by which controversies between Indians and between Indians and white men can be settled without appealing to physical force. . . . Indians . . . understand the operation of laws, and if there were any statutes the Indians would be perfectly content to place themselves in the hands of a proper tribunal, and would not take the righting of their wrongs into their own hands or retaliate, as they now do, without the law.

How many of my readers have ever read that wonderful, most moving story of this same Chief Joseph, sent by Bishop Hare to the North American Review, and published there in April 1879? In introducing it the bishop expressed his own appreciation of it by saying, "I wish that I had words at command in which to express adequately the interest with which I have read the extraordinary narrative which follows." The emphasis that Joseph lays upon the need of law is striking. "There need be no trouble," he declares.

> Treat all men alike. Give them all the same law. Give them all an even chance to live and grow. . . . I only ask of the government to be treated as all other men are treated. . . . I know that my race must change. We cannot hold our own with the white race as we are. We only ask an even chance to live as other men live. . . . We ask that the same law shall work alike on all men. If the Indian breaks the law, punish him by the law. If the white man breaks the law, punish him also.

Bishop Hare enforces this request. "Indian chiefs," he says, "however able and influential, are really without power, and for this reason, as well as others, the Indians . . . should at the earliest practicable moment be given the support and protection of our government and of our law." In March of the same year, (1879) General [Nelson] Miles printed an article on The Indian Problem in the North American Review, in which he pressed the need of establishing law and courts of justice among the Indians. He quoted Chief Joseph's words that "the greatest want of the Indians is a system of law," etc., and added, "Do we need a savage to inform us of the necessity that has existed for a century?"

In 1881 General Crook, General Miles, and others, as commissioners appointed by the President to investigate certain matters relating to the Ponca tribe, closed their report as follows:

> In conclusion we desire to give expression to the conviction forced upon us by our investigation of this case that it is of the utmost importance to white and red men alike that all Indians should have an opportunity of appealing to the courts for the protection and vindication of the rights of person and property. Indians cannot be expected to understand the duties of men living under the forms of civilization until they know, by being subject to it, the authority of stable law as administered by the courts, and are relieved from the uncertainties and oppression frequently attending subjection to arbitrary personal authority.

In 1884 Miss Alice Fletcher said, in a public address wholly devoted to the need of law on the Indian reservations: "Were the Indians as keen for crime as many believe them to be, not a human being could be safe in their midst during the present hiatus between the old tribal law and our failure to give the protection of the courts. Although matters are not at their worst, they are bad indeed, and it is almost futile to try to build up a people when the very stay and supports of industry and morality are lacking." These remarks were accompanied by convincing illustrations of their truth drawn from her experience among the Omahas. In Miss Fletcher's learned and thorough Special Report to the Bureau of Education on Indian Education and Civilization, published as a Senate Document by the United States in 1888, she comments again upon "the need for recasting the entire legal position of Indians towards the state and towards each other, and of permitting the laws of the land to be fully extended over all the various reservations and tribes."

For many years that admirable association in Philadelphia of which Mr. Herbert Welsh is secretary has urged this matter, and as early as eight or ten years ago had prepared a bill which embodied it. In a report of Mr. Herbert Welsh to his society, made in 1885, he presses (to quote his own words) "the immediate introduction of law upon the reservations." For years, also, the Boston Indian Citizenship Committee has devoted itself to efforts for accomplishing this purpose. In February last it issued a memorial, in which the following language was used:

> The Boston Indian Citizenship Committee, in view of recent events at the West, renews its solemn appeal to Congress and the country for the immediate extension of the ordinary laws of the land over the Indian reservations. . . . We desire to record our belief that this country has no duty towards the Indians so solemn and so instant as that of bringing these poor people under the protection and the control of the ordinary laws of the land.

Year after year the same appeal has come from the Mohonk Conference.

So long, so uniform, so weighty, so urgent, has been this appeal for a government of law for the Indians, and yet the thing is not done. Why? Perhaps the chief reasons are three: (1.) That there has been no one man in Congress who was deeply impressed with the importance of this particular step. Some men there appear to think the Severalty Law a finality, instead of one great step to be followed by others. (2.) That the whole Indian question gets little hold on public men, and is crowded aside by tariffs and silver, and President-making and office-jobbing and pension-giving. (3.) That so far as questions of Indian policy get any attention, this is spent on matters of detail, and in administering and patching the present system. But, I may be asked, do you call all this effort for the education of the Indians and their religious teaching, and the improvement of the civil service among them,—all these things matters of detail? Well, it would be an extravagance to say that, and yet sometimes one can best convey his meaning and best intimate the truth by an extravagance. I am almost ready to answer, *Yes, I do.* This, at any rate, I will say: It is as true now as it was fifteen years ago, when Indian Commissioner J. Q. Smith put it on record in his annual report: "That the benevolent efforts and purposes of the government have proved so largely fruitless is . . . due more to its failure to make these people amenable to our laws than to any other cause, or to all other causes combined." It is as true to-day as it was fourteen years ago when Bishop Hare said it first, and as it was eight years ago when the Indian commissioner quoted it with approval in his annual report, and seven years ago when Miss Fletcher quoted and indorsed it, that, "Wish well to the Indians as we may, and do for them what we will, the efforts of civil agents, teachers, and missionaries are like the struggles of drowning men weighted with lead as long as, by the absence of law, Indian society is left without a base." It is as true now as it was thirteen years ago, when the Indian commissioner quoted it from one of the ablest of the Indian chiefs, that "the greatest want of the Indians is a system of law by which controversies between Indians and between Indians and white men can be settled without an appeal to physical force."

Will not my reader agree with me, then, in saying that the time has come when all causes of obstruction and delay must give way; when (1) we must find or place some men at Washington who *are* profoundly impressed with the necessity of a government of law for the Indians; when (2) we must cause it to be understood that this matter is no longer to be shoved aside by any question whatever; and when (3), in dealing with the Indian question, this matter of establishing law among the Indians must take precedence for the time being of all other aspects of the subject? The Indian associations of the country and all individual friends of the Indian should now gather themselves together and concentrate their efforts for a time upon this single point. They have very great influence when they unite; they can, if they please, make such an appeal to Congress and the Executive as will speedily be heeded.

Since the spring of 1888 a carefully prepared bill for accomplishing the objects I have named has been pending in the Senate of the United States. It has the support of some of the best lawyers in the country. It was prepared by a committee of the Mohonk Conference, and has been steadily supported by the leading Indian associations. That bill, or something better, should be passed at the next session of Congress.

Source: James Bradley Thayer, "A People Without Law," *Atlantic Monthly* 68 (October 1891):540-51, and (November 1891):676-87.

4-13. Annual Message to Congress

Benjamin Harrison

December 9, 1891

Grandson of President William Henry Harrison and son of John Scott Harrison, Benjamin Harrison (1833-1901) came from a distinguished Virginia and Ohio lineage. A graduate of Miami University (Ohio), Civil War veteran, Indianapolis lawyer, and Republican political figure, Harrison, a native Ohioan, served in the U.S. Senate representing Indiana from 1881 to 1887, and as president of the United States from 1889 to 1893. The Wounded Knee massacre occurred during his administration. In his written third annual message to Congress, dated December 9, 1891, practically one year exactly since Wounded Knee in South Dakota, Harrison briefly commented on the controversy, noting that the Sioux were "naturally warlike and turbulent." A Gilded Age passive president, who fit the time, Harrison neither assumed responsibility for the incident nor offered a formal apology to grieving Native American families. Instead, he brushed over the problem, credited General Nelson A. Miles with having protected white settlers, and then concentrated on other matters pertaining to Native Americans in the United States.

. . . The work in the Bureau of Indian Affairs was perhaps never so large as now, by reason of the numerous negotiations which have been proceeding with the tribes for a reduction of the reservations, with the incident labor of making allotments, and was never more carefully conducted. The provision of adequate school facilities for Indian children and the locating of adult Indians upon farms involve the solution of the "Indian question." Everything else—rations, annuities, and tribal negotiations, with the agents, inspectors, and commissioners who distribute and conduct them—must pass away when the Indian has become a citizen, secure in the individual ownership of a farm from which he derives his subsistence by his own labor, protected by and subordinate to the laws which govern the white man, and provided by the General Government or by the local communities in which he lives with the means of educating his children. When an Indian becomes a citizen in an organized State or Territory, his relation to the General Government ceases in great measure to be that of a ward; but the General Government ought not at once to put upon the State or Territory the burden of the education of his children.

It has been my thought that the Government schools and school buildings upon the reservations would be absorbed by the school systems of the States and Territories; but as it has been found necessary to protect the Indian against the compulsory alienation of his land by exempting him from taxation for a period of twenty-five years, it would seem to be right that the General Government, certainly where there are tribal funds in its possession, should pay to the school fund of the State what would be equivalent to the local school tax upon the property of the Indian. It will be noticed from the report of the Commissioner of Indian Affairs that already some contracts have been made with district schools for the education of Indian children. There is great advantage, I think, in bringing the Indian children into mixed schools. This process will be gradual, and in the meantime the present educational provisions and arrangements, the result of the best experience of those who have been charged with this work, should be continued. This will enable those religious bodies that have undertaken the work of Indian education with so much zeal and with results so restraining and beneficent to place their institutions in new and useful relations to the Indian and to his white neighbors.

The outbreak among the Sioux which occurred in December last is as to its causes and incidents fully reported upon by the War Department and the Department of the Interior. That these Indians had some just complaints, especially in the matter of the reduction of the appropriation for rations and in the delays attending the enactment of laws to enable the Department to perform the engagements entered into with them, is probably true; but the Sioux tribes are naturally warlike and turbulent, and their warriors were excited by their medicine men and chiefs, who preached the coming of an Indian messiah who was to give them power to destroy their enemies. In view of the alarm that prevailed among the white settlers near the reservation and of the fatal consequences that would have resulted from an Indian incursion, I placed at the disposal of General [Nelson] Miles, commanding the Division of the Missouri, all such forces as were thought by him to be required. He is entitled to the credit of having given thorough protection to the settlers and of bringing the hostiles into subjection with the least possible loss of life.

The appropriation of $2,991,450 for the Choctaws and Chickasaws contained in the general Indian appropriation bill of March 3, 1891, has not been expended, for the reason that I have not yet approved a release (to the Government) of the Indian claim to the lands mentioned. This matter will be made the subject of a special message, placing before Congress all the facts which have come to my knowledge.

The relation of the Five Civilized Tribes now occupying the Indian Territory to the United States is not, I believe, that best calculated to promote the highest advancement of these Indians. That there should be within our borders five independent states having no relations, except those growing out of treaties, with the Government of the United States, no representation in the National Legislature, its people not citizens, is a startling anomaly.

It seems to me to be inevitable that there shall be before long some organic changes in the relation of these people to the United States. What form these changes should take I do not think it desirable now to suggest, even if they were well defined in my own mind. They should certainly involve the acceptance of citizenship by the Indians and a representation in Congress. These Indians should have opportunity to present their claims and grievances upon the floor rather than, as now, in the lobby. If a commission could be appointed to visit these tribes to confer with them in a friendly spirit upon this whole subject, even if no agreement were presently reached the feeling of the tribes upon this question would be developed, and discussion would prepare the way for changes which must come sooner or later.

The good work of reducing the larger Indian reservations by allotments in severalty to the Indians and the cession of the remaining lands to the United States for disposition under the homestead law has been prosecuted during the year with energy and success. In September last I was enabled to open to settlement in the Territory of Oklahoma 900,000 acres of land, all of which was taken up by settlers in a single day. The rush for these lands was accompanied by a great deal of excitement, but was happily free from incidents of violence.

It was a source of great regret that I was not able to open at the same time the surplus lands of the Cheyenne and Arapahoe Reservation, amounting to about 3,000,000 acres, by reason of the insufficiency of the appropriation for making the allotments. Deserving and impatient settlers are waiting to occupy these lands, and I urgently recommend that a special deficiency appropriation be promptly made of the small amount needed, so that the allotments may be completed and the surplus lands opened in time to permit the settlers to get upon their homesteads in the early spring.

During the past summer the Cherokee Commission have completed arrangements with the Wichita, Kickapoo, and Tonkawa tribes whereby, if the agreements are ratified by Congress, over 800,000 additional acres will be opened to settlement in Oklahoma.

The negotiations for the release by the Cherokees of their claim to the Cherokee Strip have made no substantial progress so far as the Department is officially advised, but it is still hoped that the cession of this large and valuable tract may be secured. The price which the commission was authorized to offer—$1.25 per acre—is, in my judgment, when all the circumstances as to title and the character of the lands are considered, a fair and adequate one, and should have been accepted by the Indians.

Since March 4, 1889, about 23,000,000 acres have been separated from Indian reservations and added to the public domain for the use of those who desired to secure free homes under our beneficent laws. It is difficult to estimate the increase of wealth which will result from the conversion of these waste lands into farms, but it is more difficult to estimate the betterment which will result to the families that have found renewed hope and courage in the ownership of a home and the assurance of a comfortable subsistence under free and healthful conditions. It is also gratifying to be able to feel . . . that this work has proceeded upon lines of justice toward the Indian, and that he may now, if he will, secure to himself the good influences of a settled habitation, the fruits of industry, and the security of citizenship. . . .

Source: Benjamin Harrison, Third Annual Message, December 9, 1891, in James D. Richardson, comp., *A Compilation of the Message and Papers of the Presidents 1789-1897*, 10 vols. (Washington, D.C.: Government Printing Office, 1898), 10:201-03.

4-14. The Ghost Dance and Pine Ridge

Valentine T. O. McGillycuddy

1891

A physician and agent for Native Americans, Valentine Trant O'Connell McGillycuddy (1849-1939) was born in Racine, Wisconsin, earned a degree in 1869 from the Detroit College of Medicine, worked as a recorder and surgeon with the U.S. Survey of the Great Lakes from 1871 to 1874, and accepted General George Crook's invitation in 1876 to serve as a cavalry surgeon. As assistant post surgeon at Fort Robinson, Nebraska, McGillycuddy treated Crazy Horse's wife for tuberculosis and befriended Native Americans. He also attended Crazy Horse upon the latter's death in 1877. While meeting with federal officials in Washington in 1879, McGillycuddy complained about mistreatment of Natives directly to Secretary of the Interior Carl Schurz, who immediately chose McGillycuddy as agent for the Pine Ridge Sioux reservation in South Dakota, where he remained from 1879 to 1886. These years constituted the pinnacle of his career. He built new schools, installed a Native American police force to maintain peace, and removed corrupt white traders. In 1886 President Grover Cleveland dismissed McGillycuddy, a Republican, for insubordination after he refused to replace his chief clerk with a Democrat.

McGillycuddy, active in the movement for Dakota statehood and the division of the territory into two states, signed South Dakota's constitution. He served as assistant adjutant general for South Dakota from 1889 to 1898. When a new religious fervor, the Ghost Dance, preached by Wovoka, a Paiute from Nevada, threatened to disrupt harmony, McGillycuddy counseled inaction, believing that the movement would subside on its own. General John R. Brooke spurned McGillycuddy's prudent offer to negotiate between the Sioux and the U.S. Army. The massacre at Wounded Knee occurred on December 29, 1890. Had McGillycuddy been agent at the time instead of D. G. Royer, the catastrophe might have been averted.

In 1891 McGillycuddy reported his thoughts on the Ghost Dance and Pine Ridge, commenting that had he been the agent there he would have "let them dance themselves out." He added, "What right have we to dictate to them on a religious belief founded on the teaching of the religion of the white man? If the Seventh Day Adventists get up on the roof of their houses, arrayed in their ascension robes, to meet the 'second coming,' the U.S. Army is not rushed into the field." McGillycuddy scored an important point. The Ghost Dance posed no serious or permanent threat to the stability, legitimacy, or continuation in power of the U.S. government or its duly elected leaders. McGillycuddy also mentioned the activities of various individuals, including Red Cloud, Secretary of the Interior Lucius Q. C. Lamar (1885-1887), and Republican Governor Arthur C. Mellette of South Dakota (1889-1893).

It was a pitiable, disgraceful affair forced on Indians and whites alike by politics, graft and bad management.

I was in the field all that winter from November until February, as Asst. Adj. Gen. representing Gov. Mellette of Dakota with Indians, Troops, and settlers. . . .

Well, I had a devil of a time myself that winter. It was a "free lance" going and coming among Indians, Troops, and Settlers, the Indians friendly and hostile were all my friends, as were the troops, but necessarily I felt it in the air so to speak that I was more or less a "Persona non grata." I knew the past too well, and sized up existing conditions too well, and Washington and the Harrison administration knew it.

First thing, as a matter of form, I presented my credentials, as Asst. Adj. Gen., and Colonel on the Governor's Staff of the Sovereign State of Dakota, to Gen. John R. Brooke, U.S.A., who as Commanding officer of the Department of the Platte was sent in there with a thousand men, to protect Agent [Daniel F.] Royer at Pine Ridge, but I was all alone and had no army with me, did not even have my gorgeous colonel's uniform, and when I requested from the General permission to investigate matters, the old chap looked rather cross-eyed at me, and granted the permission, with the request that I would advise him of the result, etc.

The next day, Red Cloud and the other chiefs took me out to the "hostile" village or camp in the Bad Lands, and Red Cloud addressed the council, telling them that I was "Little Beard" who had been their agent winters ago, when I was a boy, which he did not like, and also that I had come from the army which he did not like, that he and I had quarreled a great deal, and that in those days I did many things as a boy, as *he* thought, just to show my power and authority, but my answer to that was it was for their good and some day they would see it.

Then Red Cloud stated, "I see it now, and if we had in those days listened to him we would not have this trouble now."

Then the old chief turned to me with the following words:

> Little Beard, we have not behaved half badly as we did in your day, but you never sent for troops. Why have these soldiers been brought here, coming in the night with their big guns? It looks as if they have come to fight, and if it is so, we must fight, but we are tired of war, and we think of our women and children, and our property, our homes, our little farms, and our cattle we are raising. Can you not send these soldiers away, and if you will, we give you twenty-five of our young men you can take as hostages, and everything will be settled in one sleep.

My reply had to be, "My friends, I am no longer your agent, and I have no power here, I only represent the Governor, but I will take your words to the soldier chief at the Agency."

That night I went over the conditions with Gen. Brooke, and in a very pompous manner he remarked, "Do you think that you could settle this matter?" My reply was, "Yes, I think so. Take the troops over the Nebraska line, and trouble will end."

He replied in a sarcastic manner, "You have an exalted opinion of your influence over these people."

I then turned loose as follows,

> Possibly, General, but I know these people. I have known them more years than you have days; ten of the best years of my life have been spent among them. They have my confidence, and vice versa. It is now November, a cold winter is coming; this is not the time Indians go on the warpath.
>
> I took charge of these people in 1879, I organized the Indian Police, had the troops removed, and for seven years we were without troops, sometimes in harder propositions than we have today, and I won out; these Indians are not fools. I cannot but regard it as a mistake to have run troops in here in a religious excitement; but you are here, and your presence will have to be justified, and it will be, because you are going to have the biggest racket you ever had on your hands.

He went up in the air, and had I not been there representing the Governor I think I would have been removed from the reservation.

The next night The Hereditary Chief, "Man Afraid" came to my cabin, with these words,

> Father, fourteen winters have passed since the Custer Massacre. The children of those days are our warriors now. They do not know the power of the white man, as we older people do, and they think that they can hold their own. The troops came here, Sitting Bull in the North at once sent his runners through to us to stir our young men up, and unless the soldiers are taken away, we will not be able to hold our young men.

A few days later, Special Indian Agent [James A.] Cooper, who had been sent out from the Indian Office in Washington to investigate conditions, came to me and an-nounced, "Major, I have instructions from the Indian Office to investigate you on charges," and after argument showed me a copy of a telegram from Agent Royer to the Indian Commissioner, reading as follows, "[Valentine T. O.] McGillycuddy is here abusing the administration, inciting the Indians to disturbance, and doing me dirt and I want him removed."

Major Cooper was at a loss what to do. So, to expedite matters, I opened up on the Indian Office by wire through the Governor, and insisted on an immediate investigation, as it was a charge that, if true, should warrant my being led out and shot, but I heard nothing more about it.

The end of December came and with it, the "Battle of Wounded Knee."

Riding in from the battle that day, to the agency, I was intercepted by a party of blanket Indians on a cross road in a wagon, and one of them accosted me in these words, "Little Beard, eleven years ago we made an agreement and promise with you that if we would give you fifty of our young men to act as police, you would have the white soldiers taken away, the police would control, and we would have a home government. We kept our promise, and you kept yours."

Then he threw his blanket off, and showed me a bullet hole through the left arm, received that day and from which the blood was trickling, remarking, "I was one of your police. Who brought back the soldiers, and what were they brought for?"

Very reluctantly I had to reply, "I am sorry, my friend, but I am no longer your agent."...

What was back of the Ghost Dance so far as Pine Ridge was concerned?

A shortage in the beef ration, resulting hunger, and a hard winter.

The Government Indian beef contract, provided that "all beef received under this contract shall be what is known as Northern Wintered Beef, i.e., fed for not less than two winters preceding delivery, on Northern Ranges." For experience has shown that the shrinkage on "through Texas beef," by reason of the severity of the Dakota winters, would amount to about 40 [percent] to 50 [percent].

In this connection it should be remembered that hides, horns, hoofs, and bones do not shrink, but the shrinkage comes out of the edible portion of the animal.

In the previous October 5,000 head of beef had been received under the contract to be herded for issue and food during the winter.

In January following the Battle of Wounded Knee, I examined the Agency Beef Herd, remaining out of that 5,000 head, and found that the animals were all "through Texas Beef" carrying nothing but the Texas brands, and no Northern Ranch brands, hence the shrinkage and resulting hunger.

About that time [George H.] Harries, correspondent for the *Washington Star*, happened along, and interviewed me, and he referred later in his paper to the Texas Beef matter, and that *did* get me into trouble.

Late in January, the "War" being over, I returned to my home in the Black Hills.

Along came an official letter from Pres. [Benajmin] Harrison's Indian Commissioner [Thomas J.] Morgan, an ex-Baptist preacher, calling my attention to the interview in the *Washington Star*, and remarking "Your attention is called to the fact that during your incumbence as Indian Agent at Pine Ridge, many grave charges were made against you, and it is not to be presumed that with your memory of these charges, you will now make statements that you can not substantiate; hence you are called upon for an explanation."

I replied that I had a very vivid recollection of those old charges, as I had been tried before Cleveland's Secretary of the Interior [Lucius C. Q.] Lamar on the same, but not convicted; but in that connection I failed to see how those old charges had anything to do with his feeding the Indians "through Texas beef" in violation of the contract, and I would look further into the matter and advise him.

I was at that time consulting surgeon for the Union Pacific Railroad, so I got access to their books, and traced the 5,000 head of beef from the time the same was loaded on to the cars at Clayton and Amarillo Stations, Texas, the prior August, until received at Pine Ridge, and so informed the Commissioner.

Naturally I became a "persona non grata," to politicians, contractors, and others, both Republican and Democratic.

Late in November, when the storm was brewing, I induced my old friend Little Wound, a leading War Chief, to call on Gen. Brooke and Agent Royer, at the Agency Office to talk over matters.

Gen. Brooke asked Little Wound if he was Ghost Dancer. His reply was:

> No, my friend, over sixty winters have passed over me and I am too old for dancing, but now that you have asked me that question I will tell you what I know and have heard about the Messiah and the Ghost Dance.

There have lived among my people for many winters the holy men or missionaries whom the Great Father has sent to us to teach us your religion, and how much better it is than ours. They bring with them the holy book, the Bible, from that book they tell us wonderful stories, they tell us of the man who went into the den of wild animals, and was not harmed because his Great Spirit protected him.

They tell us of the men who went into the fiery furnace, hot enough to melt bullets, but their hair was not even singed.

Then they tell us a wonderful story, of how many ages ago the white men's brains got to whirling, they lost theirs ears, they would listen no more to the Great Spirit, and they strayed off on the wrong road, and finally the Great Spirit sent his Son on earth to save them.

He lived with those white men for over thirty winters, and worked hard to get you back on the road, but you denied Him, and you finally nailed Him up on a great wooden cross, tortured, and killed Him. He was known as the Messiah, and when He was dying on the cross, it was promised that He would come again some time to try and save the people. These things the missionaries tell us.

About two moons ago there came to us from the far North, from the Yellowstone country, a young Cheyenne, named Porcupine, with a strange story. He had a vision—in it he was told to go to a large lake, in the Northwest (Walkers Lake, Nevada,) and there he would meet the Messiah.

He told me that the Messiah was a tall white man with golden hair and whiskers, and blue eyes, a well spoken man, and he said, "Porcupine, I am the Messiah; my father the Great spirit, has sent Me a second time to try and save the people, but when I was here before, they denied Me and killed Me. When the Spring time comes with the green grass, I am going to visit the different Indian people, and the whites.

"But this time I have arranged a certain dance and signs, and in my travels if I am so received I will stop with them and try and help them. If I am not received in these signs, I will pass them by.

"Now Porcupine, I will give you these signs and this dance, and you go ahead of Me and teach them to your people."

Said Little Wound: "Now whether Porcupine really saw the Messiah, or only had a pleasant dream, I do not know. I got my people together and said, 'My friends, if this is a good thing we should have it; if it is not, it will fall to the earth itself. So you better learn this dance, so if the Messiah does come he will not pass us by, but will help us to get back our hunting grounds and buffalo.'"

Then the old chief turned to me with these words, “My friend Little Beard, if the Messiah is *not* coming, and by his coming he will again make us a strong people and enable us to hold our own in this land given us as a home by the Great Spirit, and the white man is not afraid of that, *why* have these soldiers been brought here to stop the dance?”

I could not but remark to Gen. Brooke as follows,

> Little Wound’s remark, “if this is a good thing we should have it, if it is not, it will fall to earth itself,” is the key to the whole situation. It means that they will dance through the winter. The green grass comes, with it no Messiah, and the thing ends.
>
> If I were agent here, I would let them dance themselves out. What right have we to dictate to them on a religious belief founded on the teaching of the religion of the white man? If the Seventh Day Adventists get up on the roof of their houses, arrayed in their ascension robes, to meet the “second coming,” the U.S. Army is not rushed into the field. . . .

P.S. Go into the highways and the byways, and spread the gospel, smite the heathen, despoil them of their lands.

I remember the remark of my old friend Mark Twain, in talking with him on the Indian question:

> Our Pilgrim Fathers were a Godly people, when they landed that day on Plymouth Rock, from off the Mayflower, they fell upon their knees, they thanked Almighty God for the many blessings he had vouchsafed them that day, in enabling them to reach the land of liberty and free thought.
>
> Later on they fell upon the aborigines.

P.P.S. Additional from Chief Little Wound: “I try hard to see goodness in the White Man’s religion, and why he killed the Messiah, for if our Great Spirit, Wakan Tonka, the Great Mystery, were to send his Son on earth to help us, we would feel honored, build a great house for him, and try and keep him with us forever.”

Source: “Dr. V. T. McGillycuddy on the Ghost Dance,” in Stanley Vestal, *New Sources of Indian History, 1850-1891: The Ghost Dance, The Prairie Sioux, A Miscellany* (Norman: University of Oklahoma Press, 1934), 81-90.

4-15. Address to the People of the United States

Philip C. Garrett and Herbert Welsh

1891

At the tragic time and aftermath of the massacre at Wounded Knee in December, 1890, Herbert Welsh, secretary of the Philadelphia-headquartered Indian Rights Association, and Philip C. Garrett, president of that association, issued a public address to the people of the United States.

. . . In the presence of grave public emergency we ask your attention.

An Indian outbreak is now in progress which has cost the lives of many of our officers, of our soldiers, of the Indians themselves, men, women and children, including both the hostiles and loyal Indian police; which has destroyed the property of settlers and of Christian Indians; which has entailed an expenditure of many hundreds of thousands of dollars, and has occasioned widespread disturbances and terror. The attention of the entire country has been fully aroused, and the question is everywhere uppermost: What are the causes of this sad state of affairs? and what is the remedy to be applied for a settlement of present trouble and for the prevention of similar conditions in the future?

As the executive body of an association which has carried on active practical work for the civilization of the Indians for many years, which possesses reliable sources of information and has no interest other than the public good, we venture to point out what we believe to be the causes of the outbreak, each in its proper relation to the other, and to suggest the remedy.

The Sioux.

The Sioux Indians, among whom the disturbance exists, number approximately twenty-eight thousand souls. They subsist mainly on rations furnished by the government, given them in payment for land ceded by them to the United States, although many of them, under the guidance of agents and missionaries, have made laudable advances toward independence, and some of them are practically self-supporting.

There are two well-defined parties among the Sioux (a fact pertinent to a consideration of the present trouble)—a progressive party, almost wholly Christian, which has been created and developed under the influence of missionaries, both white and natives of various religious bodies—Congregational, Presbyterian, Roman Catholic and Episcopalian—who for many years have labored devotedly among these Indians. This progressive party represents the "new way," new ideas and new hopes, the ideas of Christianity and of civilization. It is loyal to the government, peaceable and steadily increasing in influence, industry and vigor. A few of the native leaders of this party are educated and refined men, while its members as a whole lead exemplary moral lives.

The Heathen Party.

Second, a heathen, non-progressive party, looking backward to the days of the buffalo, predatory warfare and unrestrained freedom, hostile to the advance of civilization, whether among the whites as a menacing force outside the reservation, or among the Indians themselves as a disintegrating force within. The occupation of the heathen party since reservation life began has been the consumption of government rations, dancing, wandering from place to place on visits to friends and relatives. This party has been represented by such men as Spotted Tail, Red Cloud and Sitting-Bull, from whom nothing in the line of progress was hoped for or has been obtained. Such leaders were always openly or secretly at enmity with the government and with the best interests of their people. They have discouraged or terrorized progressive Indians—have been a thorn in the side of good Indian agents and the masters of poor ones. It is a fact that cannot be too strongly emphasized that no dangerous and powerful heathen party could have existed had the government fulfilled solemn promises and its manifest duty to provide for the education of these people.

The advance of the Christian party stimulated the non-progressive party into more and more vigorous opposition, shown in repeated attempts to check the progress of enlightened sentiment.

Broken Promises.

Recent events gave the leaders of the non-progressives powerful arguments as a leverage to move the minds of their followers and to silence the voice of their opponents.

By a recent agreement made with the Sioux, which on the whole was to their advantage and to that of the whites, about eleven million acres of land were ceded to the United States. Some of the promises of compensation to the Indians for this reduction of their territory were not fulfilled, owing to the inaction of Congress, until within the past few days. Even this fulfilment would probably not have taken place now had it not been for bloodshed on the frontier. The failure promptly to make good the promises of the government, whether implied or expressed, produced serious discontent among the pagan Indians.

There has also been at Pine Ridge, the largest and most important Indian agency in the Sioux country, extreme suffering from hunger within the past year. This was caused by a large reduction of the amount of beef issued to the Indians, by the failure of their crops owing to the drought and other causes, some of which were unavoidable, resulting in distress and unavoidable discontent.

The Messiah Craze.

In conjunction with these causes for discontent must be placed the religious fanaticism known as the "Messiah Craze," which promised to the ignorant imagination of the pagan Indian all that he longed for and lacked—food, hunting, freedom, the expulsion of the white man.

These causes, linked together, produced serious conditions; but, in our opinion, the danger might have been averted had it not been for the last, most potent and determining cause—namely, the spoils system of appointment in the management of the Indian service, which supplied at the two most critical points in the Sioux country, Pine Ridge and Cheyenne River agencies, a disastrously inadequate management and control. . . .

Under the spoils system as applied to Indian management neither the President, the Secretary of the Interior nor the Commissioner of Indian Affairs is virtually the appointing officer, but Senators, Representatives or other powerful politicians, who discharge their obligations to their henchmen by obliging the Executive or his lieutenants to give them positions in the Indian service. Thus, men are chosen, not for the best, but for the worst reasons—not for merit, but as a reward for party service. Some good men are thus obtained, but the majority are poor, and some positively bad.

Bad Appointments.

The records of this association show numerous instances of the appointment of wholly unworthy or vicious persons through the operation of this system. But even the good are rarely retained in office until their work reaches fruition, because, according to the spoils theory, a change of administration means practically a change of the incumbents of all positions in the Indian service. The folly of adopting such a system in the conduct of a service of such peculiar delicacy and responsibility as the Indian one, where human life so frequently hangs in the balance, must be manifest to any thinking mind. If civil-service reform is desirable in other branches of government service, it is imperatively necessary here.

The evil is equally serious and deep-rooted under the administration of either party, and no greater obstacle exists to its eradication than the tendency of apologists of both parties to claim that the opposite one is responsible for its baneful results.

Sweeping Changes.

Under the last Democratic administration virtually a clean sweep was made in the Indian service: upward of fifty out of the fifty-eight Indian agents were removed, and there was general change in the minor positions. Under the present administration a similar course has been pursued, with the notable exceptions of that part of the service which is under the control of the present Indian Commissioner, who, we believe, has done all in his power to secure the adoption of the merit system in the school and other branches of the Indian service.

But the appointment of Indian agents has, during this administration, under the operation of what is termed the "home-rule" system, been handed over as perquisite of Senators and Representatives of the States and Territories in which the reservations are located.

Under the administration of both parties this society has steadily pursued the same arduous and thankless task of urging upon the Executive the relinquishment of the spoils system in the management of the Indians. It has illustrated the necessity for a change by the many instances coming to its knowledge of the removal of valuable officers and the appointment of inexperienced or unworthy ones.

The Spoils System.

Our publications and our letter-files attest at once the frequency and futility of our remonstrances. The spoils system has continued on its remorseless way. Perhaps it is one of those evils from which, without shedding of blood, there is no remission.

Through the spoils system the Pine Ridge Agency became the weakest point in the Sioux country. Under the last Democratic administration a Republican agent of unusual ability, courage and success was removed to make way for an inferior appointee of the opposite party, under whom discipline of the Indian, police force and of the agency generally declined. The Democratic Secretary of the Interior was warned of the danger attending this change, owing to the power and turbulence of the non-progressive Indians at Pine Ridge. The warning was unheeded.

Under the "home-rule" system of the present administration, which this society opposed as being "unsound in theory and likely to prove disastrous in practice," the inferior Democratic agent was supplanted by a still poorer Republican one. The last incumbent was wholly unacquainted with the Indians, ignorant whom to trust and whom to suspect, as were the employes whom he brought with him.

A Frightened Agent.

A trifling incident at a moment when the excitement of the "ghost dance" was at its height brought about the complete collapse of his authority. A futile attempt to arrest a single Indian in front of the agency buildings made one day last autumn, which was the occasion of momentary excitement, alarmed the agent so that he deserted his post, fled to the neighboring town and telegraphed for the military. He did not return until they marched in ahead of him—"horse, foot and artillery." This was the spark in the powder. The turbulent Indians, wild with mingled fear and rage, thinking that they were about to be massacred, fled to the Bad Lands, plundering the houses and destroying the property of the Christian Indians on the way.

They were thus committed to a hostile course and to the bloodshed and misery which followed. Had an experienced and resolute man been in charge of Pine Ridge, possessing the confidence of the Indians, backed by a strong force of Indian police, we believe that depredations and bloodshed would have been averted. Indeed, had such men been in charge of all the Sioux agencies, such conditions as prepared for the outbreak and precipitated it could scarcely have existed.

The Causes of the War.

A brief summary of the causes of the disturbance may properly precede a statement of the remedy which we suggest:

First. Ignorance through the failure of the government to supply education, and the sway of savage ideas in the minds of the non-progressive Sioux, which fostered latent hostility to the government which made them an easy prey to religious frenzy and suggested violence as a remedy for real or fancied wrongs.

Second. Hunger and disease—the grippe among the adults and measles among the children.

Third. Distrust of the good faith of the government, based on imperfect fulfilment of former promises and delay in the carrying out of the terms of the recent agreement.

Fourth. The spoils system as applied to the management of Indian affairs, which has supplied feeble or unwise management at some of the agencies, has prevented continuity and harmony in the government's work for the civilization of the Indians.

The remedy is simple in theory, but difficult, for manifest reasons, of execution.

The Remedy.

The first and most important requisition is a single, responsible, competent head for the management of Indian affairs, and charged with that duty only, who shall report directly to the President, and who shall be looked to by the country at large for a successful Indian management.

An Indian service wholly free from the interference of partisan politics, which shall continue its policy and carry out its educational work undisturbed by changing administrations.

While we do not advocate the complete transfer of Indian management to the War Department, we believe that all the advantages which the advocates of that plan desire could be obtained by detailing many able and experienced army officers to serve as Indian agents, without the counterbalancing disadvantages which we believe would result from so radical a change.

This suggestion has especial force from the fact that a few army officers have in the past served as Indian agents with excellent results.

The appropriation of sufficient money by Congress to permit the education of all Indian youth and the maintenance of a thoroughly effective service. Manifestly, it is the part of wisdom to give enough money to do the work in hand if there be a thoroughly efficient executive officer to expend it.

A Forcible Appeal.

We have laid down what we believe to be the main lines of a reform which is by no means utopian, but wholly within the bounds of possibility.

Whether it shall or shall not be accomplished depends upon the creation of a deep and strong sense of personal responsibility among the people of the United States. To them, and to them alone, do we appeal. It is for the people to say whether the folly, the selfishness, the dishonesty which have characterized our Indian policy of the past shall continue—whether the suffering and bloodshed, the useless expenditure of money, which the past few months have witnessed in Dakota, shall recur in the future. These evils will certainly recur unless men of every shade of opinion throughout the length and breadth of the land shall unite upon some such broad, simple basis as we have outlined—men who, in view of the magnitude of the object to be obtained, can rise above the limitations of political or religious partisanship in the demand for an Indian administration that shall be representative of the intelligence and conscience of the nation. For such a demand the time is ripe.

If the people of the United States instruct both the national Executive and the national legislature, through the press and pulpit, by private letter and by word of mouth, that it is their sovereign will that there should be an immediate and complete abandonment of the spoils system in the management of the Indians, there is no one to say them nay. Popular sentiment in the United States is the court of final appeal. In demanding such a reform as this the voice of the people will be the voice of God.

Source: Philip C. Garrett and Herbert Welsh, "Address to the People of the United States," in Henry Davenport Northrop, *Indian Horrors* (Chicago: L. P. Miller and Company, 1891), 590-600.

4-16. Wynema

S. Alice Callahan

1891

Originally published in 1891, Wynema: A Child of the Forest *was the first novel known to have been written by a woman of Native American ancestry, Sophia Alice Callahan (1868-1894), who attended Wesleyan Female Institute in Virginia and worked as a Methodist teacher for the Muscogee (Creek) Nation in Oklahoma.* Wynema *was her only novel. It told the story of a lifelong friendship between Wynema Harjo, a Creek, and Genevieve Weir, a Methodist teacher from an affluent Southern family. Both heroines advocated women's rights and Native American reform; they sought to overcome prejudice and rectify injustices between sexes and races. Wanting to arouse in her readers public indignation over the crimes and outrages perpetrated against Native Americans, Callahan advocated tolerance and equality. Indeed, she dedicated the book to North America's Natives who had suffered wrongs and oppression. Callahan urged the retention of Native customs, traditions, languages, and dress.*

. . . I think it will only be a matter of time, and a short time, too, when the question as to whether our women may participate in our liberties, help choose our officers, even our president, will be settled in their favor—at least, I hope so. There is no man who is enterprising and keeps well up with the times but confesses that the women of to-day are in every respect, except political liberty, equal to the men. It could not be successfully denied, for college statistics prove it by showing the number of women who have borne off the honors, even when public sentiment was against them and in favor of their brother-competitors. And not alone in an intellectual sense are you women our equals, but you have the energy and ambition, and far more morality than we can claim. Then you know so well how to put your learning in practice. See the college graduates who make successful farmers, vintners, etc. Indeed, you women can do anything you wish. . . .

You say if the United States army would kill a few thousand or so of the dancing Indians there would be no more trouble. I judge by the above language that you are a Christian and are disposed to do all in your power to advance the cause of Christ. You are doubtless a worshiper of the white man's Saviour, but are unwilling that the Indians should have a Messiah of their own. The Indians have never taken kindly to the Christian religion as preached and practiced by the whites Do you know why this is the case? Because the Good Father of all has given us a better religion—a religion that is all good and no bad—a religion that is adapted to our wants. You say if we are good, obey the ten commandments and never sin any more, we may be permitted eventually to sit upon a white rock and sing praises to God forevermore, and look down upon our heavenly fathers, mothers, sisters and brothers in hell. It won't do. The code of morals practiced by the white race will not compare with the morals of the Indians. We pay no lawyers or preachers, but we have not one-tenth part of the crime that you do. If our Messiah does come, we will not try to force you into our belief. We will never burn innocent women at the stake, or pull men to pieces with horses because they refuse to join with us in our ghost dances. You white people had a Messiah, and if history is to be believed, nearly every nation has had one. You had twelve apostles; we have only eleven and some of them are already in the military guard-house. . . .

There was a time when my people had plenty of land, plenty of cattle and plenty of everything; but after awhile the pale-faces came along, and by partly buying, partly seizing our lands by force, drove us very far away from our fertile country, until the Government placed us on a reservation in the Northwest, where the cold wind sweeps away our tents and almost freezes us. Then the great and powerful Government promised us to supply us with bountiful rations, in return for our lands it had taken. It was the treaty with us. But one day the agent told us the Government was poor, very poor, and could not afford to feed us so bountifully as in the past. So he gave us smaller rations than before, and every day the portion of each grew smaller, until we felt that we were being starved; for our crops failed and we were entirely dependent on the Government rations. Then came the day when one cent's worth daily was issued to each of us. How we all sickened and grew weak with hunger! I saw my boy, my Horda, growing paler and weaker every day, and I gave him my portion, keeping him in ignorance of it, for he would not have taken it had he known. Our chiefs and warriors gathered around the medicine man and prayed him to ask the Great Father what we should do to avert this evil. So the medicine man prayed to the Great Father all night, in his strange, murmuring way; and the next morning he told us to gather together and dance the holy dance to the Great Father and to sing while we danced, "Great Father, help us! By the strong arm aid us! Of thy great bounty give us that we may not die." We were to dance thus until dawn, when the Messiah would come and deliver us. Many of our men died dancing, for they had become so weak from fasting that they could not stand the exertion. Then the great Government heard of our dances, and . . . sent out troops to stop us.

Source: S. Alice Callahan, *Wynema: A Child of the Forest* (Philadelphia: H. J. Smith and Company, 1891), 46, 73, 95.

➳ ● ➳

4-17. How to Bring the Indian to Citizenship and Citizenship to the Indian

Herbert Welsh

April 9, 1892

In an 1892 lecture that appeared in Boston Commonwealth *on April 9, 1892, reformer Herbert Welsh discussed some of the principal means of endeavor by which citizenship could be achieved by Native Americans.*

The first picture which the word citizen paints before the mind is that of a free man, dwelling within a city, as opposed to either a slave or a foreigner; its second and finer delineation is that of the free man of a Republic, who is endowed with all the rights necessary to control the Republic's affairs; while the fullest and last conception of the word is that of the freeman in the Republic who not only is armed with rights and privileges as an integral unit of the State, but who exercises those rights fully under a sense of deep religious obligation. Such is the citizen of whom this or any Republic, whose perpetuity must depend upon the righteousness and wisdom of its policy, has need. Upon the practical realization of this ideal of the citizen, depends the strength and glory of the State. It is with this picture in mind of what a man already endowed with the rights of the citizen should be, as well as of him who, though a foreigner, is about to assume the dignity of citizenship, that we look toward the Indian and ask the question: How shall the Indian be made a citizen?

For no one can have been engaged for a considerable time in the actual, practical work of trying to fit the ignorant, undeveloped Indian, of untutored mind and untutored body, to bear the burden—the daily rasping load—of civilized life, without seeing clearly the duplex nature of the work; that the task is not alone one of training an undisciplined intellect, or of strengthening the unaccustomed muscles for systematic labor, used hitherto only for the swift, intermittent exertion of the chase and of war, but that it is also the problem of inducing the citizenship of the Republic to exert its patriotism, its wisdom, its humanity; arousing its dormant sense of Christian pity in the conduct of so large and difficult a work. It may be said with strict accuracy, and on the basis of experience and of a careful consideration of all the facts of this complex problem, that far harder is it to arouse the conscience and intellect of the nation to the point of organized and systematic action which are necessary to secure from Congress and from the Executive a settled policy of wisdom and justice in the treatment of the Indian, whereby his begetting and his birth into citizenship is attainable, than it is to induce the Indian to accept the privilege which we offer him. Such a statement as this, which is made deliberately, does not at all presuppose that we have not an abundance of right thinking and right doing among our people, or of the spirit, of generosity and of self-sacrifice—it may well be doubted if any people has more of these qualities—it only presupposes that we have also a superabundance of unenlightened thought, of crude, false views of what is right in the administration of public affairs; and that we have also a fierce surf-line of uncontrolled greed beating upon the Indian along the borders of civilization—a line of breakers—driven onward, too frequently, as we know, by the strong tides of organized selfishness, which find their centre in the great cities of the East. "Wherever the body is, there will the eagles (let us paraphrase, in this instance, by calling them vultures) be gathered together." The weakness and ignorance of the Indian have made him the natural prey of that portion of a great nation which the Almighty has seen fit to endow with the fierce passions of acquisition and of lust, that have been as the beak and claws of the vulture to the defenseless Indian, and wholly without the balancing faculties of reason and self-control.

From the earliest colonial days until now there have been sufficient evidences of the capabilities of the North American Indian for civilization and for Christianity—the great motive power of modern civilization—but wherever that frail plant (I do not hesitate to say that it is frail) has taken root, grown upward, blossomed and borne fruit, the baser elements of the civilization which planted and matured it have in fierce gusts of brutal and revengeful passion swept over it, leaving scarcely a trace of its fair and fleeting life.

So it was with the mission work of [John] Eliot among the Indians of New England in the seventeenth century; with that of the Moravian [David] Zeisberger and his associates among the Delawares of Pennsylvania in the eighteenth; with the Stockbridge Indians under Jonathan Edwards' care; with the Mission Indians of California; with the Cherokees of Georgia. The history of all these efforts, made by Christian men of large and humane views for the elevation of the Indians, has been in substance the same sad story. In every instance there was a remarkable response on the part of the Indian to the appeal of Christian civilization. Eliot gathered his converts into various communities, at points which are now the sites of well-known towns. Here were the first fruits of American citizenship among the Indians, and, indeed, from the sparse and scattered remnants which, even under the most unfavorable circumstance, have remained until our own day, it is not too much to claim that the experiment would have been successful had not the aggressions of the wild Indians and the consequent spirit of suspicion and revenge which this aroused among the whites destroyed them.

Zeisberger's Christian Indian communities were the admiration of all who visited them. They shone as gleams of sunlight amid the sombre forests of Pennsylvania. Indians who but a short time before had been wild and revengeful men became, under the preaching and indefatigable labors of Zeisberger, peaceable and industrious. They felled the great trees, cultivated the soil, built dwellings and mission chapels, and settled into peaceful and, as they thought, permanent communities. But they were from the first regarded with envy and suspicion by the rougher elements in the rough and unrestrained colonial population. Ravaging war parties, composed of French officers and savage Indians, devastated the frontier settlements during the French and Indian War: and naturally there arose in undiscriminating and ignorant minds an intense hatred of all Indians. The Moravian missionaries and their followers were obliged to fly for the protection of the British garrison in Philadelphia to find a shelter, which was grudgingly and timidly given. But a momentary respite was obtained. New York was asked the privilege of an asylum for the Moravian Indians, but the request was refused. A year of heart-sick wandering and exile ensued. The Indians were finally permitted to make the futile attempt of creating new homes for themselves in their native regions. When the storm of the Revolution broke, they were again subjected to the same persecutions as before, culminating in the shameful tragedy known as the Massacre of Gnaddenhütten, where ninety of their men, women, and children fell unresisting victims beneath the mallets and scalping knives of American rangers. The Moravian Missions never fairly rallied from this blow. Zeisberger, one of the noblest and most Christian of men, died at Goshen, on the shores of the Tascanawas, at a great age. Strong in the testimony of a good conscience, but with the harvest of his life's work lying waste about him, his dying eyes gazed sadly on the remnant of his Indian followers who gathered to bid him farewell. From the standpoint of worldly success his life had been in vain; but not as viewed from the higher standpoint, for he had brought hundreds not only to the conception of a noble life, but to such a living of it as put the behavior of their enemies to shame.

The advance of the Cherokees from savagery to civilization in Georgia was equally remarkable. Under the guidance of missionaries, most notable among whom was Dr. Samuel Worcester, they advanced rapidly in the arts of civilization. They lived in settled communities, they built churches and schools; but Georgia determined to eject them, and, notwithstanding that the act was in violation of a treaty made with these people by the Federal Government toward the close of the last century, they were driven out, and their missionaries were imprisoned. They were conducted by United States troops across the Mississippi in a march which cost them half their numbers, and were settled in that region known now as the Indian Territory.

Quite in keeping with these instances, cited to show the apparent unwillingness of our people to permit the civilization of the red man, is the history of the Mission Indians in California, whose sufferings and incredible wrongs so touched the heart and inspired the mind of Helen Hunt Jackson. Toward the close of the last century these Indians became the objects of the religious and secular care of the Franciscan Fathers, whose missions, scattered from San Diego to San Francisco, became centres of civilizing influence. Under the paternal guidance of the Fathers these Indians were far advanced in a knowledge of the arts and customs of civilized life, when in 1832 the Mexican Government passed a law secularizing the missions. This was intended simply to convert religious parishes into civil districts. It was not intended to deprive the Indians of their homes or of the property they had accumulated; but Pio Pico, the Governor, interpreted the law adversely to the Indians, and they were consequently scattered. The unrestrained character of the American population which poured into California as a result of the discovery of gold in that region naturally operated most disastrously upon the Indians. Their defenseless condition met with scant pity from a people in whom regard for the weak is not a distinguishing trait. There is no question but that many of these Indians sadly retrograded, but on the authority of one who is thoroughly familiar with their present condition and well-fitted to form a just estimate of it, it may be said: "The great majority of them have clung to their civilized habits, and, making all due allowance for the difficulties which have beset them ever since, have made hopeful progress."

I have made these extended allusions to the history of past efforts for the civilization of the Indians, because the cases cited seem to me to contain strong evidence of two essential truths having an evident practical value in relation to the solution of our present Indian problem.

First: The comparative willingness of the Indian to accept civilization when it is offered to him by those whose character and methods win his confidence.

Second: The great and, I must admit, the hitherto insurmountable difficulty of attaining those conditions under which the work of civilizing a barbarous people can be carried to mature success, on account of the greed, violence, or prejudice of our own race.

It seems to me that these two thoughts growing out of a knowledge of the past are essential to any wise and successful handling of the present problem. They inspire a hopeful enthusiasm for the civilization of the Indian race, balanced and tempered by a due recognition of the line of weakness. Our work is to bring to bear upon the Indian the essence of Christianity—that power which alone has benefited him in the past—the Gospel of right-thinking and of right-doing, of charity, and of the moral law, with, of course, the necessary sequence of an intellectual and physical development in industry of the mind and of the body. At the same time our even more important and difficult work is to persuade a majority of the American people that the Indian has rights which the white man is bound to respect, and that the great boon of life, law, and education shall be granted him. If the public sentiment of the country will say "aye" to this second proposition, then a place, albeit a humble one, is assured to the red man in these United States, hitherto the home and refuge for all people—him only excepted.

Viewing the Indian question, then, from the standpoint of these past conditions, what may we, with a fair show of confidence, determine as to the essential nature of the work before us? It is the problem of bringing the Indian to citizenship and citizenship to the Indian; for, by couching my subject in this phrase, I endeavored to intimate that the problem is quite as much that of bringing ourselves to the point of willingness to grant the boon of civilization, as it is of inducing the Indian to accept it. I trust that the landmarks of our Indian history that I have touched upon have tended to strengthen this intimation into a conviction.

First, let us consider briefly just what is the present position of the Indian, so that we may determine at once the general features of the work in hand. The problem is a different and an easier one than it was in the past. The Indian and the white man have changed places. We are no longer few in number. The Indian is no longer to be feared. He numbers about 25,000 souls; we 60,000,000. He and his reservations might be likened to islands against which the waters of a restless sea of civilized life are steadily beating. The Indian reservations are, in fact, but a few scattered islands, running at intervals down the heart of the continent from the British Possessions to Mexico. Now the problem seems to be about this: As the reservation islands rapidly decrease in size, frayed away incessantly by the greedy gnawings of civilization, the island inhabitants remain about stationary in numbers; the forces of civilization must therefore be vigorously directed against the inertia, the ignorant barbarism of the island's inhabitant, the Indian, so that when all land more than a civilized man needs has slipped away from beneath his feet, he will be able to swim in the sea which now threatens to engulf him. To this end missionaries, school teachers, agents (if they be good ones) are forever working; and they have done much, though more still remains for the accomplishment of their object.

The work is two-fold in that it contemplates infusing new life into the Indian, arousing him to a perception of the critical position in which he is placed as the white man thunders at his gate, and at the same time it involves constant watchfulness and restraint upon the white man who wishes the Indian's land, and the best portions of it, at once. We sometimes hear much unqualified denunciation of the reservation on which the Indian has been placed, as though it were the main obstacle to his civilization. "Down with the reservation!" some friends of the Indians exclaim. But surely such remarks imply a somewhat careless and thoughtless handling of the subject. The creation of Indian reservations was an unqualified necessity at that moment when some line of separation was required between the murderous contact of whites and Indians, when the former began to occupy the Indians'—until then—illimitable hunting grounds, and the latter to resist such occupation. To have left the Indian unconfined while in his savage and warlike state would have been madness, as a moment's reflection will demonstrate.

But it is, on the other hand, quite true that to consider the reservation more than a temporary expedient, and to permit the Indian to settle down into a feeling of idle and fatuous security upon it, with the understanding that he is to remain forever separated from the swift movement of white civilization about him, is equally a grievous error. The true view to take of the reservation is that it is a nursery, the temporary shelter needful to the Indian in the days of his moral and mental childhood, and before he is fitted for unprotected contact with the world. The reservation, like the nursery, must be judiciously used, so that it shall develop and not dwarf its occupant. To eject the Indian by a stroke of the pen, and to abolish the reservation forthwith, is wholly impracticable, and in a vast majority of cases would result in the Indian's complete destruction. Such an act would be similar to turning a child of five into the streets to earn his living.

But how is the reservation to be abolished at the earliest possible moment and at the least hardship to the Indian? Manifestly by a prompt and judicious but not heedless operation of the Dawes land in severalty bill, enacted February, 1887. This bill was the result of the united efforts of Senator Dawes and the unofficial friends of the Indians, who worked through many years of popular agitation to secure its passage. The great object of the measure is to destroy tribal segregation, and to attach the Indian to the soil by a holding in fee simple; to give him 160 acres of land, which shall be inalienable for a period of twenty-five years, and to make him a citizen of the United States, charged with the responsibilities and armed with the privileges of citizenship. The granting of this land-patent to the individual Indian, with its ensuing obligations, is dependent upon the will and act of the President. The work is to be done when the President believes that any particular tribe of Indians are ready for allotment. It may readily be seen that the practical success or failure with which these allotments are made will depend almost entirely upon the character of the agents whom the President shall choose to carry out the details of the work. Not only will success depend upon those *special* agents whom the President under the law appoints to do the particular work of allotting the land, but it will depend in still larger measure upon the character of the regular Indian Agents who have permanent charge of the sixty odd Indian Agencies throughout the United States; for they are the men who should be familiar with the individual character and condition of the Indians under them, and with the capabilities of the land comprised in the reservation, from which the Indian must select his allotment. Right intentions, experience, and sound judgment, therefore, on the part of the resident Agent, are most necessary to a successful operation of the severalty law.

The dangers to which that operation is open is apparent; they are the pressure from white population contiguous to the reservations to urge the work of allotment with too great haste, so that settlers may obtain control of the Indians' surplus lands; a desire to secure the settlement of the Indians on poor land, and to have the good land thrown open to the whites; and inexperience, or ill intention, on the part of the special or resident Agents which will result in unwise selections of land for the Indians. All these are, of course, points which must be carefully guarded against, and which at the same time it is very difficult to guard against successfully, on account of the tremendous pressure of the whites to gain possession of Indian land, and on account of the poor material secured by the operation of the spoils system in the appointment of Indian Agents and their employés. The Indian Commissioner reports 2,830 patents for land approved and their issue authorized during the year, and that the work of allotment is going on rapidly upon many reservations, but concerning these no details are given. There does not seem to be sufficient data in hand to speak very positively as to the workings of the law.

In connection with the land in severalty bill, it is most important to secure the passage of an act bringing courts of law upon the Indian reservations which shall gradually supplement the arbitrary power of the Indian Agent, and teach the Indian the fundamental principles upon which law in civilized countries is based, and which shall also make him acquainted with the simpler forms of legal procedure. This important subject is now being agitated by the various Indian Associations, led by the Boston Citizenship Committee and supported by the Indian Rights Association. An act embodying the general purpose stated seems to be a necessary bridge spanning that anomalous and difficult condition in which the Indian must exist between the point in time reached by the Dawes bill and his entrance upon full citizenship. There are many practical difficulties in the way of such a measure, but the step which probably is the most judicious one to take, is to develop the germ of a law court already existing on the reservations in what is known as the Court of Indian Offenses. This is composed of an Indian jury elected by the Agent, with whom the Agent sits as judge. It is a crude make-shift, but it has served its purpose fairly well, and its usefulness might be greatly increased if it were more fully developed, and if a trained and duly appointed Judge were to preside over its proceedings in the place of the Indian Agent.

Of equal importance with the successful settlement of the Indian upon his land, by which the first great step in the process of his civilization is to be secured, and the nomadic tendencies of his past life are to be overcome, is the great question of his education—the out-drawing of his dormant powers of body and intellect and spirit. I wish to make no elaborate statement of this question of education, but simply to refer to its most salient characteristics. It used to be said not very long ago, "You can't educate an Indian," but that statement is comparatively rare now-a-days. The work of Hampton, of Carlisle, of Forest Grove, of Chilocco, of many other schools east and west have answered that question, as it was answered long before, but in a less conspicuous way, by the missionaries, very conclusively. It is hardly probable that any very serious reactionary step in the educational department of the Indian work can be made. The agitation of the last ten or twelve years has produced a deep conviction in the popular mind that the Indian can and should be educated. It is felt that this is a debt the American people owe to the red man, and one which they are fully able to pay. A spasm of pseudo-economy sometimes strikes Congress on this subject, as it has done during the past winter, but it is soon alleviated by the tonic of a prompt popular demand that educational appropriations shall be maintained.

In relation to Indian education the question often arises, "Should it be conducted in the east or in the west?" The wise answer to which is, "In both places —east and west." The eastern school is the support and standard for the western school. It is the stimulus and corrective to the latter. But the eastern schools need not be unduly multiplied. There should be comparatively few of them, and they should be of the best quality, as is the case with Hampton, Carlisle, and the Lincoln Institute. But the main force of the Indian work must be in the west, at or near the Indian, in his native climate and upon his own soil.

A great deal is made out of the alleged failure of Indian education, and it is often claimed that those who have received the best training of the east lapse upon being sent back to their homes. Of course, there is a percentage of failure, but it is not larger than the circumstances, which are in many instances very adverse, would lead us to expect. General [Samuel C.] Armstrong shows that, of his returned pupils, eighty-five per cent are doing fairly to exceedingly well. Agent [James] McLaughlin states that out of one hundred pupils returned by Hampton Institute to the Standing Rock Reservation only two have turned out badly. Of course, the importance of industrial training for the Indians is a matter of great moment. It must be so in the case of any people who have been during their past history so destitute of such training, and who up to the present moment have had so few inducements to labor.

As a necessary adjunct to the education of the Indian may be mentioned here, though it relates more to the education of adults than of children, the importance of a gradual diminution in the issue of rations, such as many tribes of Indians receive from the Government in lieu of ceded lands, and the substitution of payments in money. The receipt of rations is in its very nature degrading, and the Indian needs as a preliminary to civilized life to be taught the practical use of money. This point was very strongly urged on the present speaker very recently by Bishop [William Hobart] Hare, whose experience among the Sioux Indians of Dakota has been so widespread, and for whom he has accomplished so remarkable a work.

And now, what is the great force by which this pressing and difficult work of settling the Indian on permanent allotments of land and of providing for the education of his 40,000 children is to be accomplished? It is by public sentiment, the demand of the conscience and mind of America working through organized channels, the various societies created for that purpose, upon Congress and the Executive. It is this force alone which has brought about the results thus far attained, and it is this which must accomplish the remainder of the task. Popular agitation has already raised appropriations for Indian education from $20,000 in 1877 to $2,291,250 during the past year. But still out of forty thousand Indian children only one-half are receiving any education. It is to public sentiment that we must look for the completion of this educational work which General [Thomas J.] Morgan, the present Indian Commissioner, has so well planned, and which he is so vigorously executing.

Let me now refer to a still more difficult task that remains for us to do in the solution of the Indian problem. It is the destruction of the spoils system in the management of Indian affairs, and the maintenance, in its integrity, of the great policy of which the Dawes bill is the exponent, that the Indian shall no longer be driven from fertile lands capable of supporting him, but that he shall be encouraged, or required, if need be, to settle upon and to cultivate them.

What is the spoils system in relation to the Indian service? Alas! Those who know that service are but too familiar with it. It is an "abomination" standing in that place of all others where it ought not to stand! It is the principle of appointment to office for bad reasons and dismissal for reasons equally unsound. Under the spoils system the Indian Agent is not chosen because he is fitted, either by nature or education, for the care and training of Indians, but because he has done political service for some leading politician of the State or Territory in which his reservation is located. Not only is very poor material obtained in this way, but the accumulation of experience and knowledge which would result from retaining faithful men in office, and which would be of great benefit to the service, is effectually prevented. The loss to the country and to the Indian entailed by the persistence of both political parties in upholding so vicious a system is incalculable.

The Sioux outbreak—if it may be so called—was undoubtedly precipitated by the cowardice and inexperience of an Indian Agent stationed at a critical point in the Indian country. Had there been reasonably strong and experienced men at all the Sioux Agencies, and had such men held their positions continuously for a few years previous to the troubles, the crisis of the ghost dance and other causes of irritation no doubt could have been safely passed, and the serious loss of life and of property that occurred might have been avoided. For ten years the Indian Rights Association has pleaded with Presidents and people, pointing to innumerable cases of injury and loss resulting from this selfish and cruel system, but until last winter the plea was largely in vain; then, indeed, after the massacre of Wounded Knee, and the great public outcry which that event occasioned, the President extended the Civil Service rules to some seven hundred places in the Indian service. For this important act he deserved and received the public's thanks.

But the Agents still continue to be appointed under the old plan, and are chosen from the henchmen of western Senators, with disastrous results, as many letters received at the Indian Rights Association's office in Philadelphia testify. One missionary writes in substance: Can you not do something to favor the proposition for the appointment of army officers as Indian Agents, and so put an end to the wretched administration of affairs which exists under the spoils system? If a judicious selection of army officers could be made with a view to securing the experience, the high personal qualities which many men in the military service preeminently possess, the chance would be most advantageous, and would be welcomed by all friends of the Indians—of course, there are army officers and army officers! If the proposed change were made without the assurance of such judicious selection, it is problematical whether the good results looked for would be obtained.

That the spoils system must be abandoned, and that speedily, if the service is to do the work expected of it, and if we seriously propose to fit the Indian for citizenship, is patent to all well-informed students of the Indian question. I would lay greater emphasis on this than upon any other point:—The Indian Agent is the key to the Indian problem; it behooves us then to see that he shall be a man of integrity, of administrative capacity, of sympathy for his people, of enthusiasm for the work of their civilization. We may tolerate the spoils system with its false appointments and its wanton removals in our post-offices and custom houses, but in the Indian service, which concerns the welfare of a people, where the fortunes of human beings—even life and death—hang in the balance, it is wholly intolerable!

In conclusion I would allude briefly to the necessity for a strong dominating public sentiment which shall prevent the removal of Indians from their homes and lands, which shall curb that predatory spirit that will not permit the operation of the severalty bill in their favor, but would drive them from one place to another whenever the greed of the land speculator demands it. A notable illustration of the kind of wrong to which I allude has been brought prominently before the public in the determined attempt to remove the Southern Ute Indians from their reservation in Colorado to a new reservation in Utah, during the present session of Congress. The removal is wholly without justification. It will be simply an attempt of Colorado to dump a handful of Indians, about nine hundred in all, upon Utah, and so relieve herself of what she considers an undesirable element in her population. But the main object of the removal is the acquisition of fertile and desirable land; for it is proposed to put the Indians on a wild, inaccessible tract in Utah where there will be every inducement to them to lead a wild and predatory life. The Indian Rights Association, basing its demand on the Dawes bill, urges that the Utes should be settled on land in severalty, where they are, and given education and a capable, progressive Agent. This has not hitherto been done. Then let their surplus lands be opened up to white settlement. The decision of this yet unsettled question will determine whether the Government will be true to its own fundamental policy, or whether it will establish another precedent for a continuance of the wrongs and mistakes of the past.

I have endeavored to point out in this lecture some of the principal lines of effort by which citizenship may be brought to the Indian, and he to citizenship. It is for us to determine whether by the strength of our own patriotism, our enthusiasm for the elevation of humanity, glowing zeal and untiring patience, those lines shall be effectually followed, and the wrongs which we have wittingly and unwittingly inflicted on a defenseless people be redressed at last.

Source: Herbert Welsh, "How to Bring the Indian to Citizenship, and Citizenship to the Indian," *Boston Commonwealth*, April 9, 1892, 1-14.

4-18. Henry B. Whipple to Benjamin Harrison

August 22, 1892

Episcopal Bishop Henry Benjamin Whipple of Minnesota used correspondence, travels, and lectures to urge federal officials to improve Native American conditions. His 1892 letter from Faribault, Minnesota, to President Benjamin Harrison dealt with religion and the appointment of Indian agents, among other matters.

. . . I have spent two weeks at White Earth with these Brown children of Our Father. My eyes are blinded with tears and my heart full, as I have seen what the Blessed Gospel has done for some of them whom when I first met them were the most wretched & degraded people on the Earth. There are thousands still in the thick darkness of heathenism. No one sympathizes more deeply than I do with you, who bear for us the delegated trust, from God who alone has the right to govern, of . . . a chief ruler of sixty millions of souls.

You are a Christian. You do love the Saviour. You do look to Him for salvation. It is you who appoint the Indian agent for this people. May I not as your brother in Jesus Christ ask you if the man you appoint is one who has not faith, who never prays, who hallows no Sunday, whose example teaches these poor heathens to refuse the hand which is reached out to save them for time and for eternity. Will it not give you sorrow if they are lost. I know the President has to regard the voice of those who are of his party, but surely you may and you can say I will not appoint any man as agent who will not be a leader to lead these heathens to the right. There [are] plenty of such men who will not only care & care well for temporal things & by a pure honest Christian life be a brother to these children of our Father.

I don't care to what body of Christians he belongs, but I do ask & plead for these poor souls whose cry I have heard over 30 years. . . . I am an old man. . . . [Y]ou will I know pardon my earnest plea. . . .

Source: Henry B. Whipple to Benjamin Harrison, August 22, 1892, Benjamin Harrison Papers, Manuscripts Division, Library of Congress, Washington, D.C.

4-19. Fighting, Feeding, or Educating Native Americans

Thomas J. Morgan

1892

At the tenth annual meeting of the Lake Mohonk Conference of Friends of the Indian, held in 1892, Commissioner of Indian Affairs Thomas J. Morgan addressed the group, citing specific examples of Native American situations. He contended that fighting Native Americans was cruel but that educating them was humane, economic, and Christian.

We must either fight the Indians, or feed them, or educate them. To fight them is cruel; to feed them is wasteful; to educate them is humane, economic, and Christian. We have forced upon them—I use the term not in any offensive sense—citizenship, and we are limiting severely the period of preparation. Unless they can be educated for the proper discharge of their duties and for the enjoyment of their privileges as citizens, they will fail to be properly benefited by the boon that we are conferring upon them. The government of the United States has at large expense provided accommodation for from twenty to twenty-five thousand of their children in schools maintained wholly or in part by the government. The people will not long continue to expend these two and a quarter million dollars a year for the education of these children if those to whom it is offered are unwilling to accept it. If they refuse to send their children to school, these schools will be closed; and the people who have been made citizens will be thrown upon themselves, and be left to survive or perish, according to their individual inclination. A large body of them to-day are unwilling to send their children to school. The schools are open, they offer to them every facility for learning English, they offer them freeboard, free tuition, free clothing, free medical care. Everything is freely offered, they are urged to come, but they refuse; and there is growing up, under the shadow of these institutions of learning, a new generation of savages. We are confronted, then, with this simple proposition: Shall we allow the growth of another generation of barbarians, or shall we compel the children to enter these schools to be trained to intelligence and industry? That is practically the question that confronts the Indian Office now.

Let me illustrate: At Fort Hall in Idaho, where the Shoshones and the Bannacks are, there is a school population of about two hundred and fifty. The people are degraded. They wander about in the mountains. Their women do most of what little work is done. They live in a beastly way (I use the term thoughtfully, I have seen it); and they are refusing to send their children to school. We have spent thousands of dollars in making the school at Fort Hall one of the most attractive reservation schools that is anywhere to be found. We have two thousand acres under fence. We have a large herd of cattle, and we have a noble body of employees. We are pleading with these people to put their children in school on the reservation, almost within sight of their own homes, within twenty or thirty miles' ride of any part of the reservation; but they say: "No. The medicine men say it is bad medicine." Now, shall we compel them?

In Fort Yuma the Indians live in the sand, like lizards, and have till recently gone almost naked. They send their children to the school till they reach the age of ten or eleven years. Then they are out, the girls roaming at will in that vicinity, the boys loafing about the miserable village of Yuma, wearing their hair long and going back to the ways of the camp. One of the saddest things I ever attended was an Indian mourning feast on that reservation, within sight of that school. Now, the question for me is, Shall I compel those children to enter school, to receive a preparation for citizenship?

At San Carlos are the Apaches, who are regarded as the most vicious of the Indians with whom we have to deal. They are held practically as prisoners, the San Carlos Agency being under control of the military. For years there has been a military officer in command, supported by two or three companies of colored soldiers. The conditions on that reservation are simply deplorable, and I would not dare in this audience to more than allude to the conditions existing there. These people decline to send their children to school; but I have within the last twelve months taken from that reservation about two hundred of them. They are to-day well fed and properly clothed, are happy and contented, and making good progress. Did I do right?

. . . I must illustrate by numerous other instances. We have provided these schools for the benefit of the children, not, primarily, for our own benefit. We have done it in order that they may be brought into relationship with the civilization of the nineteenth century. It is an expression of the sentiment that is generated here on these mountains. It comes, I believe, from God. Now, then, the question is simply, Shall we say that, after having made this abundant provision and having offered it to the children, we will allow those who are still savages in their instincts, barbarians in their habits, rooted to their conservatism,—that we will allow them to keep their children out of these institutions of learning, in order that they may be prevented from becoming like white men and women?

I say, No; and I say it for these reasons: We owe it to these children to see to it that they shall have the advantages of these schools. We owe it to their children that are to come after them that they shall be born of educated parents, and not of savages. We owe it to the old people themselves. The most pitiful things that I have been confronted with on the Indian reservations are the old men and old women, wrinkled, blind, and wretched, living on the ash-heap, having no care, with no protection, turned out to die. The other day, as I stood by the side of that little Santee girl, her father said to me, as he pointed out an old wrinkled woman, "My mamma"; and a most horrible creature she was. We owe it to these people to educate their children, so that they can go back to their homes and take care of the fathers and mothers who are no longer able to take care of themselves. We owe it to ourselves. We have undertaken to do this work; we have laid aside sentiment; we have laid aside everything except regard for the welfare of the children, and simply said, This thing ought to be done. Now, I say the one step remaining is for us to say that it shall be done.

I would first make the schools as attractive as they can be made, and would win these children, so far as possible, by kindness and persuasion. I would put them first into the schools near home, into the day schools, if there are any, or into the reservation boarding-schools, where there are such. Where it is practicable, I would allow them large liberty as to whether they shall go to a government school or a private school. I would bring to bear upon them such influences as would secure their acceptance voluntarily wherever it could be done. I would then use the Indian police if necessary. I would withhold from them rations and supplies where those are furnished, if that were needed; and when every other means was exhausted, when I could not accomplish the work in any other way, I would send a troop of United States soldiers, not to seize them, but simply to be present as an expression of the power of the government. Then I would say to these people, "Put your children in school"; and they would do it. There would be no warfare. At Fort Hall to-day, if there were present a sergeant or a lieutenant, with ten mounted soldiers, simply camped there, and I sent out to those Indians and told them that within ten days every child of school age must be in school, they would be there. Shall it be done? It *will* be done if public sentiment demands it: it will not be done if public sentiment does not.

Source: Thomas J. Morgan, "Compulsive Education," in *Proceedings of the Tenth Annual Meeting of the Lake Mohonk Conference of Friends of the Indian*, 1892, 51-54.

⋙→ ● ←⋘

4-20. Jerome Commission Report

March 3, 1893

Sponsored by Congressman William M. Springer (1836-1903), an Illinois Democrat, the Springer Bill, passed by Congress in 1889, authorized the formation of the Cherokee Commission to negotiate the purchase of huge areas of land from the Cherokees, Ioways, Pawnees, Poncas, Tonkawas, Wichitas, Cheyennes, Arapahos, Kickapoos, Sac and Fox, and others. The agreement with the Kickapoos appears below.

The three-man commission consisted of presidential appointees who worked under the supervision of the secretary of the interior. This group included Warren G. Sayre, an Indiana Republican with close ties to President Benjamin Harrison; Alfred M. Wilson, an Arkansas Democrat who had acquired experience dealing with Native Americans; and David Howell Jerome (1829-1896), head of the commission. Born in Detroit, Michigan, Jerome was a merchant and state legislator prior to holding Michigan's gubernatorial office from 1881 to 1882. A Republican in politics and Episcopalian in religion, Jerome, for whom the commission was named, died in Saginaw three years after the approval of the Jerome Commission Report. When Jerome opened the council in May, 1891, he said:

> *The Government has a plan, which if you will adopt and try your best to live up to, will give you more comforts and better living to you, and your families, than you have ever had before. . . . The Government of the United States is the only friend and the best friend that the Indian has, and it is the Government of the United States that sends this food here to feed these Indians every day. Sayre informed the Wichitas that they possessed "more land than you can use and more than anybody in this nation can use."*

Jerome, Sayre, and Wilson intimidated the Native Americans into accepting individual allotments and then selling parcels to the United States. The fifteen million acres declared surplus after allotment were added to the public domain at minimal cost. These lands went to white settlers, providing homes for thousands of pioneers and making possible the State of Oklahoma, which entered the Union in 1907.

. . . Articles of agreement made and entered into on the Kickapoo Reservation, in the Indian Territory, on the 21st. day of June, A. D. 1891, by and between David H. Jerome, Alfred M. Wilson, and Warren G. Sayre, Commissioners on the part of the United States, and the Kickapoo tribe of Indians, in the Indian Territory, and completed at the city of Washington, D. C., on this 9th day of September, A. D. 1891.

ARTICLE I. The said Kickapoo tribe of Indians in the Indian Territory hereby cede, convey, transfer, and relinquish, forever and absolutely, without any reservation whatever, all their claim, title, and interest of every kind and character in and to the lands embraced in the following described tract of country in the Indian Territory, to wit:

Commencing at the southwest corner of the Sac and Fox Reservation; thence north along the western boundary of said reservation to the Deep Fork of the Canadian River; thence up said Deep Fork to the point where it intersects the Indian Meridian; thence south along said Indian Meridian to the North Fork of the Canadian River; thence down said river to the place of beginning.

ARTICLE II. In consideration of the cession recited in the foregoing article, the United States agrees that in said tract of country there shall be allotted to each and every member, native and adopted, of said Kickapoo tribe of Indians in the Indian Territory, 80 acres of land to conform in boundary to the legal surveys of said land. Each and every member of said tribe of Indians over the age of eighteen years shall have the right to select for himself or herself 80 acres of land to be held and owned in severalty; and that the father, or, if he be dead, the mother shall have the right to select a like amount of land, under the same restrictions, for each of his or her children under the age of eighteen years; and that the Commissioner of Indian Affairs, or some one appointed by him for the purpose, shall select a like amount of land, under the same restrictions, for each orphan child belonging to said tribe under the age of eighteen years.

It is hereby further expressly agreed that no person shall have the right to make his or her selection of land in any part of said tract of country that is now used or occupied, or that has, or may hereafter be, set apart for military, agency school, school farm, religious, town site, or other public uses, or in sections sixteen (16) and thirty-six (36) in each Congressional township; provided, in cases where any member of said tribe of Indians has heretofore made improvements upon, and now occupies and uses, a part of said sections sixteen (16) and thirty-six (36), such persons may make his or her selection, according to the legal subdivisions, so as to include his or her improvements. It is further agreed that wherever, in said tract of country, any one of said Indians has made improvements and now uses and occupies the land embracing such improvements, such Indian shall have the undisputed right to make his or her selection, to conform to legal subdivisions, however, so as to include such improvements.

ARTICLE III. All allotments hereunder shall be selected within ninety days from the ratification of this agreement by the Congress of the United States, provided the Secretary of the Interior in his discretion may extend the time for making such selections; and should any Indian entitled to allotment hereunder fail or refuse to make his or her selection of land in such time, then the allotting agent in charge of said work of making such allotments, shall, within the next thirty (30) days after said time, make allotments to such Indians, which shall have the same force and effect as if the selections had been made by the Indians themselves.

ARTICLE IV. When said allotments of land shall have been selected and taken as aforesaid, and approved by the Secretary of the Interior, the titles thereto shall be held in trust for the benefit of the allottees, respectively, for a period of twenty-five (25) years, in the manner and to the extent provided for in the act of Congress entitled "An act to provide for the allotment of land in severalty to Indians on the various reservations, and to extend the protection of the laws of the United States and Territories over the Indians, and for other purposes." Approved February 8, 1887.

And at the expiration of the said twenty-five (25) years the title thereto shall be conveyed in fee simple to the allottees or their heirs free from all incumbrances, provided the President may at the end of said period extend the time the land shall be so held, in accordance with the provisions of the above-recited act.

ARTICLE V. In addition to the allotments above provided for, and the other benefits to be received under the preceding articles, and as the only further consideration to be paid for the cession and relinquishment of title above recited, the United States agrees to pay the said Kickapoo Indians, to be distributed among them per capita, under the direction of the Commissioner of Indian Affairs, for the improvement of their said allotments, and for other purposes for their benefit, the sum of sixty-four thousand and six hundred and fifty ($64, 650) dollars; provided, that the number of allotments of land provided for shall not exceed three hundred (300). But if the number of allotments shall exceed three hundred (300), then there shall be deducted from the said sum of sixty-four thousand and six hundred and fifty ($64,650) dollars, the sum of fifty ($50) dollars for each allotment in excess of the three hundred (300); provided, however, that should the Kickapoos elect to leave any or all of said money in the Treasury of the United States, it shall bear interest at the rate of five per cent per annum after the ratification by Congress of this contract.

ARTICLE VI. It is hereby further agreed that wherever, in this reservation, any religious society or other organization is now occupying any portion of said reservation for religious or educational work among the Indians the land so occupied may be allotted and confirmed to such society or organization, not however to exceed one hundred and sixty (160) acres of land to any one society or organization, so long as the same shall be so occupied and used, and such land shall not be subject to homestead entry.

ARTICLE VII. This agreement shall have effect whenever it shall be ratified by the Congress of the United States.

We, the undersigned, commissioners on the part of the United States, and Ock-qua-noc-a-sey, Kish-o-com-me, and John T. Hill, authorized by the Kickapoo tribe of Indians in the Indian Territory, hereby agree with each other as follows:

The United States commissioners aforesaid and the Kickapoos have agreed on terms of sale of their reservation, except the commissioners insist on the Indians taking lands in allotment, while the Indians insist in taking an equal amount of land as a diminished reservation, the title to be held in common.

The tribe has executed a power of attorney authorizing the above named persons to make the contract with the Commissioners, but have directed them to do so at Washington. The Kickapoos so authorized insist on going to Washington to see the Secretary of the Interior, and submit to him their claim to have a diminished reservation held in common as aforesaid, and hereby agree with the United States Commission to abide his decision in the premises, and take their lands in common or in allotment as he shall direct, and further agree that at Washington, they will sign a contract as the Secretary of the Interior may determine. This is agreed to on condition that the United States shall pay their expenses and subsist them to Washington and return. . . .

The Kickapoo tribe of Indians having agreed upon terms of sale of their reservation with the commissioners for the United States, except the commissioners insist on the Indians taking lands in allotment, while the Indians insist on taking an equal amount of land as a diminished reservation, the title to be held in common, and having further agreed to abide by the decision of the Secretary of the Interior in the premises, and that said lands shall be taken in common or in allotment as he shall direct, and that a contract shall be signed as he may determine: (All of which more fully appears by an agreement dated August 29th, 1891, and a power of attorney dated August 16th, 1891, hereunto annexed.)

And said question having been submitted to the Secretary by the commissioners in person and by said Indians, appearing by their delegates, Ock-qua-noc-a-sey, Kish-o-com-me, and John T. Hill, and having been duly considered,

Now, I, John W. Noble, Secretary of the Interior, and as said Secretary, do hereby decide that the Kickapoo Indians take their lands in allotment and not to be held in common, and I so direct.

Let the contract, so far as the question submitted is involved, be signed in accordance with this decision. . . .

*****

Therefore Be it enacted by the Senate and House of Representatives of the United States of America in Congress assembled, That said agreement be, and the same hereby is, accepted, ratified, and confirmed,

That for the purpose of carrying into effect the provisions of the foregoing agreement there is hereby appropriated out of any moneys in the Treasury of the United States not otherwise appropriated the sum of sixty-four thousand six hundred and fifty dollars. And after first paying to John T. Hill the sum of five thousand one hundred and seventy-two dollars for services rendered said Kickapoo Indians and in discharge of a written contract made with said Indians and recommended by the Secretary of the Interior, the remainder to be expended for the use of said Indians as stipulated in said contract; Provided that should said Indians elect to leave any portion of said remaining balance in the Treasury, the amount so left shall bear interest at the rate of five per cent per annum." *Provided,* That none of the money or interest thereon, which is by the terms of said agreement to be paid to said Indians, shall be applied to the payment of any judgment that has been or may hereafter be rendered under the provisions of the act of Congress approved March third, eighteen hundred and ninety-one, entitled "An act to provide for the adjudication and payment of claims arising from Indian depredations."

SEC. 2. That for the purpose of making the allotments and payments provided for in said agreement, including the preparation of a complete roll of said Indians, the pay and expenses of a special agent, if the President thinks it necessary to appoint one for the purpose, and the necessary surveys or resurveys, there be, and hereby is, appropriated, out of any moneys in the Treasury not otherwise appropriated, the sum of five thousand dollars, or so much thereof as may be necessary.

SEC. 3. That whenever any of the lands, acquired by this agreement shall, by operation of law or proclamation of the President of the United States, be open to settlement or entry, they shall be disposed of (except sections sixteen and thirty-six in each township thereof) to actual settlers only, under the provisions of the homestead and town-site laws (except section twenty-three hundred and one of the Revised Statutes of the United States, which shall not apply): *Provided, however,*

That each settler on said lands shall, before making a final proof and receiving a certificate of entry, pay to the United States for the land so taken by him, in addition to the fees provided by law, and within five years from the date of the first original entry, the sum of one dollar and fifty cents an acre, one-half of which shall be paid within two years; but the rights of honorably discharged Union soldiers and sailors, as defined and described in sections twenty-three hundred and four and twenty-three hundred and five of the Revised Statutes of the United States shall not be abridged, except as to the sum to be paid as aforesaid. Until said lands are opened to settlement by proclamation of the President of the United States, no person shall be permitted to enter upon or occupy any of said lands; and any person violating this provision shall never be permitted to make entry of any of said lands or acquire any title thereto: *Provided*, That any person having attempted to, but for any cause failed to acquire a title in fee under existing law, or who made entry under what is known as the commuted provision of the homestead law, shall be qualified to make homestead entry upon said lands.

Source: "Jerome Commission Report," in *Indian Affairs: Laws and Treaties*, comp. and ed. Charles J. Kappler, vol. 1 (Washington, D. C.: Government Printing Office, 1904); S. Ex. Doc., no. 17, 52d Cong., 2d sess., vol. 1, January 4, 1893, serial set 3055.

4-21. Speech to Woman's National Indian Association

Daniel M. Browning

December 6, 1893

During the morning session of the annual meeting of the Women's National Indian Association held on December 6, 1893, in Washington, D.C., Commissioner of Indian Affairs Daniel M. Browning addressed the group on matters pertaining to the education and civilization of Native Americans.

. . . I came here to pay my respects to the good women of this association, who are engaged in so laudable a work as that of improving the condition of the Indians.

In works of charity, benevolence and christianity women have always occupied the front rank, and are entitled to great praise. There is no better field for your labors or a cause that appeals more strongly for your help than that of educating and civilizing the Indian. The task is a difficult one and necessarily slow, but progress is being made, and with earnest, faithful work on behalf of those engaged in it, it will continue; yet all the means available are needed and must be utilized.

The educational work is important. The large non-reservation and industrial schools are doing a good work. The schools on the reservations among the Indians are doing a good work. The christian people who have established churches among them, and have sent out missionaries to instruct them, are doing a good work. The allotting agents, who are engaged in allotting lands in severalty to the Indians who are prepared for it, are doing a good work. So are farmers, who are employed to go among them and teach them how to plow and cultivate crops, and the field matrons, who go among Indian women and instruct them in household duties.

In the discharge of my official duties I shall labor earnestly and faithfully to make the Indians independent and self-supporting, and when vacancies occur in the Indian Service, I will recommend none for positions unless I believe them to be capable of rendering efficient aid. I will try to secure and retain the confidence of the Indian by protecting him in his lands and property, and faithfully and honestly carrying out our treaties with him and our pledges to him. I will be thankful for any suggestions that you may have to make at any time, and for your help. . . .

Source: Daniel M. Browning, speech to Women's National Indian Association, December 6, 1893, Grover Cleveland Papers, Manuscripts Division, Library of Congress, Washington, D.C.

4-22. The Shawnee Prophet and the Peyote Cult

John Rave

1893

A prominent member of the Bear clan and native of Wisconsin, John Rave (1855-1917), a founder of the Native American Church, introduced the Bible, Christianity, and the peyote culture to the Winnebago people, enabling them to adapt their tra-

ditional culture to new circumstances. Also known as Little Redbird, Rave, a religious reformer, was a traveler who underwent visionary experiences. He recounted happenings connected with his use of peyote and those of other peyotists. Both Rave and his wife recovered from serious illnesses after eating peyote used for medicinal purposes. Peyote cured the hemorrhage of Black Water-spirit. Walking-Priest, an alcoholic who chewed, smoked, gambled, chased women, and harbored murder in his heart, metamorphosed into an entirely different and good person upon consuming peyote. "Whoever has any bad thoughts, if he will eat this peyote he will abandon all his bad habits. It is a cure for everything bad," claimed Rave. Encouraging others to obtain knowledge and try the peyote medicine, Rave added: "No other medicine can accomplish what this has done. . . . Only by eating peyote will you learn what is truly holy."

Now this is what the Winnebago heard from the Shawnee prophet; this is what he said, it is said, by those who heard him: "Let the people give up the customs they are now observing and I will give them new ones." This is what he said.

Some of the Winnebago did this and threw away their war bundles. But he had meant their bad customs. Some also threw away their good medicines. At last they decided to go over to where he was. A man named Smoke-Walker led a number of young men over. "We will walk as the thunderbirds do," said the leader. Then a great and holy man called Dog-Head said that he also was going along. He was then an old man. The leader said, "You had better not come along for we are going to walk as the thunderbirds do, and for that reason I wish only young men." But Dog-Head said, "I am going along nevertheless, and whenever you wish to walk like the thunderbirds and walk above the earth, then I can turn back. I will go along."

There were eleven who went along. When they got to the place where the Shawnee prophet was staying they found all the other tribes (represented) there except the Winnebago.

Then the prophet said, "It is good, my younger brothers." He called the Winnebago younger brothers. "There are many tribes here, but I wanted to see you here especially. It is good you have come. I want to talk to you, but it is impossible (because I cannot speak your language)." Now the old man who had come along against the wishes of the chief could speak any Indian language, so the leader said to Dog-Head, "Older brother, you used to speak almost any language; can you still do it?" Then Dog-Head said, "My younger brother, I can understand what he is saying, but I don't know whether I could talk the language myself. I may or may not be able to speak it (enough to make myself understood). I don't know." Then the leader said, "It is good, older brother. Try to talk to him, and whatever you do will be better than nothing." Then Dog-Head said to the Shawnee prophet, "I can understand what you are saying, but I am afraid to talk to you because I don't know whether I could make myself clear to you." The prophet thanked him and said, "It is good. I want to talk to you Winnebago."

Then they had a long conversation and this is what he said, "Younger brothers, we are not doing the right thing and that is why we are not getting along very well in life."

At that time they (the other tribes) were having their night dances, so the Winnebago moved over to them. There they heard the prophet speak. He said that he had been sent by the Creator because the Indians were wandering away from their old customs. For that reason the Creator had sent him to tell them of it. He at first forgot all about it, for the devil misrepresented things to him and he believed him. The devil had told him that he would go to heaven and that he could not be killed. He had told him that he had given him a holy belt. He was a bad person. Whenever he got angry he would throw his belt down on the ground and it would change into a yellow rattlesnake and rattle. When he did this the rest of the people were afraid of him. He was very mean when drunk. They were afraid of him, not only on account of his belt, which he could turn into a yellow rattlesnake, but also because of the fact that he was very strong. If, when he was drunk, a number of people jumped on him, afterwards he would find out about it and hit them. If they would resist he would kill them.

It was utterly impossible for him to be killed. He was unkind to the women. They would go with him not because they liked him but because they were afraid of him. It was a dangerous thing to say anything about him. Whenever he wished to drink he would take some person's valuables and buy drink with it. These are the things he did. The Creator had sent him on a mission to the earth, but the devil had misled him. . . .

Now, it is four generations since the Shawnee prophet prophesied, and from that time there have been many prophets among us, as he is said to have told the people. Many have prophesied, but none have told anything that seemed reasonable. The Shawnee prophet was good, but those who have come after him have prophesied so that people might praise them, or just for the sake of talking.

It is said that the Shawnee prophet said that there would come a time when a woman would prophesy and that she should be immediately killed. The end of the world would be near then. Then he is said to have said that a little boy would prophesy and that one was to give ear to what he said.

The Peyote people claim that their ceremony is the fulfillment of this prophecy and that is true. The Shawnee prophet had said that there would be springs of water in front of the people's lodges and it is so at the present time, for the water is at our very doors. His prophecy was correct and he told the truth. Then he said that trees would travel and this is happening to-day, for trees are loaded into trains and are carried all around the country. He told the truth and he knew what was going to happen. He said that one day we would be able to write our own language and we are doing that to-day, for we have a Bible in Winnebago and we are able to write to one another in our own language. All these things he was able to foretell four generations ago.

A Winnebago by the name of Noise-Thunder had also prophesied that we would be able to write our own language. One thing that he said, however, was not correct. He said that the bad thing that has come upon us will make us forget our own ways. He meant that we should not take up with the white man's ways. "Don't do it, for if you do, we will all die." Now, he was mistaken in that. "The Creator has given two plates and they are getting empty. He gave the men a plate for them to fill and the women a plate for them to fill. The women's plate is empty." He meant that the Creator had made men to hunt and the women to dig the soil and raise vegetables, and that the latter were not doing it. That is what he meant by saying that their plates were empty. Noise-Thunder insisted that this was the white man's fault; he thought that we were being weakened by the white man's food. Quite a number of people believed him. "The birds eat what was provided for them to eat, game and vegetables, and the whites eat what was provided for them. Why should we not eat what was provided for us?" He was right, but then the Creator also created the food that the whites are eating. We are now getting accustomed to it and are getting stronger on this food.

The Winnebago were decreasing in number, so the Creator gave them a medicine which would enable them to get accustomed to the white man's food; that, also, they might know the Creator and that he is the true bread and food. This they found out by using this medicine. They are going into it deeper and deeper all the time, they who had been lost, and this has all been accomplished by the medicine (the peyote). . . .

During 1893-94 I was in Oklahoma with peyote eaters.

In the middle of the night we were to eat peyote. We ate it and I also did. It was the middle of the night when I got frightened, for a live thing seemed to have entered me. "Why did I do it?" I thought to myself. I should not have done it, for right at the beginning I have harmed myself. Indeed, I should not have done it. I am sure it will injure me. The best thing will be for me to vomit it up. Well, now, I will try it. After a few attempts I gave up. I thought to myself, "Well, now you have done it. You have been going around trying everything and now you have done something that has harmed you. What is it? It seems to be alive and moving around in my stomach. If only some of my own people were here! That would have been better. Now no one will know what has happened to me. I have killed myself."

Just then the object was about to come out. It seemed almost out and I put out my hand to feel it, but then it went back again. "O, my, I should never have done it from the beginning. Never again will I do it. I am surely going to die."

As we continued it became day and we laughed. Before that I had been unable to laugh.

The following night we were to eat peyote again. I thought to myself, "Last night it almost harmed me." "Well, let us do it again," they said. "All right, I'll do it." So there we ate seven peyote apiece.

Suddenly I saw a big snake. I was very much frightened. Then another one came crawling over me. "My God! where are these coming from?" There at my back there seemed to be something. So I looked around and I saw a snake about to swallow me entirely. It had legs and arms and a long tail. The end of this tail was like a spear. "O, my God! I am surely going to die now," I thought. Then I looked again in another direction and I saw a man with horns and long claws and with a spear in his hand. He jumped for me and I threw myself on the ground. He missed me. Then I looked back and this time he started back, but it seemed to me that he was directing his spear at me. Again I threw myself on the ground and he missed me. There seemed to be no possible escape for me. Then suddenly it occurred to me, "Perhaps it is this peyote that is doing this thing to me?" "Help me, O medicine, help me! It is you who are doing this and you are holy! It is not these frightful visions that are causing this. I should have known that you were doing it. Help me!" Then my suffering stopped. "As long as the earth shall last, that long will I make use of you, O medicine!"

This had lasted a night and a day. For a whole night I had not slept at all.

Then we breakfasted. Then I said, when we were through, "Let us eat peyote again to-night." That evening I ate eight peyote.

In the middle of the night I saw God. To God living up above, our Father, I prayed. "Have mercy upon me! Give me knowledge that I may not say and do evil things. To you, O God, I am trying to pray. Do thou, O Son of God, help me, too. This religion, let me know. Help me, O medicine, grandfather, help me! Let me know this religion!" Thus I spoke and sat very quiet. And then I beheld the morning star and it was good to look upon. The light was good to look upon. I had been frightened during the night but now I was happy. Now as the light appeared, it seemed to me that nothing would be invisible to me. I seemed to see everything clearly. Then I thought of my home and as I looked around, there I saw the house in which I lived far away among the Winnebago, quite close to me. There at the window I saw my children playing. Then I saw a man going to my house carrying a jug of whisky. Then he gave them something to drink and the one that had brought the whisky got drunk and bothered my people. Finally he ran away. "So, that is what they are doing," I thought to myself. Then I beheld my wife come and stand outside of the door, wearing a red blanket. She was thinking of going to the flagpole and was wondering which road she should take. "If I take this road I am likely to meet some people, but if I take the other road, I am not likely to meet anyone."

Indeed, it is good. They are all well—my brother, my sister, my father, my mother. I felt very good indeed. O medicine, grandfather, most assuredly you are holy! All that is connected with you, that I would like to know and that I would like to understand. Help me! I give myself up to you entirely!

For three days and three nights I had been eating medicine, and for three days and three nights I had not slept. Throughout all the years that I had lived on earth, I now realized that I had never known anything holy. Now, for the first time, I knew it. Would that some of the Winnebagoes might also know it! . . .

Whoever has any bad thoughts, if he will eat this peyote he will abandon all his bad habits. It is a cure for everything bad.

To-day the Indians say that only God is holy. One of the Winnebagoes has told me, "Really, the life that I led was a very bad one. Never again will I do it. This medicine is good and I will always use it." John Harrison and Squeaking-Wings were prominent members of the medicine dance; they thought much of themselves as did all the members of the medicine dance. They knew everything connected with this medicine dance. Both of them were gamblers and were rich because they had won very much in gambling. Their parents had acquired great possessions by giving medicines to the people. They were rich and they believed that they had a right to be selfish with their possessions. Then they ate peyote and ever since that time they have been followers of this medicine. They were really very ill and now they have been cured of it. Now if there are any men that might be taken as examples of the peyote, it is these three. Even if a man were blind and only heard about them he would realize that if any medicine were good, it is this medicine. It is a cure for all evil. Before, I had thought that I knew something but I really knew nothing. It is only now that I have real knowledge. In my former life I was like one blind and deaf. My heart ached when I thought of what I had been doing. Never again will I do it. This medicine alone is holy and has made me good and has rid me of all evil. The one whom they call God has given me this. That I know positively. Let them all come here; men and women; let them bring with them all that they desire; let them bring with them their diseases. If they come here they will get well. This is all true; it is all true. Bring whatever desires you possess along with you and then come and eat or drink this medicine. This is life, the only life. Then you will learn something about yourself, so come. Even if you are not told anything about yourself, nevertheless you will learn something of yourself. Come with your disease, for this medicine will cure it. Whatever you have, come and eat this medicine and you will have true knowledge once and for all. Learn of this medicine yourself through actual experience. . . .

It is now 23 years since I first ate peyote, and I am still doing it (1912). Before that my heart was filled with murderous thoughts. I wanted to kill my brother and sister. It seemed to me that my heart would not feel good until I killed one of them. All my thoughts were fixed on the warpath. This is all I thought of. Now I know that it was because the evil spirit possessed me that I felt that way. I was suffering from a disease. I even desired to kill myself; I did not care to live. That feeling, too, was caused by this evil spirit living within me. Then I ate this medicine and everything changed. The brother and sister I wanted to kill before I became attached to and I wanted them to live. The medicine had accomplished this.

Source: "What the Shawnee Prophet Told the Winnebago," and "John Rave's Account of the Peyote Cult and of His Conversion," in Paul Radin, *The Winnebago Tribe* (Washington, D.C.: U.S. Bureau of American Ethnology, 1923), 389-94, 69-74; Paul Radin, "The Religious Experience of an American Indian" (1950):249-90, in Paul Radin Papers, Department of Special Collections and University Archives, Marquette University Libraries, Milwaukee, Wisconsin.

⋙➝ ● ←⋘

4-23. Report of the Dawes Commission

November 20, 1894

The purpose of the Dawes Commission was to expand the provisions of the General Allotment Act of 1887 to incorporate tribes such as the Chickasaw, Choctaw, Cherokee, and others, who had not been included under the provisions of the 1887 law. Henry L. Dawes, former U.S. senator from Massachusetts and recognized champion of the reform of Native America, headed the commission from 1893 to 1900. It was he who had sponsored the 1887 measure. In the commission's 1894 report, members discussed conditions existing in the Indian Territory.

. . . The barrier opposed at all times by those in authority in the tribes, and assuming to speak for them as to any change in existing conditions, is what they claim to be "the treaty situation." They mean by this term that the United States is under treaty obligations not to interfere in their internal policy, but has guaranteed to them self-government and absolute exclusion of white citizens from any abode among them; that the United States is bound to isolate them absolutely. It can not be doubted that this was substantially the original governing idea in establishing the Five Tribes in the Indian Territory, more or less clearly expressed in the treaties, which are the basis of whatever title and authority they at present have in the possession of that Territory, over which they now claim this exclusive jurisdiction. To that end the United States, in different treaties and patents executed in pursuance of such treaties, conveyed to the several tribes the country originally known as the "Indian Territory," of which their present possessions are a part only, and agreed to the establishment by them therein of governments of their own. The United States also agreed to exclude all white persons from their borders.

These treaties, however, embraced stipulations equally clear, that these tribes were to hold this territory for the use and enjoyment of all Indians belonging to their respective tribes, so that every Indian, as is expressed in some of the treaties, "shall have an equal right with every other Indian in each and every portion of the territory," and the further stipulation that their laws should not conflict with the Constitution of the United States. These were executory provisions to be observed in the future by both sides. Without regard to any observance of them on their part, the Indians claim that these treaties are irrevocably binding on the United States. These stipulations naturally grew out of the situation of the country at the time they were made, and of the character of the Indians with whom they were made. The present growth of the country and its present relations to this territory were not thought of or even dreamed of by either party when they entered into these stipulations. These Indians were then at a considerably advanced stage of civilization, and were thought capable of self-government, in conformity with the spirit if not the forms of the National Government, within whose limits they were to remain. It was not altogether unreasonable, therefore, to conclude that it would be possible, as it was by them desirable, that these Indians could have set apart to them a tract of country so far remote from white civilization and so isolated that they could work out the problem of their own preservation under a government of their own, and that not only with safety to the Union but with altogether desirable results to themselves.

For quite a number of years after the institution of this project it seemed successful, and the Indians under it made favorable advance toward its realization. But within the last few years all the conditions under which it was inaugurated have undergone so complete a change that it has become no longer possible. It is hardly necessary to call attention to the contrast between the present conditions surrounding this Territory and those under which it was set apart. Large and populous States of the Union are now on all sides of it, and one-half of it has been constituted a Territory of the United States. These States and this Territory are teeming with population and increasing in numbers at a marvelous rate. The resources of the Territory itself have been developed to such a degree and are of such immense and tempting value that they are attracting to it an irresistible pressure from enterprising citizens. The executory conditions contained in the treaties have become impossible of execution. It is no longer possible for the United States to keep its citizens out of the Territory. Nor is it now possible for the Indians to secure to each individual Indian his full enjoyment in common with other Indians of the common property of the Territory.

The impossibility of enforcing these executory provisions has arisen from a neglect on both sides to enforce them. This neglect is largely the result of outside considerations for which neither is responsible and of the influence of forces which neither can control. These executory conditions are not only impossible of execution, but have ceased to be applicable or desirable. It has been demonstrated that isolation is an impossibility, and that if possible, it could never result in the elevation or civilization of the Indian. It has been made clear that under its operations, imperfectly as it has been carried out, its effect has been to retard rather than to promote civilization, to impair rather than strengthen the observance of law and order and regard for human life and human rights or the protection or promotion of a virtuous life. To such a degree has this sad deterioration become evident that to-day a most deplorable and dangerous condition of affairs exist in the Territory, causing wide-spread alarm and demanding most serious consideration.

All the functions of the so-called governments of these five tribes have become powerless to protect the life or property rights of the citizen. The courts of justice have become helpless and paralized. Violence, robbery, and murder are almost of daily occurrence, and no effective measures of restraint or punishment are put forth to suppress crime. Railroad trains are stopped and their passengers robbed within a few miles of populous towns and the plunder carried off with impunity in the very presence of those in authority. A reign of terror exists, and barbarous outrage almost impossible of belief, are enacted, and the perpetrators hardly find it necessary to shun daily intercourse with their victims. We are now informed that, within the territory of one of these tribes, there were 53 murders during the month of September and the first twenty-four days of October last, and not a single person brought to trial.

In every respect the present condition of affairs demonstrates that the permission to govern themselves, under the Constitution of the United States, which was originally embraced in the treaty, has proved a failure. So likewise, has the provision that requires the United States to exclude white citizens from the Territory. The course of procedure by the governments of the Five Tribes has largely contributed to this result, and they are quite as much responsible as the United States for the fact that there are 250,000 white people residing in the Territory. These citizens of the United States have been induced to go there in various ways and by various methods by the Indian governments themselves. These governments consented to the construction of a number of railways through the Territory, and thereby consented that they bring into the Territory all that is necessary in the building and operation of such railroads—the necessary depots, stations, and the inevitable towns which their traffic was sure to build up, and the large building which white men alone could develop and which these railroads were sure to stimulate and make profitable.

Besides these, they have, by their laws, invited men from the border States to become their employés in the Territory, receiving into their treasuries a monthly tax for the privilege of such employment. They have also provided by law for the intermarriage of white persons with their citizens and adopted them into their tribes. By operation of these laws large numbers of white people have become adopted citizens, participating in the benefits of citizenship. A single instance of such marriage has enabled one white man under the laws to appropriate to his exclusive use 50,000 acres of valuable land. They have, by their legislation, induced citizens of the United States to come in from all sides and under leases and other agreements with private citizens, sanctioned by their own laws, farmed out to them large ranges of their domain, as well as inexhaustible coal deposits within their respective borders, and other material interests which civilized white men alone could turn to profit. In some sections of the Territory the production of cotton has proved so feasible and profitable that white men have been permitted to come in by thousands and cultivate it and build trading marts and populous towns for the successful operation of this branch of trade alone.

In a single town of 5,000 white inhabitants, built there by their permission and also for the profit of the Indian, there were during last year marketed 40,000 bales of cotton. They have also sold off to the United States one-half of their original territory, to be opened up to white settlement on their western borders, in which, with their consent thus obtained, 300,000 white citizens have made their homes, and a

Territorial government by this means has been erected in the midst of their own territory, which is forbidden by one of the executory provisions of the treaty. The day of isolation has passed. Not less regardless have they been of the stipulations in their title that they should hold their territory for the common and equal use of all their citizens. Corruption of the grossest kind, openly and unblushingly practiced, has found its way into every branch of the service of the tribal governments. All branches of the governments are reeking with it, and so common has it become that no attempt at concealment is thought necessary. The governments have fallen into the hands of a few able and energetic Indian citizens, nearly all mixed blood and adopted whites, who have so administered their affairs and have enacted such laws that they are enable to appropriate to their own exclusive use almost the entire property of the Territory of any kind that can be rendered profitable and available.

In one of these tribes, whose whole territory consists of but 3,040,000 acres of land, within the last few years have been enacted under the operation of which 61 citizens have appropriated to themselves and are now holding for pasturage and cultivation 1,237,000 acres. This comprises the arable and greater part of the valuable grazing lands belonging to that tribe. The remainder of that people, largely the full-bloods who do not speak the English language, are excluded from the enjoyment of any portion of this land, and many of them occupy the poor and hilly country where they get a scanty living from such portions as they are able to turn to any account. This class of persons in the Territory are making little if any progress in civilization. They are largely dependent on those in control of public affairs, whose will they register at the polls and with whose bidding, in a large measure, they comply without question. Those holding power by these means oppose any change and ask only to be let alone.

In another of these tribes, under similar legislation, vast and rich deposits of coal of incalculable value have been appropriated by the few, to the exclusion of the rest of the tribe and to the great profit of those who operate them and appropriate their products to their individual use. Large and valuable plants for mining coal have been established by capitalists under leases by which, together with "discoverer's claims" authorized by the tribal governments, these coal lands are covered, and under the workings of which the rightful owners are being despoiled of this valuable property with very little or no profit to them; and it is clear that this property should be restored to the common domain and protected to the common people, and the mines worked under a system just and equitable to all who have rights therein.

The vast pine forests heretofore spoken of, which are of incalculable value, if not indispensable, in the future development of the country and the building up of homes and improvements of the agricultural lands, are being spoliated and laid waste by attempts, under laws enacted for that purpose, to grant to a few, mostly adopted white citizens, the right to cut and market for their own use whatever timber they can turn to their own profit. This is an irreparable destruction of one of the most essential elements of the progress of the country in the future and should be at once arrested.

Towns of considerable importance have been built by white persons under leases obtained from Indians claiming the right to appropriate the common property to these uses. Permanent improvements of great value have thus been made by white citizens of the United States, induced and encouraged thereto by the tribal governments themselves, and have become immovable fixtures which can not be taken away. However difficult the problem of adjusting rights thus involved, nothing can be more clear than that the step can not be retraced. Towns built under such inducements can not be removed nor their structures razed to the ground, nor can the places they occupy be restored to the conditions originally contemplated by the treaties. Ruinous as any such attempt would be to those thus induced to expend their money in building these towns, it would not be less ruinous to the Indians themselves to be, by any such attempt, forced back to the methods of life existing before the coming of these white men. The original idea of a community of property has been entirely lost sight of and disregarded in every branch of the administration of their affairs by the governments which have been permitted to control this Territory under the treaty stipulations which are now being invoked, by those who are in this manner administering them, as a protection for their personal holdings and enterprises.

The large payments of moneys to the Indians of these tribes within the last few years have been attended by many and apparently well-authenticated complaints of fraud, and those making such payments, with others associated with them in the business, have, by unfair means and improper use of the advantages thus afforded them, acquired large fortunes, and in many instances private persons entitled to payments have received but little benefit therefrom. And worse still is the fact that the places of payments were thronged with evil characters of every possible caste, by whom the people were swindled, defrauded, robbed, and grossly debauched and demoralized. And in case of further payments of money to them the Government should make such disbursements to the people directly, through one of its own officers.

We feel it our duty to here suggest that any measures looking to any change of affairs in this Territory should embrace special, strict, and effective provisions for protection of the Indian and other citizens from the introduction, manufacture, or sale of intoxicants of any kind in the Territory, with penalties therefor and for failure by officers to enforce same, sufficiently severe to cause their perfect execution. A failure to thus protect these Indians will, in a measure, work their extinction at no distant day.

It is a deplorable fact, which should not be overlooked by the Government, that there are thousands of white children in this territory who are almost wholly without the means of education, and are consequently growing up with no fitting preparation for useful citizenship. A matter of so much concern to the country should not be disregarded.

When the treaties were reaffirmed in 1866, a provision was made for the adoption and equality of rights of the freedmen, who had theretofore been slaves in the tribes, upon terms provided in the treaties. The Cherokees and Choctaws have appeared to comply with the letter of the prescribed terms, although very inadequately and tardily, and the Chickasaws at one time took some steps toward complying with the terms, but now deny that they ever adopted the freedmen, and are endeavoring to retrace the steps originally taken. They now treat the whole class as aliens without any legal right to abide among them, or to claim any protection under their laws. They are shut out of the schools of the tribe, and from their courts, and are granted no privileges of occupancy of any part of the land for a home, and are helplessly exposed to the hostilities of the citizen Indian and the personal animosity of the former master. Peaceable, law-abiding, and hard-working, they have sought in vain to be regarded as a part of the people to whose wealth their industry is daily contributing a very essential portion. They number in that tribe about 4,000, while the Chickasaws number 3,500. The United States is bound by solemn treaty to place these freedmen securely in the enjoyment of their rights as Chickasaw Indians, and can not with honor ignore the obligation. . . .

The condition of the freedmen in the Choctaw and Cherokee tribes is little better than that of those among the Chickasaws, although they have been adopted according to the requirements of the treaties. They are yet very far from the enjoyment of all the rights, privileges, and immunities to which they are entitled under the treaties. In the Choctaw tribe, the 40 acres to which they are entitled for a home has not been set apart to them and no one has any title to a single foot of land he may improve or occupy. Whenever his occupancy of land is in the way of any citizen Indian he is at once, by means sufficiently severe and threatening, compelled to leave his improvements. He consequently has no abiding place, and what he is enabled to get from the soil for his support, he is compelled to gather either furtively or by the most absolute subserviency to the will, caprices, or exactions of his former master. But meager provision is made for the schooling of his children, and but little participation in the management of the government of which he is a citizen is permitted him. He is nevertheless moral, industrious, and frugal, peaceable, orderly, and obedient to the laws, taking no part in the crimes which have of late filled the country with alarm and put in peril the lives and property of law-abiding citizens. A number of these sought an interview with us on one occasion, but were, as we were informed, warned by a prominent Indian citizen that if they called upon us they would be killed, which warning they heeded.

In the Cherokee tribe the schools provided for the freedmen are of very inferior and inefficient character, and practically their children are growing up in deplorable ignorance. They are excluded from participation in the per capita distribution of all funds, and are ignored in almost all respects as a factor in the government of a people of whose citizenship they are by the treaties in all respects made a part. Yet in this tribe the freedmen are conspicuous for their morality, industrial and frugal habits, and for peaceable and orderly lives.

Justice has been utterly perverted in the hands of those who have thus laid hold of the forms of its administration in this Territory and who have inflicted irreparable wrongs and outrages upon a helpless people for their own gain. The United States put the title to a domain of countless wealth and unmeasured resources in these several tribes or nationalities, but it was a conveyance in trust for specific uses, clearly indicated in the treaties themselves, and for no other purpose. It was for the use and enjoyment in common by each and every citizen of his tribe, of each and every part of the Territory, thus tersely expressed in one of the treaties: "To be held in common, so that each and every member of either tribe shall have an equal undivided interest in the whole." The tribes can make no other use of it. They have no power to grant it to anyone, or to grant to anyone an exclusive use of any portion of it. These tribal governments have wholly perverted their high trusts, and it is the plain duty of the United States to enforce the trust it has so created and recover for its original uses the domain and all the gains derived from the perversions of the trust or discharge the trustee.

The United States also granted to these tribes the power of self-government, not to conflict with the Constitution. They have demonstrated their incapacity to so govern themselves, and no higher duty can rest upon the Government that granted this authority than to revoke it when it has so lamentably failed.

In closing this report we may be permitted to add that we have observed with pain and deep regret that the praiseworthy efforts of the Christian church, and of benevolent associations from different parts of the country, so long continued among the tribes, are being counteracted and rendered in a large measure nugatory by the untoward influences and methods now in force among them tending directly to destroy and obliterate the beneficial effects of their good work.

Source: Report of the Dawes Commission, November 20, 1894, S. Misc. Doc., no. 24, 53d Cong., 3d sess., serial 3281, 8-12.

4-24. The Woman's National Indian Association

Amelia S. Quinton

1894

A humanitarian and teacher actively involved in the Woman's Christian Temperance Union, Amelia Stone Quinton (1833-1926), a religious and moral reformer, was a native of Jamesville, New York, who in 1878 married Richard L. Quinton, a professor of history and astronomy. In 1883 she and social reformer Mary L. Bonney, along with others, formed the Woman's National Indian Association (WNIA), although the organization traced its roots to 1879 when railroads and white settlers invaded Indian Territory in violation of federal treaties. Quinton assumed the presidency of the WNIA in 1887, serving eighteen years in that capacity. Advocating Christian education and citizenship for Native Americans, as well as the end of reservations, she helped establish libraries, schools, and missions, engaged in fund raising, delivered speeches, and wrote articles supporting her humane position toward Native Americans. In 1886 Quinton published Suggestions for the Friends of the Women's National Indian Association. *Reprinted below is a piece she put together in 1893-1894 on the story of the WNIA.*

The story of the Woman's National Indian Association is, like that of similar movements, largely a personal story. The work had its rise in individual interest in Indians, and this, communicated to and shared by others, originated a philanthropy now of national proportions. The motives were Christian, and the inspiration had its birth from the missionary spirit. The history of the Association, therefore, as is natural, is largely a history of missionary activity. Even the first movement, though for five years wholly devoted to gaining political rights for Indians, was as truly from the missionary spirit as was afterward the planting [of] missions in the tribes. In the present brief outline of the work reference must be made to the above points; to the condition of things among Indians at that date—the spring of 1879—the home circumstances of the people aided, their character as then seen, the results of the labors of the Association, and to the important work still remaining to be done.

And first a personal reference. A devoted Christian educator in Philadelphia became specially interested in the Indian race through references in the daily press, related the facts observed therein to a friend, and these two secured the interest of others; an organization was proposed by the friend referred to, and effected after two years of preparatory work which was planned, provided for, and done chiefly by these two. It was seeing "the need" which moved the "compassion," and the kindred impulse to "go tell" naturally followed. Christians were believed to be millennium bringers by the application of practical righteousness to specific needs, and this "faith justified" itself by the events which were its sequel.

The appeal of the association for united effort to move our government to grant a legal status to Indians, the protection of law, lands in severalty, and education; appeal was made to the Christian press and ministry, to ecclesiastical bodies and to patriots, and soon sixteen states were included in work to these ends. The first appeal was for covenant-keeping with tribes to which solemn pledges had been given, and that no treaty should be abrogated or broken without the free consent of the Indian tribe named in it. It was of this association's service that Senator [Henry L.] Dawes, chairman of the Senate Indian Committee, said: "The new government Indian policy was born of and nursed by this woman's association," and it was his own Severalty Bill which became the law of the land in March, 1887, that granted to the Indians of the United States the rights and privileges asked in the petitions of the association.

When it became evident that this great reform would be a success, the attention of the association was given to missionary work, to home building, hospital, educational and other work needed among the Indians on the reservations, and soon ten departments of practical work were shared by interested helpers in nearly all the states of the Union, and with encouraging success. During the last nine years, since these lines of effort were undertaken, the society has established directly or indirectly thirty-three mission stations, transferring these to permanent missionary societies when well established, giving with the mission its land, mission cottage, chapel, and all its property and improvements. The association has given special education to bright Indians, training them as physicians, nurses, teachers and missionaries to help and lead their people. It has built houses by loans, placing thus about a hundred Indians in civilized and Christian homes, and the loans are being honestly repaid. It has hospital, library and industrial departments, and has built twelve missionary cottages, chapels and schoolhouses. During its last year it expended $28,000 sending goods to tribes in special need to the amount of $3,000.

A glance at the oppressions of Indians at the beginning of this work shows them to have been practically without legal rights. They were subject to enforced removals from their own land; they were constantly robbed by marauders and ruffian frontiersmen; they were under agents possessing despotic power, who could forbid trade among them, could suspend their chiefs, and arrest or drive from the reservation any unwelcome visitor. The Indians were not permitted to sell the natural products of the soil even when in a starving condition. They might be banished to reservations where farming was impossible though farming was required, and yet under such conditions were sometimes deprived of arms and ammunition for hunting, their only source of subsistence. Our nation practically prohibited all lines of work natural to the Indian, and then falsified its promises to furnish him means for farming. To-day, by the success of the movement inaugurated under Divine Providence by the Woman's National Indian Association, the Indian is lifted out of his old helplessness into the status of a man and citizen under law, is given the privilege of education, and his home and family can now be protected from ruffians and criminals.

In the old days, as a rule, the Indian home was a tepee or tent, a wickyup, hogan, bark campooda or dug-out, destitute of furniture and with no garden, field, meadow, wells, improvements, or domestic animals. Today there are thousands of comfortable homes, built of planks, logs, or better materials; many in different places are really tasteful and complete homes, and these are now surrounded with gardens, fields, orchards and other features of civilization, all constituting a wide beginning of the better era which has really dawned for the Indian race. Nor is the change in Indian character less marked. Under the old order of things the better human impulses were hindered or throttled; manhood and womanhood were humiliated and degraded, and many a character noble by nature, and many a mind finely endowed was stultified into utter helplessness and inaction by tyrannous conditions and the inescapable bondage of the reservation system, the sum of all oppression. Today the Indian, man or woman, who is conscious of the possession of character, the impulse to action felt by ability, the aspiration of power, physical or mental, has freedom to go where he will and make his own life; while he who desires education, development, culture—and there are not a few of these in the many tribes—can find his opportunity, his work, and his reward. Indian women are at last free to express the best that is in them, to embody in deeds the noblest instincts of maternity, and bravely to ask for their children the protections and privileges which have so lately come to themselves.

The results of the great change for the race are surprising when one considers the time involved. Gradually the way was preparing by Providence, and even under the reservation-government civilized industry had a beginning; but the great facts of progress are due to the changes of the last few years. One cannot but be surprised that already more than twenty-four thousand families are engaged in agriculture; that there is provision now made for three-quarters of the Indian children of school age; that there are at least twenty-five thousand real Indian citizens of the United States; that the seventy-one military posts formerly set to control them are reduced to ten; and that of the two hundred and fifty thousand Indians of the country two hundred thousand are already self-supporting. The efficiency and excellence of the work done for and by the Indians in the schools has surprised the whole country, and one need but look over the well certified reports of these schools to see that their results compare well with those of schools for any race under like conditions. Those who have visited the schools operating for one month each within these exposition grounds need no added testimony to the natural ability of the Indian, or to his willingness to work when the usual motives of civilization are permitted him. Did time permit, many interesting illustrations might be given of the success of well-endowed Indian young men and women who have in a few years obtained a good elementary English education; of others who have graduated from colleges and institutions for special professional education; of some who have been trained by our own association as physicians and nurses, or been aided in the study of law, and even of art.

The first Indian woman physician was thus educated, and is now an honored government physician and Christian worker among her own people. The achievements of some of these Indian patriots among their own people would read like epics could they be written.

We can here cite but one case: One who followed the wild, free life of an Indian boy—happily remote from vicious rough white borderers—till fourteen years of age, when, hearing from beloved lips the story of the Christ, and being won, he followed his Divine star to an Indian school one hundred and fifty miles distant; finished his course there, entered and graduated from college, achieved a three years' medical education, again graduated with honor, and to the persuasions of white fellow-students to stay east and get rich he made answer: "Do you suppose that I have studied here seven years to stay and make money? No. I go to help my people." And back to barbarians, to isolation, to hardships, but to noble service, he returned, exposing life again and again in the emergencies of his consecrated labor.

In the fifteen years given to work for this race, and in visits to tribes in every state and territory of the Union but three, it has been my happy lot to meet not a few men and women, sometimes in blanket, paint and feathers, who were jewel souls by nature, richly worth the effort of any patriot to save and uplift them into noble manhood and womanhood; and some of these have by God's grace become jewels in Christ's crown and consecrated workers in His kingdom. Some of them have heard of Him for the first time in dying hours and have said, "Now I am not afraid," and have with the last breath asked the Divine light for their people. Reproaches that can never be forgotten have fallen from some dying lips for a gospel withheld from beloved ones; from many tribes now come earnest pleadings for schools and for Christian teachers.

Among the many noble endeavors of today, what is nobler than redemptive work among these native Americans, to whom we are under so great and so lasting obligation? There are still needed forty mission stations in order to bring the Divine light to all these native tribes, and the presence and effort of a consecrated pair of friends and helpers in each tribe would discover the jewels worth polishing; would detect and go far to remedy wrongs among them; would foster all good impulses; would evolve and strengthen manhood and womanhood, and would inspire toward industry, patriotism and Christian living the worthy men and women of the tribe. With forty-four states it should be easy to provide these needed missions; and rich in mental, moral and spiritual power, it should be easy for American Christian women to finish the solution of the Indian question.

Source: Amelia S. Quinton, "The Woman's National Indian Association," in *The Congress of Women: Held in the Woman's Building, World's Columbian Exposition, Chicago, U.S.A. 1893* (Chicago: Monarch Book Company, 1894), 71-73. See also Indian Rights Association Papers, Historical Society of Pennsylvania, Philadelphia; Amelia Stone Quinton Papers, Huntington Library, San Marino, California.

4-25. Assessment of the Cherokee Nation

S. H. Mayes

1895

Samuel Houston Mayes (1845-1927) was born in the Cherokee Nation and began his public service in 1881 when he was elected sheriff of Cooweescoowee District. He served two terms in the Cherokee Senate and as principal chief from 1895 to 1895. Mayes and other tribal members in 1895 submitted a somber but realistic assessment of the Cherokee Nation to the U.S. House of Representatives and Senate. "Could a nation of irresponsible, corrupt, criminal people produce such (improved and good) conditions?" they queried. Their commentary merited careful consideration.

. . . These are times of imminent danger to those institutions of government and tenure of property that the Cherokees have brought with them from the darkness of time immemorial, modified somewhat by the enlightened influences of your great constitution but distinctive still as Cherokee institutions. The Cherokees are fully alive to the situation, and they know that unless in some way congress shall become acquainted rapidly with their true condition, all that they hold dear of country and people will be swept away by the hands that they have heretofore confidently looked to for protection, and which have in gentleness and friendship been so often extended to them. For some reasons that we cannot explain, the Cherokees have been traduced and grievously misrepresented by persons high in authority, from whom we have had every reason to expect fair statement. It is natural to love the country one lives in, if that country protects life, promotes happiness, and insures equality. When a people are found who are intensely patriotic, it can be taken for granted that their government gives them such assurances. The Cherokees are such a people; there is not upon the face of the earth today a people more thoroughly contented with their condition than the Cherokees. In his humble western home, sequestered from the mad rush one sees in the east, you will find the Cherokee a sober, industrious, religious gentleman, earning his daily bread by honest labor upon the soil, of which he is equal owner with every one else in the nation, irrespective of superior advantage such as wealth, opportunity, or education gives.

He believes in common education; such as is natural with his ideas of common property. Therefore, under the constitution adopted in 1839, we find this provision: "Religion, morality, and knowledge being necessary for good government, the preservation of liberty, and the happiness of mankind, schools, and the means of education, shall forever be encouraged in this nation." Faithful to the idea here expressed, the history of the advancement of the educational interests of the Cherokees for the last fifty years cannot but please the mind and heart of him who loves his fellow-man for the good that he promises. Now, notwithstanding the pall that the civil war threw over the land, the progress of the Cherokee schools and facilities for common education has been marked and rapid. Now, with a population of 40,000 Cherokees, we have over one hundred common schools, running nine months a year, with capable, competent teachers, generally comfortable school houses, where all of necessary appliances, books, etc., are supplied by the Cherokee nation; a male and female college, of brick and stone, at a cost not exceeding each year over $150,000, afford to the youth of both sexes an opportunity of higher education; an orphan asylum of sufficient size to accommodate every orphan of school age in the nation, which has cost over $100,000, have now an attendance of over 2,000 orphans. We have also an asylum for the infirm and unfortunate (a home for these poor stricken people). At the male seminary this year there is over one hundred and eighty young men, at the female seminary over two hundred of our girls. The several missionary societies have not less than fifteen or twenty schools in the various parts of our country, encouraged by generous gifts of land upon the part of the Cherokees. To these earnest Christian workers in our midst we also appeal, in our time of extremity for national existence, to assist us in refuting the false charges made with no other motive, we believe, than to induce congress to withdraw its powerful protection from us, that we might become easy prey of unscrupulous avarice and greed, as the hungry beast devoured his milder companion of the forest. These religious denominations among us, who brought to us the beautiful Christian religion, who witnessed the sowing of its seeds and now behold its plant of vigorous growth in the full bearing of its fruits, can bear us witness of the many false charges of retrogression, immorality, lawlessness, and crime among the Cherokees. We ask, when our enemies traduce us and when grave charges of malfeasance in public offices and trust are hurled at us, that you will require specific proof to accompany the accusation.

Churches are everywhere, organized throughout our land, and their efficient and powerful auxiliaries, the Sabbath schools, are conducted every Sunday in our various churches and school-houses, where the same lesson papers are used that your children study throughout this land and elsewhere. All of this, with the exception of the missionary efforts among us, to which we largely contribute, is done at no expense whatever to the United States, but entirely at the expense of the Cherokees. Is it to be doubted that a people fostering and encouraging such institutions have all the finer sensibilities of education and Christian manhood that will be found among similar communities in the States? Could a nation of irresponsible, corrupt, criminal people produce such conditions? Are these the results of the evil and corruption that the Dawes Commission assert pervade the very atmosphere down there? We earnestly ask that before laying the axe to the root of the tree you yourselves have planted and carefully attended, that you examine the fruits thereof and take not the word of some persons controlled by envy, and in a moment of irritability against us for not blindly following their suggestion, consent to and advise our destruction. We submit that in the nature of things, it would have been impossible for the Dawes commission to have found no good existing in our country, yet not one redeeming word do we find in their report, if there is any. Did they not see us in the worship of the same God they worship? Did they not hear us while with bowed heads we implored the intercession of the Son of God? Then why have they with the black veil of corrupt charges obscured the good that honor would have compelled them to acknowledge if they found it?

In our governmental affairs we have followed in the footsteps of your people; our form of government is as yours, with its three departments, executive, legislative and judicial, where the same authorities govern and the same methods and rules obtain, perhaps somewhat modified, as among you. It may be that at our legislature some of your practices have been adopted, and it may be that some of our methods in the struggle for office may partake of the taint we sometimes hear charged against your legislatures. Walking in your footsteps, it could hardly be expected that, in following the good you practice, some of your evils may not have also left their mark. We pursue some short cuts in office down there sometimes that would hardly receive the approbation of a legislative reformer; but that we are one half as corrupt as the Dawes commission represent us we emphatically deny, neither can we admit that we are to any degree as corrupt as the newspapers assert of your average legislatures.

. . . The Cherokees wish to call your attention to the size of their present country. Within our country as at present bounded there are less than five million acres of land; our population is thirty thousand; the estimate of the number of acres includes river beds, and portions, and all that would be necessary for public travel and commerce. At a glance it will be seen that we have now less than one hundred and sixty acres to the head. The proportion of the arable land to that unfit for cultivation is, by the most liberal estimate, not exceeding one to four, so it will be seen that today the Cherokees have less than forty acres of tillable land to the individual. We invite your close attention to this fact, for not the least among the influences seeking the destruction of our government and the opening of the country is the hope that homes may thereby be obtained for the white people who would come in. It could not be so in the Cherokee nation; we have not now more than will suffice the immediate necessities of our people; nor could we consent to part with any more land whatever without gross injustice to our poor, who depend upon agriculture and stock-raising for subsistence. There is no necessity for a town-site law in the Cherokee nation. The statement by the Dawes commission that towns had been erected, costly business houses and residences built in the Cherokee nation by non citizens is absolutely false with not a single exception. We have half a score or more of beautiful towns in the Cherokee nation, beautifully and symmetrically surveyed, containing many substantial and even fine structures; but all has been done by citizens of the nation, and such buildings are not occupied or owned in any manner by aliens, nor have they any money in them. Our towns have good systems of municipal government, the result of liberal legislation on the part of the national council. A municipal government is run by a mayor and a board of aldermen, and called a town council. The quiet and neatness of our towns commend us to all our visitors. There are no white aliens doing business among us, other than those engaged in farming; we do not, as alleged, invite them into our country; we do not invite or use their money in building our towns; we put every impediment we can in the way of their coming among us; we do not need them in our midst, but we are a hospitable people, our friendship extends beyond the lines of our country, and in our acts of hospitality we sometimes harbor in our midst coming in the guise of friends, who, through motives of envy and covetousness, subsequently advise our undoing. Our country is indeed fair to look upon; to us its lovely valleys, limpid streams, flowing prairies, waving forests, and grand hills are an Eden. There, over fifty years ago, with specious promises of ever-lasting protection, you planted us, literally driving us from our homes in the mountains of Georgia, Tennessee, and North Carolina. "As long as the grass grows and water runs," wrote General [Andrew] Jackson, "shall the country remain yours." "No state or territorial line shall ever surround you," were the words your minister who induced us to go to that country, and his words are engrafted into the treaty. Now, after the lapse of fifty years, when the bodies of those who made these promises to us have been consigned to the tomb, and their names have taken their places in history, many of them for all time, you, their children, tell us, the children of those with whom they treated, that your parents did not mean all they said, and were only preparing a temporary solution of the questions they were pretending to settle. . . .

Source: S. H. Mayes, and others, to the Senate and House of Representatives of the United States Congress, 1895, Cherokee Nation Papers, Oklahoma Historical Society, Oklahoma City.

4-26. Modern Treaty Making with Native Americans

James McLaughlin

1895

Born in Avonmore, Ontario, Canada, James McLaughlin (1842-1923) attended common schools and was a Minnesota blacksmith when in 1871 he secured an assignment as an overseer to the Devil's Lake Indian Agency in the Dakota Territory. In 1876 he emerged as Indian agent at Devil's Lake, where he abolished the Indian Sun Dance. He became Indian agent of the Standing Rock Agency in 1881, having charge of approximately 6,000 Sioux. Known as "White Hair," McLaughlin, who in 1864 had married a mixed-blood Sioux woman (Mary L. Buisson), spoke Siouan fluently. He encouraged the education of Native Americans, advocated self-sufficiency, promoted agricultural training, and stressed the importance of learning technical skills. McLaughlin clearly understood Native American cultural traditions. "The closer the Indian is to nature," he once remarked, "the more nearly is he a spiritualist." On March 31, 1895, McLaughlin, a Roman Catholic, was appointed U.S. Indian inspector for the Interior Department. Later he managed to procure histories of the Battle of the Little Bighorn and the life of Chief Joseph. During his career, McLaughlin concluded more than forty agreements between Native Americans and the U.S. government and no doubt enjoyed greater personal acquaintances with Indians than any other Gilded Age American. In 1910 he published My Friend the Indian *in which he related his experiences, adventures, and years as an Indian agent. The following excerpt pertaining to treaty making comes from that poignant memoir.*

. . . Treaty-making with the Indians has been my business very generally since my appointment as inspector [in 1895]. I have made all the treaties—or agreements, as they are designated now, legally—with two exceptions, that have been entered into in the past thirteen years. There was a treaty-making commission that was organized in President [Grover] Cleveland's last term, but the commission made only two treaties in the several years of its existence,—one known as the Fort Hall treaty, and the other with the Crows.

This constant treating with many tribes has brought me into close personal contact with practically all of the Indian tribes of the country. From the Chippewas of Minnesota, in the northeast, to the Mission Indians in California, in the southwest, I have dealt with all the red people, consummating numerous agreements and other important negotiations. In the list of Indians who were parties to these agreements, were many tribes who would not appear in the enumeration of the agreements themselves, for it is frequently the case in the Pacific Coast agencies that remnants of many tribes are gathered on a single reservation. And I might say now that I believe the solution of the Indian problem is brought very much nearer to us by this mixing of the tribes.

I had recently occasion to visit a remote agency in California at the Round Valley school. The reservation is located in the heart of the Coast Range mountains, forty-odd miles from the nearest railroad point and approachable only by a mountainous and difficult road. On this reservation there were gathered during the third quarter of the last century fragments of bands belonging generally to the Digger tribe, with a couple of remnants of people that were not classified as Diggers. These bands, or sub-tribes, spoke different languages. They had been widely scattered and much persecuted. They had some traditional customs in common, and they were very far down in the scale of humanity. Being confined on the one reservation, they were compelled to adopt a common language, and they took to the English as the readiest mode for a common tongue. This necessarily broke down the Indian barrier of a language foreign to that used by the whites, and made easy their conversion to other customs of the white people.

I have no hesitancy in saying that these people, who were so far down in the scale of humanity a couple of generations ago, are now further advanced than nine tenths of the Indians in the country. They have received no government aid, have been compelled to "rustle" for subsistence, and are at least the equals of the whites who live in the country surrounding them. They demonstrate positively the tenability of my theory that the Indian problem will solve itself as soon as the Indian is shown that he must depend entirely on his own resources; that the government has nothing more in store for him. These people—Concows, Wylackies, Ukies, and several other bands—are prosperous and enlightened. Almost invariably they have attained to some sort of independence, and are rather better off than the white people among whom they live.

Indians are shrewder in diplomacy than might be expected by those who judge of their capacity from the manner in which they have been deprived of their native riches. In the hard school of adversity they have learned a great deal, and I have found among them many men who, had they been educated, would have made excellent lawyers. It is true that I have generally succeeded in making the agreements that I have offered the Indians, but this success was rather due to the manner of the negotiations than because the agreements were desired by the Indians. This I have effected by permitting the other parties to the agreement to take the position of making the terms themselves. In almost every instance, the attitude of the Indian in the beginning has been that of opposition to the proposed agreement, but they have always come around to the other point of view. It has been simply a matter of showing them, by illustrations they would understand, that what was proposed would be best for them in the long run.

They are simple-minded people, and direct arguments must be made to them; but they are no longer amenable to the argument that used to take the form of feasting them. Many successful treaty-makers used this method most effectively. General [George] Crook was known among the Sioux as "the pony-and-grub man." On one occasion, when I was negotiating an agreement with the Red Lake Chippewas of Minnesota, for the cession of a portion of their reservation, one of the chiefs, who was originally opposed to the proposition submitted, said that the beef that was piled on the porch was there for the purpose of seducing his young men. I know not if that be true, but he ate some of the beef, and signed the agreement.

Practically all of the so-called agreements made with the Indians in these latter days concern the cession of lands that have been parts of Indian reservations. Among the agreements which I have negotiated are those which opened to settlement large areas in South Dakota and other states, and with this feature of the land-openings the public is not familiar. The method of procedure in treaty-making is nearly always the same, the argument being adapted to local conditions. In the list of treaties in which I represented the government and was successful in having them accepted, the proposition in every case arising with the government, are three agreements with the Shoshones and Arapahoes, two tribes located on the same reservation in Wyoming; with the Lower Brules, the Sioux of the Rosebud agency, ceding the land that caused the rush to Bonesteel, South Dakota, in 1904, and again in 1909; with the Otoes and Missourias; with the Klamaths and Modocs; with the Northern Cheyennes; with the Grande Rondes; with the Yanktons for the Pipestone quarry; with the Sioux of Devils Lake, North Dakota; with the Red Lake Chippewas; with the Mille Lacs Chippewas; with the Sioux of the Cheyenne River agency, for grazing leases and cattle-trails, also for a large cession of lands, in 1908; with the Standing Rock Sioux, the Pah-Utes of Walker River, Nevada; with the Port Madison Indians, Washington, and with the Mormons of Tuba City, Arizona,—the latter being an agreement for the relinquishment of land held by them, and necessary for the extension of the Moqui reservation. . . .

Source: "Modern Treaty-Making," in James McLaughlin, *My Friend the Indian* (Boston: Houghton Mifflin Company, 1910), 291-95. See also James McLaughlin Papers, Archives of Assumption Abbey, Richardton, North Dakota, and Louis L. Pfaller, *James McLaughlin: The Man with an Indian Heart* (New York: Vantage Press, 1978).

4-27. Songs of the Ghost Dance

1896

During a solar eclipse in 1889, Wovoka (ca 1858-1932), also known as Jack Wilson, a native of Nevada and a Paiute messiah, envisioned his death and transformation to heaven, where he recognized deceased relatives and friends and conversed with God, who counseled him to live peacefully with white people. There he was shown a special form of dance to be preformed for five consecutive nights until a new world crystallized that replaced Anglo domination. In this idyllic utopia, resurrected Native American ancestors and others would once again live the good life as in the former glorious days. For geographically isolated and economically deprived Native Americans, this new religion, which blended elements of Shakerism, Mormonism, Catholicism, and Presbyterianism, offered hope for the future. Regrettably, federal government officials overlooked the cultural benefits and philosophical qualities of the Ghost Dance, concentrating instead on misguided notions that it constituted a prelude to militancy and war. In reality, this movement posed no military, political, religious, or social threat to the federal government. The entire imbroglio, consisting of overzealous participants and exceptionally nervous, irrational officials, culminated tragically in the December, 1890, massacre at Wounded Knee in South Dakota.

One of the early anthropologists to research and report on the Ghost Dance and the Sioux outbreak of 1890 was James Mooney (1861-1921), a reformer and author. Born in Richmond, Indiana, he undertook important cultural studies of Native Americans. For thirty-six years, beginning in 1885, Mooney maintained affiliation with the Bureau of Ethnology of the Smithsonian Institution in Washington, D.C. The following Ghost Dance songs came from Arapahos, Paiutes, Sioux, and Kiowas.

Songs of the Arapaho

My children, when at first I liked the whites,
My children, when at first I liked the whites,
I gave them fruits,
I gave them fruits.

My father, My father,
While he was taking me around,
While he was taking me around,
He turned into a moose
He turned into a moose.

Father, now I am singing it–*Hi'ni'ni!*
Father, now I am singing it–*Hi'ni'ni!*
That loudest song of all,
That loudest song of all–
That resounding song–*Hi'ni'ni!*
That resounding song–*Hi'ni'ni!*

Our father, the Whirlwind,
Our father, the Whirlwind,
Now wears the headdress of crow feathers,
Now wears the headdress of crow feathers.
I circle around–
I circle around
The boundaries of the earth,
The boundaries of the earth–
Wearing the long wing feathers as I fly,
Wearing the long wing feathers as I fly.

My children, my children,
Look! the earth is about to move,
Look! the earth is about to move.
My father tells me so,
My father tells me so.

My father, my father–
I am looking at him,
I am looking at him.
He is beginning to turn into a bird,
He is beginning to turn into a bird.

The rock, the rock,
I am standing upon it,
I am standing upon it.
By its means I saw our father,
By its means I saw our father.

My children, my children,
I am about to hum,
I am about to hum.
My children, my children.

Father, have pity on me,
Father, have pity on me;
I am crying for thirst,
I am crying for thirst;
All is gone–I have nothing to eat,
All is gone–I have nothing to eat.

The crow has called me,
The crow has called me.
When the crow came for me,
When the crow came for me,
I heard him,
I heard him.

The crow is circling above me,
The crow is circling above me,
The crow having come for me,
The crow having come for me.

I hear everything,
I hear everything.
I am the crow,
I am the crow.

There is a good river, There is a good river,
Where there is no timber–
Where there is no timber–
But thunder-berries are there,
But thunder-berries are there.

My children, my children,
I am flying about the earth,
I am flying about the earth.
I am a bird, my children,
I am a bird, my children,
Says the father,
Says the father.

My father, I am poor,
My father, I am poor.
Our father is about to take pity on me,
Our father is about to take pity on me.
Our father is about to make me fly around,
Our father is about to make me fly around.

I am going around the sweat-house,
I am going around the sweat-house.
The shell lies upon the mound,
The shell lies upon the mound.

My children, my children,
It is I who wear the morning star on my head,
It is I who wear the morning star on my head;
I show it to my children,
I show it to my children,

Says the father,
Says the father.

Father, the Morning Star!
Father, the Morning Star!
Look on us, we have danced until daylight,
Look on us, we have danced until daylight.
Take pity on us–*Hi'i'i'!*
Take pity on us–*Hi'i'i'!*

Thus says our father, the Crow,
Thus says our father, the Crow.
Go around five times more–
Go around five times more–
Says the father,
Says the father.

Songs of the Paiute

The snow lies there–*ro'răni'!*
The snow lies there–*ro'răni'!*
The snow lies there–*ro'răni'!*
The snow lies there–*ro'răni'!*
The Milky Way lies there,
The Milky Way lies there.

A slender antelope, a slender antelope,
A slender antelope, a slender antelope,
He is wallowing upon the ground,
He is wallowing upon the ground,
He is wallowing upon the ground,
He is wallowing upon the ground.

The black rock, the black rock,
The black rock, the black rock,
The rock is broken, the rock is broken,
The rock is broken, the rock is broken.

The wind stirs the willows,
The wind stirs the willows,
The wind stirs the willows,
The wind stirs the grasses,
The wind stirs the grasses,
The wind stirs the grasses.

Fog! Fog!
Lightning! Lightning!
Whirlwind! Whirlwind!

The whirlwind! The whirlwind!
The whirlwind! The whirlwind!
The snowy earth comes gliding, the snowy earth comes gliding;
The snowy earth comes gliding, the snowy earth come gliding.

There is dust from the whirlwind,
There is dust from the whirlwind,
There is dust from the whirlwind.
The whirlwind on the mountain,
The whirlwind on the mountain,
The whirlwind on the mountain.

The rocks are ringing,
The rocks are ringing,
The rocks are ringing.
They are ringing in the mountains,
They are ringing in the mountains,
They are ringing in the mountains.

The cottonwoods are growing tall,
The cottonwoods arc growing tall,
The cottonwoods arc growing tall.
They are growing tall and verdant,
They are growing tall and verdant,
They are growing tall and verdant.

Songs of the Sioux

Who think you comes there?
Who think you comes there?
Is it someone looking for his mother?
Is it someone looking for his mother?
Says the father,
Says the father.

I love my children–*Ye'ye'!*
I love my children–*Ye'ye'!*
You shall grow to be a nation–*Ye'ye'!*
You shall grow to be a nation–*Ye'ye'!*
Says the father,
Says the father.
Haye'ye' Eyayo'yo'! Haye'ye' E'yayo'yo'!

Mother, come home; mother, come home.
My little brother goes about always crying,
My little brother goes about always crying.
Mother, come home; mother, come home.

Now they are about to chase the buffalo,
Now they are about to chase the buffalo,
Grandmother, give me back my bow,
Grandmother, give me back my bow,
The father says so, the father says so.

The whole world is coming,
A nation is coming, a nation is coming,
The Eagle has brought the message to the tribe.
The father says so, the father says so.

Over the whole earth they are coming.
The buffalo are coming, the buffalo are coming,
The Crow has brought the message to the tribe,
The father says so, the father says so.

It is I who make these sacred things,
Says the father, says the father.
It is I who make the sacred shirt,
Says the father, says the father.
It is I who made the pipe,
Says the father, says the father.

Songs of the Kiowa

The father will descend,
The father will descend.
The earth will tremble,
The earth will tremble.
Everybody will arise,
Everybody will arise.
Stretch out your hands,
Stretch out your hands.

The spirit army is approaching,
The spirit army is approaching,
The whole world is moving onward,
The whole world is moving onward.
See! Everybody is standing watching,
See! Everybody is standing watching.
Let us all pray, Let us all pray.

My father has much pity on us,
My father has much pity on us.
I hold out my hands toward him and cry,
I hold out my hands toward him and cry.
In my poverty I hold out my hands toward him and cry,

In my poverty I hold out my hands toward him and cry.

That wind, that wind
Shakes my tipi, shakes my tipi,
And sings a song for me,
And sings a song for me.

God has had pity on us,
God has had pity on us.
Jesus has taken pity on us,
Jesus has taken pity on us.
He teaches me a song,
He teaches me a song.
My song is a good one,
My song is a good one.

Source: Ghost-Dance Songs, in *American Poetry: The Nineteenth Century* (New York: The Library of America, 1993), 2:727-735; Thomas E. Sanders and Walter W. Peek, eds., *Literature of the American Indian* (Beverly Hills, Calif.: Glencoe Press, 1976), 186-87; James Mooney, "The Ghost-Dance Religion and the Sioux Outbreak of 1890," *Fourteenth Annual Report of the Bureau of American Ethnology*, 1896.

4-28. Home Life Among the Indians

Alice Cunningham Fletcher

June 1897

The daughter of New England parents, Alice Cunningham Fletcher (1838-1923) was a reformer, author, musicologist, and anthropologist. Like several others of her generation from New England and the North, where the antislavery crusade had prevailed, Fletcher in the post–Civil War period turned her energies toward improving the lives of Native Americans. Influenced by Frederic Ward Putnam and by Francis and Susette La Flesche, Fletcher conducted surveys and engaged in other activities pertaining to Native Americans for the federal government. She also lived for a time among the Omahas, publishing Indian Story and Song from North America *in 1900. Her vivid description of home life among Native Americans occupied eleven pages in the June, 1897, copy of* Century Magazine.

There are no locks and keys in an Indian tribe. In the tent there is no closet: in the home there can be no secret, for the family skeleton, if there is one, is also public property. This lack of privacy in personal and social affairs becomes a definite factor in the education of the people; its exigencies are potent in the fixing of external habits and in the formation of personal character. The constant exposure to observation, the impossibility of wrestling alone with his petty faults during the formative period of life, develops in the Indian two extremes of feeling—obtuseness as to the interest of others, and over-sensitiveness to blame or approbation of himself. There is no covering up of the follies of youth; every lapse from the tribal standard of rectitude in known to all; and when once fixed in the indelible Indian memory, it is not easy to outgrow one's shortcomings. Reformation of a lost character becomes a discouraging task where there is not forgetting, and where criticism is a common privilege and ridicule a weapon. Reserve is the Indian's only defense, and self-restraint his only safeguard; and these virtues are the earliest lessons which the child receives. Indian reserve, often mistaken for sullenness, is susceptible of philosophical explanation.

Living among the people, I could not fail to be soon impressed by their peculiarities. Occasionally an Indian would unaccountably become silent, would refuse to answer when spoken to, and would turn away from the other inmates of the lodge. His conduct did not seem to surprise or disturb anybody; the voluntary exile to Coventry was allowed to take his own way unmolested, and to return to society when and how he chose. After I had been for several weeks living in the lodge, never away from the sight and sound of the people, one day I suddenly found myself with my back to all the world, not wishing to speak to, or even to look at, any one. This discovery of my own behavior set me to thinking why I had been guilty of precisely the same conduct which in the Indian I had attributed to savagery. I found that the constant enforced presence of others produced such mental fatigue that exhausted nature's demand for relief must be met in some way, and was met in the only way open to me. This expression of my own mood enlightened me as to many phases of Indian character, and helped me to appreciate all the more the many invariable sunny natures of my acquaintance, among men and women, whose charity raised them above their fellows; who were able to shut their eyes to that which could not be concealed in the lives of those less strong than themselves to resist temptation.

The necessity which we feel of individualizing our living-place, of having some one spot sacred from intrusion, has been partly recognized and provided for in the Indian dwelling. It is true that all live upon the ground, sitting, sleeping, eating there; yet the space within the lodge is divided—not by visible partitions, but by assigning certain places by long-established custom to the several members of the family.

Entering the lodge from the east, one finds the fire burning in the center. All tents, except in rare instances, are pitched facing the east. To the left, near the door, is the particular domain of the mother. Here are kept the stores in immediate use and the dishes and utensils for cooking. The location is convenient. The woman can slip in and out of the tent, disturbing no one, can bring in the wood and water, prepare the food and cook it at the fire unmolested, except by the toddling children or the voracious puppy. Beyond the mother's place, in the middle of the south side of the lodge, is the space set apart for the father. In the angular space behind him, made by the slant of the tent and the ground, he keeps his personal belongings and his tools. The father's place in the tent is never intruded upon by a stranger; but when a lodge is prepared for a ceremony, it is this place which is occupied by the host of the evening. The rear of the lodge, opposite the entrance, is where all guests are made welcome. It would be as discourteous for a visitor to pass between his host and the fire, and sit down anywhere he chose, as it would be to enter the private apartments of our homes, ignoring the reception-room. When a guest enters an Indian home he turns to the right, passes around the fire to the back of the tent, and seats himself silently where the place is always ready for him, furnished with mats, robes, or blankets. On the other side of the fire, opposite the father's seat, is the place reserved for the older members of the family: it may be the grandfather or the grandmother. By the door on the right the grown sons are to be found. They are supposed to be on the alert to serve their parents, to attend to the horses, or, if occasion require, to protect the family from harm. The children are tucked in among the elder folk, the girls being placed beyond their parents toward the back of the lodge, where they sit and play or sew, unmolested and unnoticed by the visitors who come and go. This order within the tent is so universal that were one to pass into a strange lodge in the dark, he could be reasonably sure of knowing the person he aroused by noting his location.

In the large communal houses, such as the Omaha earth-lodges of the last generation, where more than one family lived and in the long houses of the Iroquois and of the Pacific tribes, where many groups of kindred were gathered together under one roof, and each family had its separate fire, a like etiquette regarding place was observed within each separate allotted space.

In the Indian family all property is individual; even the small children have their own belongings. Nothing is owned in common, nor does any one ever attempt to interfere in the control of another's possessions. The man owns his weapons and his tools, his own clothing and his horses; to the wife belongs the tent with the robes, and she owns the domestic utensils and her own particular horses, and all property used in common by the family is hers, over which she holds unquestioned right of disposition.

One day at a festival an Indian acquaintance of mine gave away a valuable horse. I was surprised at her act, knowing something of the circumstances of the family; and I privately asked her, as we sat together, if her husband was willing to part with the animal. She looked at me blankly for a moment, and then said: "The horse was mine; what had he to say about it?" I ventured to explain that a white woman would first have asked her husband's consent. "I wouldn't be a white woman," she said, after a little reflection, as she sprang up to join the dance, her snapping necklaces and ear-pendants emphasizing her opinion as she kept time to the rhythm of the song.

One would hardly suppose that there could be particular rules as to the manner of sitting upon the ground; but here, as in every other part of Indian life, there is rigid observance of custom. Men may properly sit upon their heels or cross-legged, but no woman may assume these attitudes. She must sit sidewise, gathering her feet well under her, and make a broad, smooth lap. When working she may kneel or squat, and when resting she, as well as the men, may sit with legs extended; but at all other times men and women must observe the etiquette of posture distinctive of sex. To rise without touching the ground with the hand, springing up lightly and easily to the feet, is a bit of good breeding very difficult for one not to the manner born. Careful parents are particular to train their children in these niceties of behavior. Among the Winnebagos the little girls are drilled in the proper way of standing when under observation on dress occasions. Their position of feet and hands is also the proper one for the women in certain religious dances. While among the Sioux, a mother with a good-sized family of boys and girls propounded to me the question whether white women did not find their daughters more trouble than their sons; she was sure she did. "Look at those girls," said she; "I have their clothes to make, their hair to braid, and to see that they learn how to behave. Now, my boys are no trouble." As I glanced at the group of children, the glossy braids of the girls falling over their single smock, and the boys, naked but for the breech-clout, their miniature scalp-lock ornamented with a brass sleigh-bell surmounting a snarl of frowzy hair, I recognized the kinship of maternal perplexities the world over.

Indian good breeding forbids that a newly arrived guest should be spoken to until he has rested, collected his thoughts, and at his own pleasure opened the conversation. The talk at first is always upon light, common topics; if there is any matter of weight to be presented or discussed, though it may be the special object of the visit, it is reserved until the last, often one or two days passing before it is even mentioned.

The guests of an Indian home who are not relatives are generally elderly persons; young people seldom make visits outside their family circle, which, however, is never narrow, owing to the far-reaching recognition of Indian relationships. Sometimes a young man of prominence is the bearer of a message from one chief to another, and then he is ceremoniously received, and after transacting his business he departs as he came, unknown even by name to the younger members of the family.

In the Indian household, as in our own, children bear an important part. The baby is the constant companion of its mother; not that other members of the family do not share in the care of it, but the little one is kept closely under the maternal eye. Soon after birth it is laid in its own bed, which is often profusely ornamented, and is always portable. A board about a foot wide and three feet long is covered with a feather pillow or with layers of soft skins. Upon these the baby is fastened by broad bands of skin, flannel, or calico. When asleep the child's arms are bound under cover, but they are released when it awakens. A great portion of the infant's time is spent lying upon a soft robe or blanket, where it can kick and crow to its heart's content. If, however, the mother should be so engaged as to be frequently called out of the tent, the baby is laced upon its board, and hung up under a tree, or placed where there is no danger of falling. Should the mother have to go any distance from home, she will slip the strap of the board over her head, and the baby goes along, winking at the great world from its mother's back. Long journeys on horses are made by babies snugly packed and hung from the horn of the mother's saddle.

There is something to be said in favor of the *tekas*, as the Nez Percés call the babies' cradle-board, as a safe means of handling and carrying infants. The child is not lifted by its arms or weighted by long garments, nor is its feeble back strained in balancing on the arm of its nurse. By this simple, comfortable device Indian babies are secured from tumbles and the many other mishaps which come to the child in civilization.

Each tribe has its peculiar fashion in the construction and ornamentation of the cradle-board. The head of the infant is generally so arranged as to rest upon the back, so that nearly all Indian heads show a slight flattening of the occiput. In a large family where I was a familiar guest, I noticed that the youngest child had not this peculiarity, and calling the mother's attention to it, she laughingly said: "I never could keep that boy on the board. The older ones would always take him off to play with him. His head was always rolling, and I think that is what makes him so mischievous now."

Swinging cradles are made by setting two crotched sticks in the ground, between which are stretched ropes made of withes, over which a skin or blanket is folded. The father is often seen, as he fashions or mends his implements, swinging the little one to keep it asleep.

Children when five or six months old, and until they are able to walk firmly, are often carried on the back. The mother's blanket is drawn up over the child, which during the adjustment clings closely about its mother's neck. She crosses the upper corners of the blanket over her breast, tucking them in her girdle, which also holds the blanket close at the back; then the mother gives a gently but decided shrug, and the child loosens its arms and settles into its bag-like bed, peering comfortably over its mother's shoulder.

The crying of infants is always prevented, if possible; but I have never heard a little one put to sleep with a song. Both men and women make a weird sound for a lullaby. It is like the wind in the pine-trees. Who knows what far-away echoes of ancient migrations by forest and ocean may linger in this bit of nursery lore?

When the Omaha infant is four or five days old, the father calls together to a feast the principal men of his gens. On this occasion those who belong to the father's sub-gens act as hosts, and, according to Indian custom, cannot partake of the food. After the repast, an old man, selected by the father from his near of kin, bestows upon the child a *ne-ke-ae* name—one belonging to the father's sub-gens, but not borne by any living person.

In some gentes there is the additional ceremony of placing the peculiar objects of taboo beside the infant, or of painting their symbols upon it, as in the Tapa, a deer gens, when the child is decorated with spots like those of the fawn. The penalties attached to any disobedience of the rules of its gens respecting the use of proscribed articles are then recited over the new-born Omaha child.

There is a belief in the tribe that certain persons understand the language of infants. When a baby cries persistently, as if in distress, some one of these knowing folk is sent for to listen to the child and find out its trouble. So, also, there is a notion that an infant can be impressed by the instruction imparted to it when its tribal name is bestowed.

In olden times no Omaha child put on moccasins or had its hair cut until these acts were first performed ceremonially by an old man of the *In-shtá-sunda* gens, to whom had descended this tribal duty. In the spring, when the grass was well up and the corn planted, the parents took their three-year-old boy, who could now "walk steadily," to the tent of the In-shtá-sunda. The mother carried with her a little pair of embroidered moccasins, wherein she had stitched many hopes and plans for her son, while gifts for the old man were borne in the arms of the child's little playmates. On entering the tent the mother said, "Venerable man, I desire my child to wear moccasins." The boy was then led up to the old man, who gathered in his hand the hair on the top of the child's head, tied it in a bunch, then cut it off and laid it away. This done, he clothed the little feet in the new moccasins, and grasping the boy by the arms near the shoulders, lifted him from the ground, turned him slowly to the left, lowering him at each point of the compass until his feet touched the earth, and in this way completed the circle. This was repeated four times, and when the feet of the boy rested on the ground at the completion of the final circuit, he was gently urged forward with this invocation:

> May Wakanda have compassion upon you.
> May your feet rest long upon the earth.
> Walk forth now into the path of life.

When the boy reached home his hair was trimmed by his father in the symbolic manner of his gens, and every spring until he was seven or eight years old his hair was cut in this symbolic style. After that it was suffered to grow, and was dressed in the general tribal fashion. Now and ever after through life a small lock was parted off in a circle upon the crown of the head, and kept carefully braided. Upon this scalp-lock the decorations of youth and the talisman of maturity were tied, and to braid these locks in fine strands was the duty and pride of the sister or wife.

There was a belief among the Omahas that there exists a subtle relation between a person and the things which he has worn or used. A father who was ambitious for his son to achieve a valorous career would take with him on some warlike expedition the moccasins of his boy. When the farthest part of his journey had been reached he would lay the little shoes upon the prairie, saying: "So shall my child walk far and bravely over the land": and he would leave the moccasins there "to draw their owner after them."

If grief for the loss of a child drove a man forth to kill or be killed, he carried in his belt the little moccasins of the dead. If he slew an enemy, he placed the moccasins beside the slain, in the belief that thenceforth his child would have a brave companion in the spirit-world to guide his faltering feet.

The summer days are none too long for Indian children at their play. They mimic the occupations of their elders. Miniature tents are set up, and the mother's shawl is sometime purloined from her pack to serve as tent-covering. If the boys are inclined to gallantry, they will cut tall sunflower-stalks for poles, and there will be fine sport with a tent large enough to creep into; no matter if feet and legs protrude, heads are under cover, and children are children all the world over in the delight of "make-believe." Boys and girls sometimes join in playing "going on the hunt"; the play tents are taken down, and poles and bundles tied upon the boy ponies, who are obedient or fractious, as the case may be, obstinate when fording streams, and stampeding when attacked by enemies. Some boys carry their pony reputations through life. Women have laughingly pointed out to me certain elderly men who were in childhood their "very bad" or their "very good ponies."

Playthings are improvised by the Indian youngster with no small power of invention. Fine war-bonnets are made from corn-husks, at the expense of much time and labor, and everything that children see is modeled in clay: dishes, pipes, ponies, whole villages, show their imitative faculty, while coffins with a bit of glass set in the lid covering a pinched-up baby indicate their keen observation of new customs. Dolls vary as much as the children and their surroundings. Stone babies are not uncommon among the Alaskans, dull enough in appearance, but evidently responsive in the fancy of the small Northwesterner. Dollies made of fawn-skin, with painted eyes and cheeks and real hair, having hands with wonderfully tapering fingers, and clad in gala garments and moccasins fitting well their diminutive feet, are the delight of the children of the plains. One woman who was skilful in the manufacture of dolls made a pair for me, but refused to duplicate them, because she had already used nearly all her own hair in the construction of dolls. Hobby-horses for boys are as universal as dolls for girls. The sunflower-stalk with one nodding blossom left on the end is a favorite pony. In their races the boys ride one stalk and trail two or three others after them as "fresh horses," thus increasing the dust and excitement of the play.

When the Omaha tribe is in camp, a boy of either side of the *Hoó-thu-ga*, or tribal circle, dares not venture to cross the invisible line which divides the In-shtá-sunda from the *Hun-ga-chey-nú*. If he were sent across on an errand, he would secure the company of several other boys of his own side, for a fight is as apt to take place as at the meeting of "gangs" in our own towns and villages. In general their sports are not characterized by quarrelsomeness, for Indian children are remarkably peaceable, and seldom require punishment.

Among Indians, as elsewhere, there are games with songs, which are traditional among the children; and "follow my leader" carries many a boy into plights full of rough-and-tumble fun, while ball, throwing sticks, hoop-catching, hunting the moccasin, and guessing-games delight the young and the old. Indeed, at an early age the love of chance games leads to the gambling away of all sorts of articles, from the varied treasures of a small boy's pockets to the entire property of the man. During winter there is coasting, with cakes of ice for sleds; or, placing one foot before the other upon a smooth stick curved like a barrel-stave, holding on to a string tied to the forward end with one hand, and with a long balancing-pole in the other, a lad will shoot down a bluff at fearful speed, avoiding disaster with wonderful skill.

The Nez Percé Indians during the winter formerly lived in communal lodges, which were from 100 to 150 feet in length and about 20 feet wide. The depressions in the earth where these dwellings stood are still visible at abandoned village sites on the borders of the Clearwater River. Twenty or more families occupied one of these long lodges; their fires were about ten feet apart, and between every two fires an elongated entrance projected from the side of the structure, with closely woven mats hung at the outer and inner openings.

The discipline of the children of a village was delegated to certain men called *Pe-wet-tá-te-pats* (the whippers). They were appointed by the chiefs, and inspired a wholesome awe in quarrelsome and disobedient boys and girls, and, indeed, in the whole juvenile population; for when any children in a lodge were reported as needing punishment, all the little folk were forced to share in it. The hour for this exercise was just at dark; and when the well-known step of the whipper was heard approaching, and the mat was lifted and fell behind him, every youngster began to howl in anticipation of approaching woe. The last one to lie down on his face and receive his thrashing was the really guilty one, that he might have the benefit of prolonged anticipation. The hubbub in the lodge at the hour of discipline is easier to fancy than to describe. Parents of an innocent child frequently contrived his absence at this time; he would be sent upon some errand, perhaps to catch a pony, and the little fellow would gladly plunge through snow and travel far to be beyond the reach of the rod. If, however, a really guilty child absented himself, the whipping was administered on his return. That many a boy, in his wrath, resolved to thrash the grandchildren of the Pe-wet-tá-te-pats when he grew up to be a man and was himself the whipper, is not to be wondered at. There may have been little philosophizing in the Nez Percé's mode of discipline, but he copied the methods of Nature, and his rules were as indiscriminating as her laws.

There is a general belief among Indians that children should be made hardy so as to be capable of great endurance later in life. In some tribes the training is severe, but the old men and women subjected to it when young are examples of vigor and activity when threescore and ten and even at fourscore years of age.

It was the rule among the Nez Percés that all boys and girls about thirteen years old, in good health, should plunge into the river every morning, and remain a given time up to their necks in water. The rapid stream was frequently filled with broken ice, and to prevent the body from being cut, a mat was tied about the neck and adjusted over the part most exposed to the running ice. The arms and legs were to be kept in violent motion, and the child must shout at the top of his lungs. Should he shirk or try to get out of the water too soon, the switch of the whipper would be sure to add to his torment; and should any one succeed in escaping the morning plunge, he took his whipping at night. On returning to the lodge, the children were wrapped in blankets and kept away from the fire during the period of reaction. A certain white pole in the lodge was the tally-post upon which every child marked in black each of his baths.

The Omahas are very careful to protect their children from cold when asleep. In the winter the mercury remains for a long time below zero, and the nights are often bitterly cold; then the little ones are put into robes, and laced up so that they cannot uncover themselves; two or three are sometimes thus tied up together by the watchful mother of the family.

In the Indian home no one is addressed by his personal name. It is very bad manners even to mention the name of a man or woman in his or her presence. Persons are spoken of by terms of relationship only, and I shall never forget my first practical introduction to the intricacies of the Indian system of consanguinity; the result of all my study upon the subject was as nothing before the incongruous complications that faced me. One day, determined to master my perplexities, I went to an Indian friend. "Do you think," I said, "you can make me understand why you call the young man who was here yesterday 'grandfather,' and the little girl who ran in this morning 'mother'?"

"I never thought about it," she answered; "but it must sound queer to you. The young man was father's uncle, so he is my 'grandfather,'"

"I don't see why. I wish you would begin at the beginning."

"Where is the beginning?"

Taking out my note-book, and writing as I spoke: "You call your father and mother as we do, and their brother and sister 'uncle' and 'aunt.'"

"No, I don't," she interrupted. "Mother's brother I call 'uncle,' and father's sister I call 'aunt'; but mother's sister I call 'mother,' and father's brother I call 'father.'"

"Wait! I must write it down and look at it. You have no 'uncles' on your father's side, not 'aunts' on your mother's. What do you call your cousin?"

"I haven't any. Those you call cousins I call 'brothers' or 'sisters,' except the children of my uncle; these, if girls, are 'mothers,' and if boys are 'uncles.'"

"Why?"

"I don't know that I can explain it." Then, after a pause, she added: "A man has a right to marry his wife's niece,—that is, his wife's brother's daughter,—and we always speak of relations which might come about just as if they existed; so the daughter of my uncle might become my father's wife; therefore I call her 'mother.'"

"I see. You call the girl 'mother' because your father has the right to marry her, and the boy 'uncle' because he is the brother of a possible 'mother.'"

"You have it now.

"I wonder if I can make out why you call your father's uncle 'grandfather.' The uncle's daughter might be your father's 'mother,' and you would address the father of the one your father called 'mother' as 'grandfather'?"

"That's it," she exclaimed; "I never thought it all out before. It is very simple."

"I am glad it seems so to you, but I am sure I should have to work out my might, could, or should be 'mothers,' 'uncles,' and 'grandfathers' like algebraic problems."

"It does make trouble; not that way, but about getting married. Every girl has ever so many men who have a right to marry her; all whom she calls brothers-in-law have that right."

"Talk slowly, and tell me whom you call 'brothers-in-law.'"

"All the husbands of my sisters, and these husbands' brothers, and all the husbands of my aunts."

"Why should you call all these men 'brothers-in-law'?"

"According to Indian custom, a man has a right to marry all the 'sisters' and 'nieces' of his wife; you know, polygamy used to be common."

"I understand. These 'brothers-in-law' are potential husbands of your 'sister'; but why does this make trouble in getting married?"

"Because," she answered, "a young man has to give valuable presents to satisfy the claims of all these men who have a right to the girl."

"Is that why men give presents for girls?"

"It is partly the reason. Indians always cancel a claim by a gift; and besides the young man must part with something he prizes to show that he cares for the girl he wants to marry. I have read hard things written about Indians buying and selling their women, and they seem unjust to me. Presents are a necessity, you see, according to our custom."

The uncle is a privileged character in the home circle. He can play tricks upon nephews and nieces, which they may return in kind, and no offense will be taken by either. No such familiarity exists between the children or any other relative or friend. The uncle has in some instances a control over his sister's children rivaling that of the parents. In tribes where descent is traced only through the mother the uncle is the masculine head of the family; but where, as with the Omahas, the child follows the gens of his father, the uncle occupies the place of first friend and playmate to the children.

One evening the skin hanging over the lodge entrance was lifted, and the uncle stepped in, a handsome, merry fellow, wrapped in a red blanket. Something queer in the outline of it caught the eye of the eldest son of the family, a boy about twelve years old, who ran to see what was hidden under the folds of his uncle's robe, when suddenly a gun was leveled at the lad, who jumped away in pretended terror. The uncle, throwing himself down with a laugh, began taking the gun to pieces, the boy intently watching the operation.

"You shall have this gun," said the uncle, "when you have earned it. You must dance for it."

"All right," said the boy, jerking his shoulders to make ready; then, lifting his feet, and bringing them down with a thud, with his small brown hands clutching tight the sides of his shirt, he vigorously kept time to his uncle's song and improvised drum.

"The hammer is won; now you must dance for the ramrod."

All right," responded the lad, rising from the robe upon which he had dropped to regain his breath; and again his feet and body rose and fell, the ribbons on his scalp-lock fluttering, and the perspiration dropping from his brows.

"The reward is yours. Here is the barrel; I can't let you have this unless your sister dances too."

"Come," said the boy, seizing the little girl's hand; and she, nothing loath, planted her wee moccasined feet close together, and hopped lightly about, with arms dropped by her side and body erect, her bead necklace glistening, and her glossy black braids shining in the firelight.

"This is all I have left," said the saucy uncle, holding high over his head the gunstock. "You can't have this unless"—here he paused and looked about with mischievous glee—"unless grandmother dances."

Unchecked by this audacity, the boy grasped the old woman, crying breathlessly, "Oh, come, or I shall lose my gun!"

Shouts of laughter rang through the lodge as the grandmother, dropping her blanket, rose nimbly to her feet, and gallantly reinforced the excited boy. The elders recalled their youth as they watched her spirited movements, and the grandfather whispered, "The young women nowadays can't dance as the girls did when I was young."

Close to every home lodge a play-house tent was set up by the mother, and here there was uproarious fun in the bright days. Thither the children carried their spare food, and sometimes their entire meal, that the little girls might give a feast to their play-mates. Many a time, in passing among the lodges, I have heard the laughter of the children; and perhaps a merry face would peer out at the top of the baby tent, an old handkerchief bound about the head to keep in place a wig of yellow grass representing the locks of an old woman.

In the long winter evenings story-telling delighted both young and old. No one told tales in the summer, for the snakes would hear and make trouble. These folk-tales of the Indians resemble those found among all peoples the world over: men and animals involved in a common fate, befriending or opposing one another. Some of the myths were interspersed with songs, which the children teased their mothers to sing; and those constituted the only nursery music in the tribe. The adventures in the myths, with their songs, were sometimes turned into games by the little folk, who greatly enjoyed representing the birds or animals of the stories.

There are home duties as well as pleasures for the children. Boys are required to look after the ponies, to lend a hand in planting, to help in the harvest; and they are often made to do active duty as scarecrows in the newly planted field, where, like little Bo-peep, they fall fast asleep. The girls help to gather wood, bring water, and look after the younger ones. As they grow older they are taught to cut, sew, and make garments. In former days, the old Omahas say, no girl was considered marriageable until she had learned to tan skins, make tents and clothing, prepare meat for drying, and could cultivate corn and beans; while a young man who had not learned to make his own weapons and to be a skilful hunter was not considered fitted to take upon himself the responsibilities of the provider of a family.

In the olden times the Omahas pounded their corn into a coarse meal, a few grains at a time, between two round stones, or reduced it to powder in a mortar made from a section of the trunk of a tree, which was hollowed out by burning. The bottom was sharpened to a point so it could easily be driven into the ground and the mortar made firm and steady. The pestle was a long stick shaped not unlike our ordinary pestle; but the blow was struck by the small end entering the mortar, the weight of the larger end adding effectiveness to the stroke.

On the Pacific coast and among the mountain tribes the *kaus* and other roots are still pounded fine on a flat stone, over which is placed a flaring basket, open at the bottom, and held in place by forked sticks catching the edge and driven into the ground. Into this basket mortar the roots are poured, after having been dried in a sort of oven made in the earth and lined with stones. The rapidity of stroke of the woman, lifting the stone pestle weighing several pounds, and bringing it down with precision on the foundation-stone, while with her left hand she sorts the roots within the basket, must be seen to be realized. These pestles, made from basaltic rock, are sometimes well shaped and finished with an ornamentation at the top, and are not infrequently preserved through several generations.

Among the Omahas I collected a score of receipts for preparing and cooking corn; but for all that, there was little variety in Indian food. In the absence of any native animals producing milk and eggs, the cuisine was necessarily limited, and opportunities for an elaborate menu were wholly wanting. The mother served the food to the family, but before partaking of it the ceremony of acknowledging that all is from Wakanda was usually observed. A bit of meat was raised, turned to the four points of the compass, and dropped into the fire. (In some feasts given by societies this remembrance became elaborate in form.) If any guests were invited, it was usual for them to bring their own dishes. As all families had to be ready to move camp upon short notice, it was useless to accumulate goods and chattels that could neither be transported nor left behind in safety; consequently there was no great number of extra dishes in any family. Indian custom obliged one to eat or to carry away all that was served him. The idea underlying this form of hospitality was that no one should travel hungry, the extra food serving for refreshment on the journey.

This custom, so unlike our own, has led to queer misunderstandings and criticisms as when an Indian has been offered a platter containing the family supply of food, and he has gravely appropriated the whole. On the other hand, Indians have told me of their discomfort, when visiting white folk, at being forced to eat so much, not knowing that we permit a person to decline food without giving offense.

There is another custom, in violation of which a good missionary once became the subject of Indian criticism. Among the Sioux, if a kettle is borrowed, it must be returned with a portion of what was cooked in it remaining in the bottom. The missionary, desirous of setting an example of neatness, returned the borrowed vessel nicely cleaned, and was charged with being stingy and covetous, "like her race."

The tribe, as has been shown, is made up of groups of kindred, and the life within these groups reveals a bond of affection strong and vital. Although words of endearment are seldom, if ever, spoken openly, there are other signs that betray the warm heart beneath the cold exterior. The Indian hazards his life for his friend. The cords of love between parent and child are the warp upon which are woven every feeling and every act. The love of country amounts to a passion, men and women longing with a fervor we cannot understand for the familiar scenes of their youth, clinging even to bits of detail in the never-to-be-forgotten landscape. Said an exiled Indian to me: "Oh, how I miss the color in the grass of my home!"

Banished from his native soil, or bereft of his dear ones, the Indian easily falls into listlessness, or plunges into deeds that may end a life he no longer cares to cherish.

The entrance of death into the family circle rends the veil of silence that infolds the Indian. In the presence of his dead the Omaha breaks forth into terms of endearment that custom forbade should ever be poured into the ear of the living—words which bear the burden of a love stronger than death, but which must be heard only by the released spirit.

Long ago, in his mountain fastnesses, the heartbroken, aged Nez Percé gathered his dead son in his arms, and found comfort only in the opened grave, which closed over the dead and the living together.

Looking upon my experience of Indian life, against a background of poverty and rude circumstance stands forth the picture of unfailing family affection and faithfulness, of unhesitating hospitality and courtesy toward strangers, a modesty of demeanor at all times, and a spirit of happiness and content that left little room for ambition or envy.

Source: Alice Cunningham Fletcher, "Home Life Among the Indians: Records of Personal Experience," *Century Magazine* 54, n.s., 32 (June 1897):252-63.

4-29. Future of the Red Man

Simon Pokagon

1897

Simon Pokagon (1830-1899) was a Potawatomi leader, orator, and writer. Born in Michigan, Pokagon studied at Notre Dame (Indiana), Oberlin Collegiate Institute, and Twinsburg Academy in Ohio. Christened a Roman Catholic, he demonstrated interests in theology, research, writing, poetry, and playing the organ. He wrote *articles for magazines, spoke five languages fluently, published his poems, and addressed groups on the history, culture, and conditions of Native Americans. As principal chief, Pokagon persuaded the U.S. government to pay his tribe an old treaty land claim of $150,000. He met twice with President Abraham Lincoln and once with President Ulysses S. Grant in an endeavor to improve relations between the Potawatomi and whites and assert Native American rights. His booklet,* The Red Man's Greeting, *printed on birchbark, was exhibited in 1893 at the World's Columbian Exposition in Chicago, where he delighted visitors with descriptions of Native American life. The publication of his book* Ogimawkwe Mitigwaki: Queen of the Woods, *which retold the courtship with his first wife, appeared in 1899. Pokagon quite possibly was the most educated Native American of his time.*

Often in the stillness of the night, when all nature seems asleep about me, there comes a gentle rapping at the door of my heart. I open it; and a voice inquires, "Pokagon, what of your people? What will their future be?" My answer is: "Mortal man has not the power to draw aside the veil of unborn time to tell the future of his race. That gift belongs to the Divine alone. But it is given to him to closely judge the future by the present and the past." Hence, in order to approximate the future of our race, we must consider our natural capabilities and our environments, as connected with the dominant race which outnumbers us—three hundred to one—in this land of our fathers.

First, then, let us carefully consider if Mis-ko-au'-ne-ne-og' (the red man) possesses, or is devoid of, loyalty, sympathy, benevolence, and gratitude,—those heaven-born virtues requisite for Christian character and civilization. But, in doing so, let us constantly bear in mind that the character of our people has always been published to the world by the dominant race, and that human nature is now the same as when Solomon declared that "He that is first in his own cause seemeth just; but his neighbor cometh and searcheth him." In our case we have ever stood as dumb to the charges brought against us as did the Divine Master before His false accusers; hence all charges alleged against us in history should be cautiously considered, with Christian charity. There have been, and still are, too many writers who, although they have never seen an Indian in their lives, have published tragical stories of their treachery and cruelty. Mothers, for generations past, have frightened their children into obedience with that dreaded scarecrow, "Look out, or the Injuns will get you!"; creating in the infant mind a false prejudice against our race, which has given birth to that base slander, "There is no good Injun but a dead one." It is therefore no wonder that we are hated by some worse than Satan hates the salvation of human souls.

Let us glance backward to the year 1492. Columbus and his officers and crew are spending their first Christmas on the border-islands of the New World. It is not a merry, but a sad, Christmas to them. They stand crowded on the deck of the tiny ship "Nina." Four weeks since, Pinson, with the "Pinta" and her crew, deserted the squadron; and last night the flagship, "Santa Maria," that had safely borne the Admiral across an unknown sea to a strange land, was driven before the gale and stranded near the shore of Hispaniola. Deserted by her crew and left to the mercy of the breakers, she lies prostrate on the perilous sands, shivering and screaming in the wind like a wounded creature of life responsive to every wave that smites her.

It is early morning. Columbus sends Diego de Arna and Pedro Guthene to the great Chief of the Island, telling him of their sad disaster, and requesting that he come and help to save their goods from being swept into the sea. The Chief listens with all attention to the sad news; his heart is touched; he answers with his tears; and orders his people to go at once, with their canoes well manned, and help to save the stranger's goods. He also sends one of his servants to the Admiral with a message of sincere regrets for his misfortunes, offering all the aid in his power. Columbus receives the servant on shipboard; and, while he listens with gratitude to the cheering message delivered in signs and broken words, he rejoices to see coming to his relief along the shore a hundred boats, manned by a thousand men, mostly naked, bearing down upon the wrecked "Santa Maria," and swarming about her like bees around their hive. The goods disappear from the ship as by magic, are rowed ashore, and safely secured. Not one native takes advantage of the disaster for his own profit. Spanish history declares that in no part of the civilized world could Columbus have received warmer or more cordial hospitality.

Touched by such tender treatment, Columbus, writing to the King and Queen of Spain, pays this beautiful tribute to the native Carib race:

> They are a loving, uncovetous people, so docile in all things that I swear to your Majesties there is not in all the world a better race, or more delightful country. They love their neighbors as themselves; their talk is ever sweet and gentle, accompanied with smiles; and though they be naked, yet their manners are decorous and praiseworthy.

Peter Martyr, a reliable historian, has left on record the following:—

> It is certain the land among these people is as common as sun and water, and that "mine and thine," the seed of all misery, have no place with them. They are content with so little that in so large a country they have rather a superfluity than a scarceness, so that they seem to live in the golden world, without toil, living in open gardens not intrenched or defended with walls. They deal justly one with another without books, without laws, without judges. They take him for an evil and mischievous man who taketh pleasure in doing hurt to another; and although they delight not in superfluities, yet they make provision for the increase of such roots whereof they make bread, content with such simple diet wherewith health is preserved and disease avoided.

Does not this quotation most emphatically show that the red men of the New World did originally possess every virtue necessary for Christian civilization and enlightenment?

The question is often asked, What became of the numerous Caribs of those islands? They seemed to have vanished like leaves in autumn; for within a few years we find them supplanted by foreign slaves. The noble Bishop [Bartolome] Las Casas tells us, in pity, "With mine own eyes, I saw kingdoms as full of people as hives are of bees; and now, where are they?" Almost all, he says, have perished by the sword and under the lash of cruel Spanish taskmasters, in the greedy thirst for gold.

Certain it is that in those days, which tried the souls of the Carib race, some fled from the lust and lash of their oppressors by sea to the coast of Florida, and reported to the natives there that Wau-be-au'-ne-ne-og' (white men), who fought with Awsh-kon-tay' Au-ne-me-kee' (thunder and lightning), who were cruel, vindictive, and without love, except a thirsty greed for gold, had come from the other side of Kons-ke-tchi-saw-me' (the ocean) and made slaves of Mis-ko-au-ne-ne-og' (the red man) of the islands, which was reported from tribe to tribe across the continent.

Scarcely a quarter-century passes since the enslavement of the Carib race, and Ponce de Leon, a Spanish adventurer, is landing from his squadron a large number of persons to colonize the coast of Florida. A few years previously, while in pursuit of the fountain of youth, he had been here for the first time, on the day of the "Feast of Flowers." Then, he was kindly received and welcomed by the sons of the forest. Now, as then, the air is perfumed with the odor of fruits and flowers; and all on shore appears pleasing and inviting. The Spaniards land, and slowly climb the terrace that bounds the sea. Here they pause, planting side by side the Spanish standard and the cross. But hark! War-whoops are heard close by. And there they come, —long lines of savages from the surrounding woods, who, with slings and darts, with clubs and stones, fall upon the dreaded Spaniards. The onslaught is terrible. Many are killed; and Ponce de Leon is mortally wounded. He now begins to realize that among the savage hosts are Caribs who have escaped from slavery and death. He well knows the bitter story of their wrong, and that this bloody chastisement is but the returning boomerang of Spanish cruelty. They flee from the avengers of blood to the ships. The report they give of the savage attack, on their return to Spain, is so terrible that years pass before another attempt is made to colonize the land of fruits and flowers.

I deem it unnecessary to explain why these peaceful natives so soon became so warlike and vindictive. Suffice it to say: "Enslave a good man and, like the wasp which stings the hand that holds it fast, he will make use of all the means which nature has placed in his power to regain his liberty." During the first century of American history, many adventurers from different European countries sailed along the eastern coast of North America,—all reporting the natives peaceable and kind when not misused.

There was a tradition among our fathers that, before the colonization of North America, an armed band of Wau-be-au'-ne-ne-og' (white men), gorgeously clad, came on the war-path from the East, reaching the Dakotas, which then extended south as far as the mouth of the Arkansas River; that they were vindictive and cruel, destroying the natives wherever they went with Awsh-kon-tay' Au-ne-me-kee' (thunder and lightning). They were looking for gold, their Man-i-to (god), and, not finding him, went down Mi-che-se-pe (the great river) and were seen no more. Those cruel adventurers, who came among us by sea and land, must have awakened hatred and revenge in the hearts of our fathers, which may have been transmitted to their children.

It should be borne in mind that several European Powers colonized this continent about the same period, among whom the English and French took the lead. Settlements were mostly made along the Atlantic coast, which was then occupied by the Algonquin family, to which my tribe—the Pottawattamies—belong: they seem to have had a common origin and common language. For a time the two races lived in peace. The French in Canada seemed naturally to assimilate with our people, many of whom received the Catholic faith. In course of time there were many marriages between the two races; and we began to look upon the great King of France as our invincible sovereign: for we were taught that he was king of all kings except the King of Wau-kwing' (heaven). Their priests were devoted to their work; visiting all the tribes of the south and west, followed by French traders, planting the cross, the lilies, and the shield side by side. The tribes firmly believed that the land belonged to their great king who loved them and would, if necessary, fight their battles for them. With the exception of William Penn, who settled Pennsylvania, the English who colonized the United States did not seem to have the tact of the French in their dealings with us. They were less liberal with presents, and apparently less united in their religious belief. They were not so successful as the French in obtaining native converts; although some good ministers, like Roger Williams, did much to unite the races in brotherhood, and thereby delayed the final struggle.

Inroads were being continually made into Taw-naw-ke-win' (our native land); and in seeking new homes we found ourselves invading the hunting-grounds of other tribes. The warlike Iroquois of New York would not even allow the eastern tribes to pass through their country,—as a result, our forefathers seemed compelled to make a stand against the advance of the incoming race. In doing so, our villages were laid waste with fire, our people slaughtered and burned by white warriors who seemed without number for multitude. Our fathers finally gave up the contest. Some, to avoid the Iroquois, went West through Canada. Others went West through Pennsylvania, meeting in Indiana, Michigan, and Wisconsin, then known as Indian Territory, where we found French priests and traders, who gave us a hearty welcome, assuring us that we should remain safe with them. In course of time the English, finding the French traders posted along the western frontier, gave them to understand that the land they occupied belonged to the English, as well as the right to buy fur from the natives. Hence the so-called French and Indian War was inaugurated, in the course of which many outrages were committed on the frontiers,—*all of them being charged to the Indians.* During this war a manifold tin box of curious make was found in a large village called Wa-gaw-naw-kee-zee', which lay along Lake Michigan, between Little Traverse Bay and the Straits of Mackinaw. The unsuspecting Indians opened it, and in the innermost box found a mouldy substance. Soon after, the smallpox—a disease unknown to our fathers—broke out among them; and O-daw-yo-e-waw' Da-dodse- ses' (their medicine men) all died. In fact every one taking the disease died. Lodge after lodge was filled with unburied dead. The great village was entirely depopulated. Our fathers thought the disease was sent among them by the English because the Indians had helped the French during that war. I have passed over the ancient site of this village. Its bounds are clearly marked by second-growth forests, which now cover it. It is fifteen miles long and from one to two miles wide.

Almost on the heels of this war, after France had ceded her rights to the English, came the Revolutionary war. Our people had just begun to learn that they owed allegiance to the British, who had conquered our invincible French King. They had seen the Bourbon flag taken down from the western forts, and replaced by the red cross of St. George; and they were compelled to shout, "Long live the King, —King George who rules from the Arctic Ocean to the Gulf of Mexico."

We now began selling furs to our new masters; receiving in exchange dry-goods and Awsh-kon-tay' Ne-besh (fire-water), when we were called upon again to take the war-path, to aid our new king in subduing his rebellious colonies. We could not serve two masters at the same time; hence remained loyal to our new king, while the Iroquois of New York and Canada were divided. And so it was that all the dirty, cruel work of war between the revolutionists and the mother country was laid at the door of our people, whose mouths were dumb to defend or justify themselves in respect of the outrages charged against them. These outrages were generally planned, and frequently executed, by white men, as was, in after years, the Mountain Meadow Massacre, of Mormon notoriety, for which also we were persecuted and suffered untold disgrace.

I always think of my people in those days as the dog kept by the schoolmaster to be whipped whenever a child disobeyed. During the war of 1812 we were again incited through English influence to take the war-path. Proctor, the English general of the Northwest, said to our heroic Tecumseh, "Assemble all your warriors together, join forces with us, and we will drive the Americans beyond the Ohio River, and Michigan shall be yours forever." Such a promise, from so high an authority, awakened all the native energies of our being to regain our liberty and homes, for which we had been contending against overpowering forces.

The Ottawas and Chippeways of the north, the Pottawattamies and Miamies of the south, and other tribes gathered themselves together to make the last desperate effort to regain the promised land. In this war our cause was far more sacred to us than was the Americans' to them. They had drawn the sword in defence of one of their rights; we, *for all of ours*; for our very existence, for our native land, and for the graves of our fathers, most sacred to our race.

The last engagement in which the confederated Algonquin tribes fought the Americans was at the battle of the Thames in Canada, on October 5, 1813, where we and the English were defeated by General [William Henry] Harrison, and General Tecumseh, our brave leader, was killed.

After this battle our fathers became fully convinced that the small remnant of their tribes must either accept extermination, or such terms as their enemy saw fit to give. So they sued for peace; and the American warriors, uplifted by victory, and our Algonquin fathers, bowed down by defeat, stood around the grave of the hatchet —buried forever—and smoked the pipe of peace together.

At one time I felt that our race was doomed to extermination. There was an awful unrest among the western tribes who had been pushed by the cruel march of civilization into desert places, where subsistence was impossible. Starvation drove many to steal cattle from adjacent ranches; and when some of our people were killed by the cowboys, their friends were determined to take the war-path. I never failed on such occasions to declare most emphatically, "You might as well march your warriors into the jaws of an active volcano, expecting to shut off its fire and smoke, as to attempt to beat back the westward trend of civilization. You must teach your sons everywhere that the war-path will lead them but to the grave."

Having briefly reviewed some of our past history, the fact must be admitted that, when the white men first visited our shores, we were kind and confiding; standing before them like a block of marble before the sculptor, ready to be shaped into noble manhood. Instead of this, we were oftener hacked to pieces and destroyed. We further find in our brief review that the contending Powers of the Old World, striving for the mastery in the New, took advantage of our trustful, confiding natures, placing savage weapons of warfare in our hands to aid us in butchering one another.

It is useless to deny the charge, that at times we have been goaded to vindictive and cruel acts. Some of my own tribe, however, were soldiers in the Northern army during the civil war. Some of them were taken, and held prisoners in the rebel prisons, and the cruelty which, according to the tales they tell, was witnessed there was never outdone in border warfare with the scalping-knife and tomahawk. And yet I believe that, had the Northern people been placed in the South under like circumstances, their prisoners of war would have been treated with similar cruelty. It was the result of a *desperate* effort to save an expiring cause. I believe there is no reasonable person, well grounded in United States history, who will not admit that there were ten times as many who perished miserably in Southern prisons as have been killed by our people since the discovery of America. I recall these facts not to censure, but to show that *cruelty and revenge are the offspring of war, not of race*, and that nature has placed no impassable gulf between us and civilization.

It is claimed that the United States have paid out five hundred million dollars in trying to subdue the red man by military force. But now—thank Heaven!—through the influence of good men and women who have thrown the search-light of the golden rule into the great heart of the nation, her policy is changed. Where hundreds of thousands of dollars were paid out annually to fight him, like sums are now being paid yearly to educate him in citizenship and self-support; that his children may not grow up a race of savages to be again fought and again cared for at the expense of the nation. I rejoice in the policy now being pursued. If not perfect, it is certainly on the right trail to success.

While a guest at Chicago, during the World's Fair, I spent much time at the United States Indian School. There I met many delegations from different governmental schools. I was particularly interested in the delegation from Albuquerque, New Mexico, composed of Navajos, Pinas-Mojaves, Pueblos, and others. With pride I examined the articles which they had made, their clean, well-kept writing-books, and listened to their sweet vocal and instrumental music. I then and there said, in my heart: "Thanks to the Great Spirit, I do believe the remnant of our race will yet live and learn to compete with the dominant race; proving themselves worthy of the highest offices in the gift of a free people."

The Indian school at Carlisle, Pennsylvania, has done wonders in showing what can be effected for the education of our children. The test there made is a reliable one, inasmuch as that school is made up of pupils from more than sixty different tribes, from all parts of the United States. I was highly gratified a few months ago to learn that the football team from that school was able to defeat the champion Wisconsin team at Chicago, receiving many compliments from the immense crowd for their tact and self-control as well as for their physical development,—showing conclusively that our race is not, as some claim, becoming enfeebled and running out.

While I most heartily indorse the present policy of the Government in dealing with our people, I must admit—to be true to my own convictions—that I am worried over the ration system, under which so many of our people are being fed on the reservations. I greatly fear it may eventually vagabondize many of them beyond redemption. It permits the gathering of lazy, immoral white men of the worst stamp, who spend their time in idleness and in corrupting Indian morality. I do hope the Government will provide something for them to do for their own good, although it should pay her little or nothing. Again: I fear for the outcome of the Indian nations. Our people in their native state were not avaricious. They were on a common level; and, like the osprey that divides her last fish with her young, so they acted toward each other. But I find, to my sorrow, that, when you associate them with squaw men, and place them in power, they develop the wolfish greed of civilization, disregarding the rights of their less fortunate brothers. I must admit that it staggers my native brain to understand what reason, equity, or justice there is in allowing independent powers to exist within the bounds of this Republic. If the "Monroe doctrine," which has been so much petted of late years, should be enforced anywhere, it would certainly be in the line of good statesmanship to carry it out, at least in principle, at home.

Lastly, Pokagon must admit that he feels very deeply the ravages made among his people by the "intoxicating cup." Were it an open enemy outside our lines, we might meet it with success. But alas! it is a traitor within our camp, cunning as Wa-goosh (the fox). It embraces and kisses but to poison like the snake—without the warning rattle. Before I associated with white men, I had supposed that they were not such slaves to that soulless tyrant as the red man. But I have learned that the cruel curse enslaves alike the white man in his palace and the red man in his hut; alike the chieftain and the king; the savage and the sage. I am indeed puzzled to understand how it is that the white race, whose works seem almost divine, should not be able to destroy this great devil-fish, which their own hands have fashioned and launched upon the sea of human life; whose tentacles reach out into the halls of legislature and courts of law, into colleges and churches,—doing everywhere its wicked work.

As to the future of our race, it seems to me almost certain that in time it will lose its identity by amalgamation with the dominant race. No matter how distasteful it may seem to us, we are compelled to consider it as a probable result. Sensitive white people can console themselves, however, with the fact, that there are to-day in the United States thousands of men and women of high social standing whose forefathers on one side were full-blooded so-called savages; and yet the society in which they move, and in many cases they themselves, are ignorant of the fact. All white people are not ashamed of Indian blood; in fact, a few are proud of it.

At the World's Fair on Chicago Day, after ringing the new Liberty Bell, and speaking in behalf of my people, I presented Mayor [Carter] Harrison, [Sr.], according to the programme of the day, with a duplicate of the treaty by which my father, a Pottawattamie chief, in 1833, conveyed Chicago—embracing the fair-grounds and surrounding country—to the United States for about three cents per acre. In accepting the treaty, the venerable Mayor said,

> Grateful to the spirit of the past, I am happy to receive this gift from the hand of one who is able to bestow it. Chicago is proving that it recognizes the benefits conferred through this treaty. I receive this from an Indian all the more gratefully because in my own veins courses the blood of an Indian. Before the days of Pokagon, I had my origin in the blood that ran through Pocahontas. I stand to-day as a living witness that the Indian is worth something in this world.

I have made diligent inquiries of the headmen of different tribes as to what estimate they place on the half-breeds among them. Their general reply has been, "They are certainly an improvement on the pale face, but not on the red man." Which no doubt is the case; for it is a lamentable fact that criminals, outlaws, and vagabonds are generally the first who seek homes among us, bringing with them nearly all the vices and diseases, and but few of the virtues, of civilization. Yet, notwithstanding such an unfortunate mixture, we find some grand characters who have been able to rise high above the sins of parentage. I have further found, by close observation, that those tinctured with our blood are far less subject to nervous diseases; but whether at the expense of intellectual force or otherwise, I am not so certain. Be that as it may, we cannot safely ignore the fact, that it is the physical development of the people of a nation that gives it strength and stability; that physical decay brings loss of executive ability, and has proved the overthrow of ancient kingdoms. I do not wish it to be understood that I advocate or desire the amalgamation of our people with the white race. But I speak of it as an event that is almost certain; and we had much better rock with the boat that oars us on than fight against the inevitable. I am frequently asked, "Pokagon, do you believe that the white man and the red man were originally of one blood?" My reply has been: "I do not know. But from the present outlook, they surely will be."

The index-finger of the past and present is pointing to the future, showing most conclusively that by the middle of the next century all Indian reservations and tribal relations will have passed away. Then our people will begin to scatter; and the result will be a general mixing up of the races. Through intermarriage the blood of our people, like the waters that flow into the great ocean, will be forever lost in the dominant race; and generations yet unborn will read in history of the red men of the forest, and inquire, "Where are they?"

Source: Simon Pokagon, "The Future of the Red Man," *Forum* 23 (1897):698-708.

4-30. Assessment of the Dawes Commission

G. M. P. Turner

1897

In 1893 Congress enacted legislation providing for the presidential appointment of a commission to the Five Civilized Tribes (Cherokee, Choctaw, Chickasaw, Muskogee (Creek), and Seminole of the Indian Territory) with the intention to work toward abolishing tribal governments and settling their estates. The first authorized commission, known as the Dawes Commission, consisted of former U.S. Senator Henry L. Dawes of Massachusetts, Archibald S. McKennon of Arkansas, and Meredith H. Kidd of Indiana. The purpose of the Dawes Commission revolved around expanding the provisions of the General Allotment Act of 1887 to incorporate these tribes. Opposed to the possible dissolution of their governmental entities, division of lands, and extinguishment of tribal title to these areas, the Natives declined to greet the commissioners enthusiastically.

George M. P. Turner also found fault with the purposes and tactics of the threefold commissionership. A Tennessee lawyer and attorney general for the Memphis district during the late 1880s and early 1890s, Turner had assisted in establishing the News Scimitar, *a Memphis evening newspaper. In 1897 he relocated to Muskogee, Indian Territory, practicing law until his death in the early twentieth century. His son, Hamner George Turner, was a farmer, stockraiser, and first mayor of Checotah. The elder Turner in 1897 issued a verbal statement about the Dawes Commission, an excerpt of which appears below.*

Egypt had its locusts, Asiatic countries their cholera, France had its Jacobins, England had the black plague, Memphis had the yellow fever, Texas had her Middle-of-the-road Populists, the world had McKinley and prosperity, Kansas had its grasshoppers, but it was left for the unfortunate Indian Territory to be afflicted with the worst scourge of the Nineteenth century, the Dawes Commission. When God, in the medieval days of His divine administration, first conceded the great idea of building worlds, making governments and creating judiciaries, He never contemplated the Dawes Commission. If He had, He would have shrunk with horror, quit His job and left the world in chaos.

Source: John D. Benedict, *History of Muskogee and Northeastern Oklahoma*, 3 vols. (Chicago: S. J. Clarke Publishing Company, 1922), 1:142.

➳ ● ⇜

4-31. Curtis Act

June 28, 1898

Vice president of the United States from 1929 to 1933 during the administration of Herbert Hoover, Charles Curtis (1860-1936) was born in Topeka, Kansas. He practiced law in Topeka, worked as prosecuting attorney for Shawnee County (1885-1889), held a seat as a Republican in the U.S. House of Representatives from 1893 until 1907, and served in the U.S. Senate from 1907 to 1913 and again from 1915 to 1929. Curtis chaired the Committee on Indian Depredations during the Fifty-ninth through Sixty-first Congresses and functioned as Republican whip from 1915 to

1924, when he was elected Senate majority leader, holding that post from the Sixty-eighth through the Seventieth Congresses. He advocated Republican regularity, prohibition, woman's suffrage, benefits for farmers and veterans, protective tariffs, fair labor standards for children, economy in government, and federal allotment policies for Native Americans.

Curtis was America's only vice president of Indian blood. His mother, Ellen Gonville Pappan, was a quarter-blood member of the Kansa (Kaw) tribe. He traced his maternal ancestry to Kansa chief White Plume, who had married a daughter of Pawhuska, an Osage chief. Following the death of his mother in 1863 and the wandering exploits of his father, Curtis as a boy lived for a time at the Kaw Indian Reservation in Kansas with his maternal grandmother, Julie Gonville Pappan, before eventually residing with his paternal grandmother, Permelia Hubbard Curtis. Although expelled from Kaw membership in 1878 because of nonparticipation in tribal affairs, Curtis nevertheless used his ancestry to political and social advantage, especially after 1903 and his chairmanship of the House Committee on Indian Affairs.

Representative Curtis sponsored the Curtis Act, which Congress passed on June 28, 1898, during the William McKinley presidency, for the protection of people of the Indian Territory and other purposes. This legislation provided the foundation for Oklahoma's eventual statehood, started the dissolution of the Five Civilized Tribes, and abolished tribal courts. A lengthy and highly detailed measure, it laid the framework for establishing and regulating townsites, managing leases of mineral rights, authorizing the Dawes Commission to set up rolls and allot lands to Native Americans on these rolls, and providing for certain other technical matters. Printed here are various sections of the Curtis Act.

. . . SEC. 11. That when the roll of citizenship on any one of said nations or tribes is fully completed as provided by law, and the survey of the lands of said nation or tribe is also completed, the commission heretofore appointed under the Acts of Congress, and known as the "Dawes Commission," shall proceed to allot the exclusive use and occupancy of the surface of all the lands of said nation or tribe thereof, as shown by said roll, giving to each, so far as possible, his fair and equal share thereof, considering the nature and fertility of the soil, location, and value of same; but all oil, coal, asphalt, and mineral deposits in the lands of any tribe are reserved to such tribe, and no allotment of such lands shall carry the title to such oil, coal, asphalt, or mineral deposits; and all town sites shall also be reserved to the several tribes, and shall be set apart by the commission heretofore mentioned as incapable of allotment. There shall also be reserved from allotment a sufficient amount of lands now occupied by churches, schools, parsonages, charitable institutions, and other public buildings for their present actual and necessary use, and no more, not to exceed five acres for each school and one acre for each church and each parsonage, and for such new schools as may be needed; also sufficient land for burial grounds where necessary. When such allotment of the lands of any tribe has been by them completed, said commission shall make full report thereof to the Secretary of the Interior for his approval. . . .

SEC. 17. That it shall be unlawful for any citizen of any one of said tribes to inclose or in any manner, by himself or through another, directly or indirectly, to hold possession of any greater amount of lands or other property belonging to any such nation or tribe than that which would be his approximate share of the lands belonging to such nation or tribe and that of his wife and his minor children as per allotment herein provided; and any person found in such possession of lands or other property in excess of his share and that of his family, as aforesaid, or having the same in any manner inclosed, at the expiration of nine months after the passage of this Act, shall be deemed guilty of a misdemeanor. . . .

SEC. 19. That no payment of any moneys on any account whatever shall hereafter be made by the United States to any of the tribal governments or to any officer thereof for disbursement, but payments of all sums to members of said tribes shall be made under direction of the Secretary of the Interior by an officer appointed by him; and per capita payments shall be made direct to each individual in lawful money of the United States, and the same shall not be liable to the payment of any previously contracted obligation. . . .

SEC. 26. That on and after the passage of this Act the laws of the various tribes or nations of Indians shall not be enforced at law or in equity by the courts of the United States in the Indian Territory. . . .

SEC. 28. That on the first day of July, eighteen hundred and ninety-eight, all tribal courts of Indian Territory shall be abolished, and no officer of said courts shall thereafter have any authority whatever to do or perform any act theretofore authorized by any law in connection with said courts, or to receive any pay for same; and all civil and criminal causes then pending in any such court shall be transferred to the United States court in said Territory by filing with the clerk of the court the original papers in the suit: *Provided*, That this section shall not be in force as to the Chickasaw, Choctaw, and Creek tribes or nations until the first day of October, eighteen hundred and ninety-eight. . . .

Source: Curtis Act, June 28, 1898, *U.S. Statutes at Large*, 30:497-98, 502, 504-05. See also William E. Unrau, *Mixed Bloods and Tribal Dissolution: Charles Curtis and the Quest for Indian Identity* (Lawrence: University Press of Kansas, 1989); Leonard Schlup, "Charles Curtis: The Vice President from Kansas," *Manuscripts* 35 (Summer 1983):183-201; and Charles Curtis Papers, Kansas State Historical Society Library, Topeka.

4-32. General Custer's Last Fight as Seen by Two Moons

Hamlin Garland

September 1898

An American dramatist, novelist, and writer of short stories and essays, Hamlin Garland (1860-1940) was born near West Salem, Wisconsin, grew up in an agricultural environment, worked on a farm, taught school, and lived in Iowa and South Dakota before settling in Boston in 1884. Using impressionist techniques, he explored the sordid side of life and scored points as a political activist. Founder and first president of the Cliff Dwellers Club (Chicago), Garland wrote Main-Traveled Roads *(1891) and* Prairie Folks *(1893), among others. An activist in the Indian reform movement, Garland regarded Native American culture as a national resource and opposed attempts to destroy indigenous identity.*

Near the end of the Gilded Age, Garland sojourned to the great American West, where he met Two Moons (1847-1917), also known as Two Moon and Ishi'eyo Nissi, a Northern Cheyenne leader in the War for the Black Hills, an army scout, and the model for the "buffalo" or "Indian head" U.S. nickel designed by James Fraser and released in 1913. Two Moons was present at the Battle of the Little Bighorn in June, 1876. The following year, after surrendering in Montana, he served under

Colonel Nelson A. Miles in the Nez Perce War. Two Moons acted as a research informant to Garland, whose article, "General Custer's Last Fight as Seen by Two Moons," made its debut in the September, 1898, number of McClure's Magazine.

. . . As we topped the low, pine-clad ridge and looked into the hot, dry valley, Wolf Voice, my Cheyenne interpreter, pointed at a little log cabin, toward the green line of alders wherein the Rosebud ran, and said: "His house—Two Moon."

As we drew near we came to a puzzling fork in the road. The left branch skirted a corner of a wire fence, the right turned into a field. We started to the left, but the waving of a blanket in the hands of a man at the cabin door directed us to the right. As we drew nearer we perceived Two Moon spreading blankets in the scant shade of his low cabin. Some young Cheyennes were grinding a sickle. A couple of children were playing about the little log stables. The barn-yard and buildings were like those of a white settler on the new and arid sod. It was all barren and unlovely—the home of poverty.

As we dismounted at the door Two Moon came out to meet us with hand outstretched. "How?" he said, with the heartiest, long-drawn note of welcome. He motioned us to be seated on the blankets which he had spread for us upon seeing our approach. Nothing could exceed the dignity and sincerity of his greeting.

As we took seats he brought out tobacco and a pipe. He was a tall old man, of a fine, clear brown complexion, big-chested, erect, and martial of bearing. His smiling face was broadly benignant, and his manners were courteous and manly.

While he cut his tobacco Wolf Voice interpreted my wishes to him. I said, "Two Moon, I have come to hear your story of the Custer battle, for they tell me you were a chief there. After you tell me the story, I want to take some photographs of you. I want you to signal with a blanket as the great chiefs used to do in fight."

Wolf Voice made this known to him, delivering also a message from the agents, and at every pause Two Moon uttered deep-voiced notes of comprehension. "Ai," "A-ah," "Hoh,"—these sounds are commonly called "grunts," but they were low, long-drawn expulsions of breath, very expressive.

Then a long silence intervened. The old man mused. It required time to go from the silence of the hot valley, the shadow of his little cabin, and the wire fence of his pasture, back to the days of his youth. When he began to speak, it was with great deliberation. His face became each moment graver and his eyes more introspective. [He then began]:

> Two Moon does not like to talk about the days of fighting; but since you are to make a book, and the agent says you are a friend to (George B.) Grinnell, I will tell you about it—the truth. It is now a long time ago, and my words do not come quickly.
>
> That spring (1876) I was camped on Powder River with fifty lodges of my people—Cheyennes. The place is near what is now Fort McKenney. One morning soldiers charged my camp. They were in command of Three Fingers (Colonel [Ranald S.] McKenzie). We were surprised and scattered, leaving our ponies. The soldiers ran all our horses off. That night the soldiers slept, leaving the horses one side; so we crept up and stole them back again, and then we went away.
>
> We traveled far, and one day we met a big camp of Sioux at Charcoal Butte.
>
> We camped with the Sioux, and had a good time, plenty grass, plenty game, good water. Crazy Horse was head chief of the camp. Sitting Bull was camped a little ways below, on the Little Missouri River.
>
> Crazy Horse said to me, "I'm glad you are come. We are going to fight the white man again."
>
> The camp was already full of wounded men, women, and children.
>
> I said to Crazy Horse, "All right. I am ready to fight. I have fought already. My people have been killed, my horses stolen; I am satisfied to fight."

Here the old man paused a moment, and his face took on a lofty and somber expression.

> I believed at that time the Great Spirits had made Sioux, put them there,"— he drew a circle to the right—and white men and Cheyennes here,—indicating two places to the left—expecting them to fight. The Great Spirits I thought liked to see the fight; it was to them all the same like playing. So I thought then about fighting.

As he said this, he made me feel for one moment the power of a sardonic god whose drama was the wars of men.

About May, when the grass was tall and the horses strong, we broke camp and started across the country to the mouth of the Tongue River. Then Sitting Bull and Crazy Horse and all went up the Rosebud. There we had a big fight with General [George] Crook, and whipped him. Many soldiers were killed—few Indians. It was a great fight, much smoke and dust.

From there we all went over the divide, and camped in the valley of Little Horn. Everybody thought, "Now we are out of the white man's country. He can live there, we will live here." After a few days, one morning when I was in camp north of Sitting Bull, a Sioux messenger rode up and said, "Let everybody paint up, cook, and get ready for a big dance."

Cheyennes then went to work to cook, cut up tobacco, and get ready. We all thought to dance all day. We were very glad to think we were far away from the white man.

I went to water my horses at the creek, and washed them off with cool water, then took a swim myself. I came back to the camp afoot. When I got near my lodge, I looked up the Little Horn towards Sitting Bull's camp. I saw a great dust rising. It looked like a whirlwind. Soon Sioux horseman came rushing into camp shouting: "Soldiers come! Plenty white soldiers."

I ran into my lodge, and said to my brother-in-law, "Get your horses: the white man is coming. Everybody run for horses."

Outside, far up the valley, I heard a battle cry, *Hay-ay, hay-ay!* I heard shooting, too, this way (clapping his hands very fast). I couldn't see any Indians. Everybody was getting horses and saddles. After I had caught my horse, a Sioux warrior came again and said, "Many soldiers are coming."

Then he said to the women, "Get out of the way, we are going to have hard fight." I said, "All right, I am ready."

I got on my horse, and rode out into my camp. I called out to the people all running about: "I am Two Moon, your chief. Don't run away. Stay here and fight. You must stay and fight the white soldiers. I shall stay even if I am to be killed."

I rode swiftly toward Sitting Bull's camp. There I saw the white soldiers fighting in a line ([Marcus] Reno's men). Indians covered the flat. They began to drive the soldiers all mixed up—Sioux, then soldiers, then more Sioux, and all shooting. The air was full of smoke and dust. I saw the soldiers fall back and drop into the river-bed like buffalo fleeing. They had no time to look for a crossing. The Sioux chased them up the hill, where they met more soldiers in wagons, and then messengers came saying more soldiers were going to kill the women, and the Sioux turned back. Chief Gall was there fighting, Crazy Horse also.

I then rode toward my camp, and stopped squaws from carrying off lodges. While I was sitting on my horse I saw flags come up over the hill to the east like that (he raised his finger-tips). Then the soldiers rose all at once, all on horses, like this (he put his fingers behind each other to indicate that Custer appeared marching in columns of fours). They formed into three bunches (squadrons) with a little ways between. Then a bugle sounded, and they all got off horses, and some soldiers led the horses back over the hill.

Then the Sioux rode up the ridge on all sides, riding very fast. The Cheyennes went up the left way. Then the shooting was quick, quick. Pop—pop— pop very fast. Some of the soldiers were down on their knees, some standing. Officers all in front. The smoke was like a great cloud, and everywhere the Sioux went the dust rose like smoke. We circled all round him—swirling like water round a stone. We shoot, we ride fast, we shoot again. Soldiers drop, and horses fall on them. Soldiers in line drop, but one man rides up and down the line—all the time shouting. He rode a sorrel horse with white face and white fore-legs. I don't know who he was. He was a brave man.

Indians keep swirling round and round, and the soldiers killed only a few. Many soldiers fell. At last all horses killed but five. Once in a while some man would break out and run toward the river, but he would fall. At last about a hundred men and five horsemen stood on the hill all bunched together. All along the bugler kept blowing his commands. He was very brave too. Then a chief was killed. I hear it was Long Hair (Custer), I don't know; and then the five horsemen and the bunch of men, may be so forty, started toward the river. The man on the sorrel horse led them, shouting all the time. He wore a buckskin shirt, and had long black hair and mustache. He fought hard with a big knife. His men were all covered with white dust. I couldn't tell whether they were officers or not. One man all alone ran far down toward the river, then round up over the hill. I thought he was going to escape, but a Sioux fired and hit him in the head. He was the last man. He wore braid on his arms (sergeant).

All the soldiers were now killed, and the bodies were stripped. After that no one could tell which were officers. The bodies were left where they fell. We had no dance that night. We were sorrowful.

Next day four Sioux chiefs and two Cheyennes and I, Two Moon, went upon the battlefield to count the dead. One man carried a little bundle of sticks. When we came to dead men, we took a little stick and gave it to another man, so we counted the dead. There were 388. There were thirty-nine Sioux and seven Cheyennes killed, and about a hundred wounded.

Some white soldiers were cut with knives to make sure they were dead; and the war women had mangled some. Most of them were left just where they fell. We came to the man with big mus-

> tache; he lay down the hills towards the river. The Indians did not take his buckskin shirt. The Sioux said, "That is a big chief. That is Long Hair." I don't know. I had never seen him. The man on the white-faced horse was the bravest man.
>
> That day as the sun was getting low our young men came up the Little Horn riding hard. Many white soldiers were coming in a big boat, and when we looked we could see the smoke rising. I called my people together, and we hurried up the Little Horn, into Rotten Grass Valley. We camped there three days, and then rode swiftly back over our old trail to the east. Sitting Bull went back into the Rosebud and down the Yellowstone, and away to the north. I did not see him again.

The old man paused and filled his pipe. His story was done. His mind came back to his poor people on the barren land where the rain seldom falls.

> That was a long time ago. I am now old, and my mind has changed. I would rather see my people living in houses and singing and dancing. You have talked with me about fighting, and I have told you of the time long ago. All that is past. I think of these things now: First, that our reservation shall be fenced and the white settlers kept out and our young men kept in. Then there will be no trouble. Second, I want to see my people raising cattle and making butter. Last, I want to see my people going to school to learn the white man's way. That is all.

There was something placid and powerful in the lines of the chief's broad brow, and his gestures were dramatic and noble in sweep. His extended arm, his musing eyes, his deep voice combined to express a meditative solemnity profoundly impressive. There was no anger in his voice, and no reminiscent ferocity. All that was strong and fine and distinctive in the Cheyenne character came out in the old man's talk. He seemed the leader and the thoughtful man he really is—patient under injustice, courteous even to his enemies.

Source: Hamlin Garland, "General Custer's Last Fight as Seen by Two Moon," *McClure's Magazine* 11 (September 1898):443-48.

4-33. Our Indian Problem

Lyman Abbott

December 1898

Lyman Abbott (1835-1922), a clergyman, was born in Roxbury, Massachusetts, and graduated from New York University in 1853. After passing the bar examination three years later, he settled in Brooklyn, New York, where he came under the influence of Henry Ward Beecher, a preeminent preacher. In 1859 Abbott abandoned his law practice to study theology in Maine. The next year he began serving as the pastor of the Congregational church in Terre Haute, Indiana, but returned to New York after the Civil War. In 1888 he began serving as pastor of the Plymouth Congregational Church in Brooklyn. He also was editor of The Illustrated Christian Weekly *(1870) and of* Christian Union *(1876), in 1893 changing the name of the latter to* Outlook, *which became a widely circulating paper. Abbott advocated Protestant progressivism and social reform. His most significant book was* The Evolution of Christianity *(1892). Readers of the December, 1898, issue of* North American Review *learned his views about Native America. He suggested six possible remedies for reform, including the removal from politics of the Indian Bureau.*

Helen Jackson has written the history of a hundred years of our nation's dealing with the Indians, under the title of "A Century of Dishonor." Her specifications seem to make the indictment of her title good. Yet I am persuaded that the dishonor which justly attaches to the history of our dealing with the North American Indians is due rather to a lack of prophetic vision, quite pardonable, in the nation's leaders, and an ignorance and indifference, not pardonable, in the nation at large, rather than to any deliberate policy of injustice adopted by the nation. Bad as has been our treatment of the Indians, it is luminous by the side of Russia's treatment of the Jews, Turkey's treatment of the Armenians, Spain's treatment of the Moors, and, if we include the war of Cromwell against the Irish, the English legislation against Irish industry, Irish education, and the Church of Ireland's choice, it compares favorably with England's treatment of Ireland.

When thirteen States—a fringe of civilization on the eastern edge of an unknown wilderness—constituted the American Republic, there was no prophet to foresee the time when the Republic would stretch from the Atlantic to the Pacific, and from the Lakes to the Gulf of Mexico, and would include seventy million people. If there were any such prophet he was as a voice crying in the wilderness; no one heard or heeded. The politician is almost invariably an opportunist, perhaps necessarily so, since no great prevision is granted to the children of men. The infant republic did not know and took little pains to ascertain either the extent of the domain which stretched to the west, or the number or character of the people who roamed over it. Each decade was satisfied to provide for its own necessities and leave the next decade to take care of itself. As the boundary line was pushed steadily westward new treaties were made, by which all territory west of a given boundary was reserved for the Indians forever. I think it was in 1800 that such a treaty was made, securing to them for all future time the land west of the Mississippi River. All future time is a long while, and each new treaty was made only to be broken, as increase of population and incoming immigration made new demands on the continent for support. Thus gradually grew up without design the so-called reservation system. Less and less land was reserved to the Indians; more and more was taken up by the whites; until at last certain relatively small sections were deeded to separate Indian tribes. In these, according to the treaties made, the several tribes were at liberty to remain forever hunters and trappers, freed from the obligations and without the advantages and perils of civilization.

These reservations have been practically prison yards, within which the tribes have been confined. If any member passed beyond the boundaries of the reservation without leave he was liable to arrest. If he raised crops or manufactured goods he could not carry them for sale to the open market; if he wished to buy he could not go to the open market to purchase. The land was owned by the tribe in common, and the idle and industrious shared alike its advantages and disadvantages. Industry received no reward; idleness involved no penalty. Money due the tribe under the treaty was paid with more or less regularity, generally in rations, sometimes in guns and ammunition to fight the white man with, or scalping knives to take from his head a trophy of the battle. The forms of industry to which the men were accustomed—

hunting and trapping—gradually disappeared; little or nothing was done to teach new forms of industry or to inspire the men to undertake them. From the reservation all the currents of civilization were excluded hy Federal law. The railroad, the telegraph, the newspaper, the open market, free competition—all halted at its walls. By favor of the government, generally freely granted, the missionary was allowed to establish a church, or Christian philanthropy to plant a school. But as an educated Indian was rather impeded than aided in the tribal community by education, neither the church nor the school could do more than save individuals from a population shut up by law to the general conditions of barbarism. No courts sat in these reservations; no law was administered by those judicial methods familiar to the Anglo-Saxon; no warrants from local courts outside could be executed; no Indian, if wronged, could appeal to any court for redress. Such law as existed was administered by an Indian agent, a person of ill-defined, and to the Indian mind, of illimitable power. He was as nearly an absolute despot as can be conceived existing on American soil. He was sometimes an intelligent and beneficent despot, sometimes an ignorant and incompetent one; but in either case a despot.

Thus there has grown up in America, by no deliberate design, but by a natural though mischievous opportunism which has rarely looked more than ten years ahead, a system as inconsistent with American principles and the American spirit as could easily be devised by the ingenuity or conceived by the imagination of man. It has denied to the Indian, often under the generous desire to do more for him than mere justice, those rights and prerogatives which the Declaration of Independence truly declares to belong inalienably to all men. It has made a prisoner of him that it might civilize him, under the illusion that it is possible to civilize a race without subjecting them to the perils of civilization. It has endeavored to conduct him from the relative innocence of barbarism to the larger and more perilous life of a free and civilized community, and to guard him from the dangers of temptation and the consequences of his own ignorance *en route*. The reservation system is absolutely, hopelessly, incurably bad, “evil and wholly evil and that continually.” It was never framed by anyone. It has grown up under the commingled influence of careless indifference, popular ignorance, local prejudice and unthinking sentimentalism. The Indian problem is, in a sentence, how to get rid of it in the easiest and quickest way possible, and bring the Indian and every Indian into the same individual relation to the State and Federal governments that other men in this country are, with the least possible violence of rupture with the past and the greatest possible regard for the rights and the welfare of those who are the least responsible for the present conditions—the Indians themselves.

The reservation system, I say, is wholly bad. The indictment against it is fourfold.

In the first place, the Indian Bureau is, and always has been, a political machine, whose offices are among the spoils which belong the victors. In the twenty years during which I have had some familiarity with Indian affairs, not a single Commissioner of Indian Affairs has been appointed because he was familiar with the Indians or an expert in the Indian problem, and only one who was an expert in that work of education which is, of course, one of the chiefest elements in the Indian problem. They have been, I think, all of them, men of excellent character—honest, able, ambitious to do the best that could be done for the Indian. Some of them have made notable contributions toward the solution of the problem. But each one of them has come into office with little or no familiarity with the problem, has had to acquaint himself with it, and has hardly had more than enough time to do so before his term or office has expired and he has been replaced by a successor who has had to take up the work subject to the same disadvantages. The same policy of political removal and political appointment has characterized the whole Indian administration. Sometimes, the appointments have been made by the Commissioner of Indian Affairs, sometimes by the Secretary of the Interior, sometimes, practically by local politicians; but in all cases alike not for expert knowledge of Indians but for political service rendered or to be rendered, or from reasons of personal friendship. The notion that there is a continuous and consistent policy to be pursued toward the Indians, and that this requires continuity of service and expertness of knowledge in the administration, has not entered the head of our public men, or, if so, has not been allowed to obtain lodgment there. That so bad a system has secured so many good Indian agents and subordinate officials is a matter for surprise. It is not surprising that it has in more than one instance sent a drunken official to keep the Indians sober, an ignorant official to superintend their education, and a lazy official to inspire them with industry. One recent illustration of the result of this method of administration is to be seen in the removal of Dr. [W. N.] Hailman, the Superintendent of Indian Education, an expert educator, whose retention in his office was urged upon the administration by substantially all those familiar with the work which he had done. An even more striking object lesson is afforded by the outbreak among the Pillager Indians, largely due to three successive appraisals of their timber lands, two of which appraisals have been set aside as inadequate, through the incompetence of the appraisers, the enormous cost of each appraisal having been charged to the Indians.

But even if the Indian Bureau could be taken out of politics and kept out of politics, the reservation system would still be incurably bad. It assumes that the Federal executive can administer a paternal government over widely scattered local communities. For such a function it is peculiarly unfitted. The attempt to engraft a Russian bureaucracy on American democracy is a foredoomed failure. The Federal government does exercise paternal authority over the District of Columbia. But on the decent government of the district the well being, the health and perhaps the lives of the members of Congress depend; the relation between the government and the governed is thus direct, close, intimate. Local communities in the United States exercise some paternal functions, as in the case of the insane, the sick, and the paupers. But here again those directly interested have an opportunity of exercising an immediate supervision over the work and calling the public officials to account. But it is in the nature of the case impossible that a President, a Secretary of the Interior, or even a Commissioner of Indian Affairs, can personally supervise the innumerable details involved in the paternal administration of communities scattered from Minnesota to New Mexico, and from Michigan to California.

An aristocratic government, composed of men who have inherited political ability from a long line of governing ancestry, and who have been especially trained for that work from boyhood, so that both by inheritance and training they are experts, may be supposed fitted to take care of people weaker, more ignorant, or less competent than themselves, though the history of oligarchic governments does not render that supposition free from doubt. But there is nothing in either philosophy or history to justify the surmise that seventy millions of average men and women, most of whom are busy in attending to their own affairs, can be expected to take care of a people scattered through a widely extended territory—a people of social habits and social characteristics entirely different from their care-takers; nor is it much more rational to expect that public servants, elected on different issues, for a different purpose, can render this service efficiently. Our Government is founded on the principle of local self-government; that is, on the principle that each locality is better able to take care of its own affairs than any central and paternal authority is to take care of them. The moment we depart from this principle we introduce a method wholly unworkable by a democratic nation. It may be wide of the present purpose, yet perhaps not as an illustration, to say, that if the United States assumes political responsibility for Cuba and the Philippines, as I personally think it is bound to do, it must fulfill that responsibility not by governing them as conquered territory from Washington, but by protecting and guiding, but not controlling them, while they attempt the experiment of local self-government for themselves. We have tried the first method with our Indians, and it has been a continuous and unbroken failure. We have tried the second method with the territory west of the Mississippi River, ours by conquest or by purchase, and it has been an unexampled success. If the Indian is the "ward of the nation" the executive should not be his guardian. How that guardianship should be exercised I shall indicate presently.

This political and undemocratic paternalism is thoroughly bad for the Indian, whose interests it is supposed to serve. It assumes that civilization can be taught by a primer in a school, and Christianity by a sermon in a church. This is not true. Free competition teaches the need of industry, free commerce the value of honesty; a savings bank the value of thrift; a railroad the importance of punctuality, better than either preacher or pedagogue can teach them. To those, and there are still some, who think we must keep the Indian on the reservation until he is prepared for liberty, I reply that he will never be prepared for liberty on a reservation. When a boy can learn to ride without getting on a horse's back, or to swim without going into the water, or to skate without going on the ice—then, and not before, can man learn to live without living, The Indian must take his chance with the rest of us. His rights must be protected by law; his welfare looked after by philanthropy; but protected by law and befriended by philanthropy he must plunge into the current of modern life and learn to live by living. The tepee will never fit him for the house, nor the canoe for the steamboat, nor the trail for highways and railroads, nor trapping and hunting for manufactures and husbandry. Imagine—the illustration is Edward Everett Hale's, not mine—imagine that we had pursued toward our immigrants the policy we have pursued toward the Indians; had shut the Poles, the Hungarians, the Italians, the Germans, the Scandinavians, each in a reservation allotted to them, and forbidden them to go out into the free life of America until they had Americanized themselves—how long would the process have taken?

But the capital objection to the reservation system is that it is one impossible to maintain; and it is impossible to maintain because it ought not to be maintained. The tide of civilization, surging westward, comes some day to a fair and wealthy but unused and idle territory. There are forests which no woodsman's axe has ever touched; rivers where waterfalls turn no mill wheels; mountains whose treasures of gold or silver, iron or copper or coal no pickaxe has uncovered; prairies whose fertile soil is prolific only in weeds. "Come," cries the pioneer, eager to develop this useless territory, "let us go in and make those acres rich by our industry." "No!" replies the law; "you cannot. "Why not?" "It belongs to the Indians." "Where are they?" "Hunting, trapping, sleeping, idling, and fed on rations." "When are they going to use this land; to convert this timber into boards; these rivers into mill-streams; when are they going to excavate these minerals and turn these weedy prairies into fruitful farms?" "Never! This land in the heart of a civilized community is forever consecrated to barbarism." The pioneer's impatience with such a policy is fully justified, though his manner of manifesting it is not. Barbarism has no rights which civilization is bound to respect. The question on what basis the right to land rests is one of the most difficult which political economy has to answer. Many scholars who do not accept Henry George's conclusions accept his premise, that the soil belongs to the community, and that individual ownership rests not on any indefeasible right, but on the express or implied agreement of the community. Certain it is that the half a million, more or less, of Indians who roamed over this continent in the seventeenth century, had no right by reason of that fact to exclude from it the several hundred million industrious men and women whom eventually it will support. As little have a tribe of a few hundred Indians a right to keep in unproductive idleness a territory which if cultivated would provide homes for as many thousands of industrious workers. No treaty can give them that right. It is not in the power of the Federal Government to consecrate any portion of its territory thus to ignorance and idleness. It has tried, again and again, to do so; it has always failed; it always ought to fail; it always will fail. English parks kept untitled, yet ministering to taste and refinement, have always been regarded by political economists as difficult to justify; nothing can be said to justify American reservations, kept untilled only that they may minister to idleness and barbarism.

The editor of the NORTH AMERICAN REVIEW, in asking me to write this article, indicated his desire that I should write "on the probable future of the Indians in their relations with the Government, and the reforms necessary in the administration of their affairs." It may seem that I have been a long time coming to any definite answer to this question; but in order to set forth succinctly a reform it is first necessary to set forth as clearly and forcibly as possible the evil to be reformed. That evil, I believe, is the reservation system. The reform is all summed up in the one word, abolish it. Cease to treat the Indian as a red man and treat him as a man. Treat him as we have treated the Poles, Hungarians, Italians, Scandinavians. Many of them are no better able to take care of themselves than the Indians; but we have thrown on them the responsibility of their own custody, and they have learned to live by living. Treat them as we have treated the negro. As a race the African is less competent than the Indian; but we do not shut the negroes up in reservations and put them in charge of politically appointed parents called Agents. The lazy grow hungry; the criminal are punished; the industrious get on. And though sporadic cases of injustice are frequent and often tragic, they are the gradually disappearing relics of a slavery that is past, and the negro is finding his place in American life gradually, both as a race and as an individual. The reform necessary in the administration of Indian Affairs is: Let the Indian administer his own affairs and take his chances. The future relations of the Indians with the Government should be precisely the same as the relations of any other individual, the readers of this article or the writer of it, for example. This should be the objective point, and the sooner we can get there the better. But this will bring hardship and even injustice on some individuals! Doubtless. The world has not yet found any way in which all hardship and all injustice to individuals can be avoided. Turn the Indian loose on the continent and the race will disappear! Certainly. The sooner the better. There is no more reason why we should endeavor to preserve intact the Indian race than the Hungarians, the Poles, or the Italians. Americans all, from ocean to ocean, should be the aim of all American statesmanship. Let us understand once for all that an inferior race must either adapt and conform itself to the higher civilization, wherever the two come in conflict, or else die. This is the law of God; from which there is no appeal. Let Christian philanthropy do all it can to help the Indian to conform to American civilization; but let not sentimentalism fondly imagine that it can save any race or any community from this inexorable law.

This general and radical reform involves certain specific cures. For example,

1. The Indian Bureau ought to be taken at once and forever out of politics. The Government should find the man most expert in dealing with the Indians—he may be the present Commissioner of Indian Affairs—and instruct him to bring the Indian Bureau to a close at the earliest possible moment. Once appointed to office for that purpose he should stay there till the work is completed. I believe that in one respect an army officer would be the best fitted for such a post, because he would be eager to bring the work to a close, while the civilian would see a hundred reasons why it should be continued from year to year. His subordinates should be Indian experts, and removed only for cause, never for political reasons.

2. There are, it is said, ten or a dozen reservations in which the land has already been allotted in severalty and the reservations broken up. The agents in such cases should be dismissed. If the Indian still needs a guardian, if there is danger that his land will be taxed away from him, or that he will be induced to sell it for a song, the courts, not the executive, should be his guardian. Guardianship is a function the courts are accustomed to exercise. It ought not to be difficult to frame a law such that an Indian could always appeal to a Federal judge to have his tax appraisal revised, and always be required to submit to a Federal judge any proposed sale of real estate.

3. The Indian and every Indian should be amenable to the law and entitled to its protection. I believe that, despite occasional injustice from local prejudice, it would be quite safe to leave their interests to be protected by the courts of any State or Territory in which they live; for I believe that the American people, and certainly the American judiciary, can be trusted. The policy of distrust has intensified the local prejudice against the Indian. But it would be easy, if it be necessary, to provide that any Indian might sue in a United States court, or if sued or prosecuted might transfer the suit to a United States court. I assume there is no constitutional provision against such a law.

4. All reservations in which the land is capable of allotment in severalty should be allotted as rapidly as the work of surveying and making out the warrants can be carried on. The unallotted land should be sold and the proceeds held by the United States in trust for the Indians. How to be expended is a difficult question. Not in food and clothing, which only pauperize. The first lesson to be taught the Indian is, if he will not work, neither shall he eat. Perhaps in agricultural implements; perhaps in schools; perhaps in public improvements; perhaps in all three. When the land is of a kind that cannot be allotted in severalty, as in the case of extended grazing lands, for example, it would seem as though a skillful lawyer should be able to devise some way in which the tribe could be incorporated and the land given to the corporation in fee simple; in which case the shares of stock possibly for a time should be inalienable, except by approval of the court; or possibly the property might even be administered for a time by a receiver appointed by and answerable to the court.

5. Every Indian should be at once free to come and go as he pleases, subject as every other man is to the law of the locality and the processes of the courts where he is, and under their protection. The Indian with his blanket should have the privilege of travelling where he will, as much as the Italian with her shawl.

6. Finally, as fast and as far as the tribal organization is dissolved and the reservation is broken up, the Indian should have a ballot, on the same terms as other citizens; not so much because his vote will add to the aggregate wisdom of the community as because the ballot is the American's protection from injustice.

The reform is very simple, if it is very radical. It is: Apply to the solution of the Indian problem the American method; treat the Indian as other men are treated; set him free from his trammels; cease to coddle him; in a word, in lieu of paternal protection, which does not protect, and free rations, which keep him in beggary, give him justice and liberty and let him take care of himself.

Source: Lyman Abbot, "Our Indian Problem," *North American Review* 167 (December 1898):719-28.

4-34. Rising Wolf: Ghost Dancer

Hamlin Garland

January 1899

A native of Wisconsin, writer, and political activist, Hamlin Garland (1860-1940) gained fame during the Gilded Age for his literary realism in Main-Travelled Roads *(1891), veritism in* Prairie Folks *(1893), and romantic portrayal in* Her Mountain Lore *(1901). His essay on a description of the Ghost Dance by Rising Wolf (the "white Blackfoot" Hugh Monroe) appeared in* McClure's Magazine *for January, 1899.*

. . . One night there came into our midst a Snake messenger with a big tale. "Away in the west," he said to us in sign talk,

> a wonderful man has come. He speaks all languages and he is the friend of all red men. He is white, but not like other white men. He has been nailed to a tree by the whites. I saw the holes in his hands. He teaches a new dance, and that is to gather all the Indians together

> in council. He wants a few head men of all tribes to meet him where the big mountains are, in the place where the lake is surrounded by pictured rocks. There he will teach us how to make mighty magic and drive away the white man and bring back the buffalo.

All that he told us we pondered long, and I said: "It is well, I will go to see this man. I will learn his dance. . . ."

A day passed, and he did not come; but one night when we sat in council over his teachings, he suddenly stepped inside the circle. He was a dark man, but not so dark as we were. He had long hair on his chin, and long, brown head-hair, parted in the middle. I looked for the wounds on his wrists; I could not see any. He moved like a big chief, tall and swift. He could speak all tongues. He spoke Dakota, and many understood. I could understand the language of the Cut-throat people, and this is what he said:

> My people, before the white man came you were happy. You had many buffalo to eat and tall grass for your ponies. You could come and go like the wind. When it was cold, you could go into the valleys to the south, where the healing springs are; and when it grew warm, you could return to the mountains in the north. The white man came. He dug the bones of our mother, the earth. He tore her bosom with steel. He built big trails and put iron horses on them. He fought you and beat you, and put you in barren places where a horned toad would die. He said you must stay there; you must not hunt in the mountains.
>
> Then he breathed his poison upon the buffalo, and they disappeared. They vanished into the earth. One day they covered the hills, the next nothing but their bones remained. Would you remove the white man? Would you have the buffalo come back? Listen, and I will tell you how to make great magic. I will teach you a mystic dance, and then let everybody go home and dance. When the grass is green, the change will come. Let everybody dance four days in succession, and on the fourth day the white man will disappear and the buffalo come back; our dead will return with the buffalo. . . .
>
> You have forgotten the ways of the fathers; therefore great distress is upon you. You must throw away all that the white man has brought you. Return to the dress of the fathers. You must use the sacred colors, red and white, and the sacred grass, and in the spring, when the willows are green, the change will come. . . .

Then he taught us the song and the dance which white people call the ghost dance, and we danced all together, and while we danced near him he sat with bowed head. No one dared to speak to him. The firelight shone on him. Suddenly he disappeared. No one saw him go. Then we were sorrowful, for we wished him to remain with us. . . .

At last we reached home, and I called a big dance, and at the dance I told the people what I had seen, and they were very glad. "Teach us the dance," they cried to me. . . .

Then they did as I bid, and when the moon was round as a shield, we beat the drum and called the people to dance. . . .

The agent came to see us dance, but we did not care. He was a good man, and we felt sorry for him, for he must also vanish with the other white people. He listened to our crying, and looked long, and his interpreter told him we prayed to the great Spirits to destroy the white man and bring back the buffalo. Then he called me with his hand, and because he was a good man I went to him. He asked me what the dance meant, and I told him, and he said, "It must stop." "I cannot stop it," I said. "The Great Spirits have said it. It must go on.". . .

On the fourth night, while we danced, soldiers came riding down the hills, and their chiefs, in shining white hats, came to watch us. All night we prayed and danced. We prayed in our songs.

But the agent smiled, and the soldiers of the white chiefs sat not far off, their guns in their hands, and the moon passed by, and the east grew light, and we were very weary, and my heart was heavy. I looked to see the red come in the east. "When the sun looks over the hills, then it will be," I said to my friends. "The white man will become as smoke. The wind will sweep him away."

As the sun came near we all danced hard. My voice was almost gone. My feet were numb, my legs were weak, but my heart was big. . . .

But the sun came up, the soldiers fired a big gun, and the soldier chiefs laughed. Then the agent called to me, "Your Great Spirit can do nothing. Your Messiah lied.". . .

All day I lay there with my head covered. I did not want to see the light of the sun. I heard the drum stop and the singing die away. Night came, and then on the hills I heard the wailing of my people. Their hearts were gone. Their bones were weary.

When I rose, it was morning. I flung off my blankets, and looked down on the valley where the tepees of the white soldiers stood. I heard their drums and their music. I had made up my mind. The white man's trail was wide and dusty by reason of many feet passing thereon, but it was long. The trail of my people was ended.

Source: Hamlin Garland, "Rising Wolf: Ghost Dancer," ***McClure's Magazine*** **12 (January 1899):241-48.**

➳ ● ⬸

4-35. The Indian on the Reservation

George Bird Grinnell

February 1899

George Bird Grinnell (1849-1938) was born in Brooklyn, New York, and earned an undergraduate degree and a Ph.D. from Yale University. He was a zoologist, ethnologist, ornithologist, explorer, naturalist, historian, anthropologist, and prolific writer. Grinnell edited Forest and Stream *from 1876 to1911, served as president of Forest and Stream Publishing Company (1880-1911), and emerged as president of Bosworth Machine Company after 1887. Throughout this time and later, he maintained close associations with Native Americans of the northern plains. President of the National Parks Association and active in various professional organizations, Grinnell participated in sojourns to the West, including George Custer's 1874 trip to the Black Hills, William Ludlow's reconnaissance to Yellowstone Park in 1875, and the Harriman Alaska Expedition in 1899. Grinnell's highly focused analysis of Native Americans on reservations appeared in the February, 1899, issue of* Atlantic Monthly.

When an Indian tribe had given up fighting, surrendered to the whites, and taken up a reservation life, its position was that of a group of men in the stone age of development, suddenly brought into contact with modern methods, and required on the instant to renounce all they had ever been taught and all they had inherited; to alter their practices of life, their beliefs, and their ways of thought; and to conform to manners and ways representing the highest point reached by civilization. It is beyond the power of our imagination to grasp the actual meaning to any people of such a condition of things. History records no similar case with which one can compare it. And if it is hard for us to comprehend such a situation, what must it have been for the savage to understand it, and, still more, to act it out?

On no two reservations was life precisely the same, yet on all of them it was the same in this: that it was different from old times; that the people no longer came and went at their own pleasure, but were confined by metes and bounds, and were subject to the orders of persons whom they themselves had not chosen to obey as chiefs. With the irksomeness of confinement came a change in physical conditions and health. The toils of the warpath and the hunting trail had ceased. Men who had been active in all the ordinary pursuits of their earlier life had now no occupation. They took no exercise, but sat about grieving over the good old times which were gone, and brooding over the present.

Cut off from their old free life of roving hunters, the Indians were forced to endure an existence without interest or occupation, and to see their people, old and young, dying about them faster than they had ever died in former days. They saw before them no prospect save of an indefinite continuance of the same state of things. They had nothing to look forward to nor anything to hope for. They were like men sentenced to life imprisonment, with blank walls all about them,—walls which they could never hope to pass. Yet, as the years went by, the Indians grew more or less accustomed to these miseries and felt them less acutely, though to the older men and women memory still made life a bitter thing. But the people came to regard the hardships as unavoidable, and accepted them with a sad stoicism as a part of the new and incomprehensible situation.

The Indians had been brought to a reservation and were to be civilized. Let us see how they were handled,—what sort of men were set to instruct these grown-up children; to persuade, to urge, and to command them to do white men's work; to perform the difficult and delicate task of changing wild savages and roaming hunters to civilized laborers. To be successful, such work calls for infinite patience and tact, together with the constant realization that the tasks required of these people are wholly new and uncomprehended by them. Before they can perform them, they must understand why and how their work is to be done.

It is obvious that the Indians can be taught the white man's ways only by actual contact with white men, and that this contact can be had only with those living on the reservation to which the Indians are confined. Such white men are the employees of the Indian Bureau and the missionaries.

The task of civilizing the Indians really depends almost wholly upon the agent who is set over them. He represents the Great Father; he alone has authority. It is for him to explain to them the benefits of toil, to reward the industrious, to punish the refractory, to encourage the unsuccessful, and to direct the ambitious. He can lead the tribe to see that work is necessary, and can induce them to work; or he can let the Indians take their own way, and face their problems without assistance. If he has enthusiasm for his work and a real desire to see the people advance, he can infuse into them some part of his own energy, and make them believe that actual benefits to themselves and to their children will follow their efforts.

An Indian agent has absolute control of affairs on his reservation, subject only to the approval of the Department of the Interior at Washington, which two or three times a year may send out an inspector to look after him. His position is one of great responsibility, for he has to administer a business representing each year from $50,000 to $200,000. His power on the reservation is more nearly absolute than anything else that we in this country know of. He has not the authority to order out his Indians to instant execution, but in practice this is the only power that he does not possess. Over property, liberty, and the actions of every-day life he has absolute authority. No Indian can receive food, no Indian can obtain a tool, no Indian can live in his home, unless the agent is willing. He holds in the hollow of his hand the welfare of the tribe and of each one of its individuals.

The man who bears these responsibilities and is clothed with these powers over his fellow men should be of high character and good abilities, such as one as would be chosen for the manager of a considerable business. He should feel the responsibility of his position, and not be satisfied merely to get along as easily as possible and to draw his salary regularly. The good agent really stands in the relation of a parent toward his Indians; and as a father instructs, punishes, and rewards his children, so the agent should firmly, but kindly, govern the people who are under him. They recognize this relation, and often speak of the agent as their father. In the ordinary pursuits of life, a man qualified by training and temperament for such a place would receive a good salary; he ought to receive it here,—at least thrice the pittance that is now paid to Indian agents. Such a man ought to be retained in office so long as he would remain, and should not be turned out with the coming in of each new administration.

But the Indian service long constituted an important part of the spoils which until recently belonged wholly to the victors in the political contest. The position of agent is still a part of these spoils, and at present most of the offices are portioned out to the Senators and Congressmen of the various states. There are a few army officers acting as Indian agents,—among whom there has rarely been one who was incompetent,—but a large share of the civilian officials have been political appointees, minor ward or county politicians who obtain the office as a reward for vote-getting, or else "good fellows" who have failed in every business that they had undertaken, and now fall back on this place for a living. Men of this class cannot be expected to care for their people; often they are concerned only for their pay and their perquisites. Perhaps, in a vague way, they advise the Indians "to follow the white man's road," and then leave them to find out for themselves what that road is and whither it leads. Some Indian agents are men of high character, but none are well paid; for they receive only from $1500 to $2000 per annum—small compensation for the never ending worries and detail of their position, to say nothing of the isolation of life at any Indian agency. The unwisdom of paying so poorly men who have such important work to do has long been understood, and many years ago, during President [U. S.] Grant's administration, some of the religious denominations, to which the control of the Indians has been intrusted, chose as Indian agents men fitted for the task, and themselves added to the government salary a further compensation from their own funds.

The position of Indian agent is one full of annoyances, full of temptations. He should be a man of patience and shrewdness, kindly yet firm; a man of character, absolutely truthful. He must be willing to make over and over again the same elaborate explanations of the simplest matters; to resist attempts to impose on or to frighten him; to take a decided stand and never recede from it; to incur the lasting hostility of the white men, Indians, and men of mixed blood who received special favors from the previous agent, and who now expect the same from him. Most agents appear to imagine that their position is one which calls especially for office work, and much of their time, therefore, is spent in the office, overseeing the making out of papers; giving out orders for flour, sugar, coffee, sacks, and other things requested by the Indians; acting, in fact, much like a retail country storekeeper. The truth is that an agent should spend the greater part of his time in the saddle or in his wagons traveling about among his people; learning the personality of each; finding out how each family lives, what improvements the man has made on his place, what property he has, how he is taking care of it and what use he is putting it to. The agent thus learns what each man requires and how far he is deserving. He also appears to his Indians to be talking an active interest in their welfare and to be more or less in sympathy with them; and there is nothing that an Indian appreciates more, nothing which is to him a stronger incentive to try to do well, than the exhibition of such sympathy.

The agent is assisted by a force of clerks, farmers, and other employees, each of whom is brought into closest contact with the Indians, and thus may wield a tremendous influence for good or for evil. These men, as a rule, take their tone from the agent. If he is energetic and enthusiastic, they follow his lead at the pace he sets. If he is rough, brutal, and profane in his dealing with the Indians, they are so too. If he is dishonest, they are dishonest. If he is weak, a stronger man soon gains an ascendency over him, and becomes practically the ruling power on the reservation. Often the clerks appear to regard it as an imposition that they have to attend to the Indians' wants, and are harsh in their intercourse with them, cursing them freely and treating them with the greatest indignity. Often, too, the agency farmers, whose immediate duty it is to instruct the people in the pursuits of civilization, do anything rather than that. They potter about the agency, or they are stablemen, or they work in the blacksmith shop, or put up new buildings, or paint and whitewash old ones, or spend much of their time at the butchering and the issue,—do anything, in fact, except to teach the Indians farming and oversee their work.

The United States army has given us by far the best class of men who have ever held the position of Indian agents; they have usually had a training in military business, and work on a system; they have no private ends to serve, and no affiliations with the white population adjacent to the reservation. When detailed to the service, they go to the posts assigned them to do their duty as they understand it; that duty being to make the Indians self-supporting and civilized, to protect them from white aggression, and, in general, to govern them according to the principles of justice and right. This view is different from that held by the average Indian agent, and so the work done by army officers is very different from that of most civilians, and very much better. Among the civilians are notable exceptions to the rule,—a few men who have done work that could hardly have been excelled; but for all that such men are the exceptions; the rule remains. Among the army officers, on the other hand, a careless or incompetent agent is rare.

First and last, much has been done for the Indians by missionaries sent out by the various denominations. Many are earnest men who try hard to do their whole duty by the Indians; but as missionaries, after all, are only men, some of them are careless, lazy, and inefficient, while a considerable portion lack any understanding of how to handle men. Of the least efficient among them it may be said that if they do no good, they at least do little harm, while there are many whose services to Christianity and to civilization are very great. I have in mind an army chaplain whose work among some Indians who incidentally came within the sphere of his influence was so effective that it will never be forgotten by them. The man was a true follower of the Master, and instead of attempting at once to force upon the Indians the acceptance of religious doctrines, he showed them only sympathy and friendliness. When he had won their good will, they readily gave ear to the simple religious precepts that he taught. Admirable missionary work is done, too, by the Roman Catholic priests and sisters who are stationed on many of the Western reservations. They accomplish in a silent, unsuspected way a great deal of good.

It may obviously be objected to all purely religious work among the Indians that it is caring for the soul before the body is cared for. It is hard for a man to pray with a good heart when he is hungry, nor is it easy to concentrate the attention on the doctrine of the Trinity when his little ones are crying for food. Before the Indian can be Christianized he must be civilized and taught how to earn his living; after he has learned this lesson, and has acquired some of the mental habits of civilized people, the ground will have been prepared for the sowing of the seeds of religion.

There is a practical form of missionary work seldom seen, which cannot be too highly applauded. I have seen it practiced on the Blackfoot reservation by the Rev. E. S. Dutcher. This good man preaches on Sunday to those who come to hear him in the little church which his own hands built, and on other days of the week he takes his tools—for he has learned the carpenter's trade—and goes about over the reservation, helping the Indians to hang the doors and set the window frames in their houses, or to set the fence posts and stretch the wire for their pasture fences. Often his wife goes with him; and while he works out of doors with the men, she is busy within, teaching the women how to bake good bread or make the family clothing. Missionary work such as this, where practical religion is made a part of the daily life, and soul and mind and body are cared for at once, accomplishes lasting results.

For many years good people have been endeavoring to devise plans which should at once transform the Indian from a rover and a warrior to a sedentary laborer. Men of various trades and professions, from the soldier to the theologian, have studied the Indian problem and many different methods have been suggested for rendering the wild man civilized and self-supporting. The author of each has had most perfect confidence that his remedy was the one certain to cure all ills brought to the Indians by contact with the white man. Some of these projects have had fair trial; yet the progress of the race has not been so rapid as to justify the faith that any of these means of civilization—except when engineered with unusual energy and wisdom—would do the work claimed for it, while in some cases the experiments have brought disaster to the Indians.

The sincerity and earnestness of a majority of such philanthropists cannot be doubted, but in all their reasoning about Indians there has been one point of weakness: they had no personal knowledge of the inner life of the people they were trying to help. Their theories appear to have assumed that Indians are precisely like white men, except that their minds are blank and plastic, ready to receive any impression that may be inscribed on them. These friends of the Indians had little acquaintance with Indian character; they did not appreciate the human nature of the people. They did not know that their minds were already occupied by a multitude of notions and beliefs that were firmly fixed there,—rooted and grounded by an inheritance of a thousand years. Still less did they comprehend the Indian's intense conservatism, the tenacity with which he clings to the beliefs which have been handed down to him by uncounted generations.

The plans of the philanthropists who were anxious to benefit the race were based on the general proposition that all Indians should become farmers. As most civilized men earn their living by tilling the soil, they took it for granted that the Indian could do the same, and must become civilized in that way. They were profoundly ignorant of the surroundings of the Indian and of the land he dwelt in, and did not know that over a very large part of the West no crops can be grown unless the soil is well irrigated. They seem to have imagined the great plains a fertile country—perhaps like the prairies of Illinois—where, if land were ploughed and seed sown, bounteous harvests would be sure to follow. They did not understand that many of the Indian reservations consist of the most arid and barren lands that the sun ever shone on,—a waterless, desolate, soul-withering region, whose terrors are incomprehensible to those who have never traveled over it. They did not know that many of the reservations are situated in the land of thirst, where water is the one priceless thing, and its lack the greatest horror. Many years and much effort have therefore been wasted in trying to teach the Indians how to raise crops in regions where white farmers could not possibly make a living; yet, up to a short time ago, the authorities, clinging to the antiquated notions of those who would make all Indians agriculturists, continued to insist that the Indians should sow in the desert, even though they could never hope to reap. Only within a few years has it been learned that in a country adapted for stock-raising Indians should raise stock, and in a farming country they should farm. Yet ever since these tribes have been known to us, the Pueblos and others, who have always practiced irrigation, and the Navajoes, who have long been herdsmen, have furnished examples of this adaptation to environment, and have shown us that different peoples should be treated according to the different conditions which surround them.

One civilizing idea has by this time become impressed on all the Indians of this country: they comprehend to-day that they must work if they would live. The time when food, a blanket, a gun, and some ammunition satisfied the Indians' wants has gone, never to return. Association with civilized people has brought the need for the things of civilization, which can only be had for money. The Indians see that, under the new conditions, money is as necessary to them as it is to the white men. They recognize that the government will not support them forever. So they are intensely anxious to work, to earn money. On many reservations they wear out the patience of the agent by continually asking him for work, when he has no work to give them. On the reservation of the Northern Cheyennes, for the last two or three years, there has been an opportunity for a few men to secure work as laborers on the great irrigating ditch in course of construction on the adjacent Crow reservation. So long as men were wanted for this work, the Cheyenne agent was kept busy giving out passes to his people who wished to labor on the ditch. All the able-bodied men in the tribe would have gone, if there had been work for all. On the Blackfoot reservation, agents have told me of having fifteen or twenty applications a day for the job of going into the mountains to cut wood and haul it away for fuel. The Indians are ready to hire out to anyone who will pay them, and they will work as hard, as long, and as faithfully as any laborers. Usually, there is little or no work to be had. Even the students who come back from the Eastern boarding schools equipped with knowledge of English and a trade, and fitted for a place in the blacksmith's or wheelwright's shop or for a position as industrial teacher at the agency day schools are only occasionally employed about the agency in the various positions which they might fill.

This, then, is one of the chief obstacles to the Indian's progress, the difficulty of earning a livelihood. After he has succeeded in doing this, he must learn how to keep his money when he gets it,—in other words, the lesson of thrift. The old-time Indian was hospitable, openhanded, and generous, to the last degree. The near Indian must learn to be closefisted. As he progresses toward self-support, it is not very hard for him to accumulate horses, cattle, tools, and furniture; but to deal with money merely as money is as yet a very serious problem. If he has money, it burns in his pocket, and he feels that he must spend it. The time will come when Indians will have bank accounts, but that time—except among the civilized tribes—has not yet been reached.

Under the most favorable circumstances—with instruction and encouragement—it is hard enough for the Indian to change himself into a patient laborer, willing to toil day after day at his unpleasing task. Too often, in addition to the difficulties which are inevitable, his advancement is retarded or stopped by his being robbed of his lands by methods which he is powerless to resist. The courts protect citizens; but the Indian is not a citizen, and nothings protects him. Congress has the sole power to order how he shall live, and where. Most thoughtful people believed that in the past the Indians have been greatly wronged by the whites, but imagine that this is no longer the case. Let us see.

The greatest corruption of our Indian affairs took place not very long after the close of the war of the Rebellion. In those days, to be an Indian agent, trader, or contractor was to be on a highroad to fortune, if one made the most of his advantages. The contracts for supplies of every sort were in the hands of a small group of men, who controlled them all, and, what was more important, to a great extent controlled the agents and employees of the Indian Bureau, in the field. Attacks on the Indian ring were made from time to time with more or less success, reforms in the service and its methods were gradually introduced, and the opportunities for robbery grew less. The actual wholesale stealing of the food and clothing provided by the government has ceased, for the most part or has degenerated into petty pilfering.

Nevertheless, methods are still found by which the money of the Indians may be diverted from its proper objects to find its way into the pockets of white men. One of these is the hiring of unnecessary attorneys for them. There are on file before the Court of Claims in Washington many thousands of dollars' worth of claims for alleged Indian depredations, and suits against various Indians tribes and the United States are being carried on before that court. These suits are defended by the Attorney-General's office, and any judgment recovered runs against both the Indian tribe and the United States. If the tribe has no money to pay a judgment rendered against it, the United States must do so. But of late years most of the treaties made with Indians provide that none of the money appropriated under the treaty shall be used to pay depredation claims, and the ratification by Congress of an agreement of this nature puts the money of the tribe out of the reach of the Court of Claims, and so protects the Indians. Moreover, under a ruling of the Interior Department, made a number of years ago, it was determined that no tribes, except two, have any money available for the payment of such claims, and this ruling has hitherto been sustained. Nevertheless, it is a form of legal industry recognized in Washington, for a lawyer to visit an agency and inform the chiefs that claims amounting to many thousands of dollars have been filed against the tribe, and that they may have to pay these claims. By alarming them about the safety of their money, it is not difficult for the lawyer to induce them to make a contract retaining him as their attorney to defend the suits. Contracts of this kind are invalid until approved by the Secretary of the Interior, who is constantly pestered by the lawyers and their political friends to give his assent to them. But since the Indians have no funds which can be used to pay such judgments rendered against them, since the law specifically forbids the use of their funds for such a purpose, and since, therefore, they can have no money interest whatever in the suits, it is manifestly a great wrong that these contracts should be approved by the department, and that the money appropriated for the Indians' support should go to fill the pockets of lawyers. Yet I have in mind a single law firm in

Washington which, by its contracts with different tribes of Indians, who are protected by their treaty and so in no wise need attorneys, is likely to receive this year over $8000,—and for doing nothing. There was absolutely nothing for them to do. The defense they pretended to give the Indian did not require. There was nothing for them to defend him against. The real defense he needs is against the lawyers themselves. It is hardly necessary to add that a large proportion of the depredation claims filed against the different tribes are barefacedly fraudulent.

Indians are now subject to encroachments, conducted, not by an Indian ring, but by the government, which, in its ignorance, does injury to this race as serious as ever was done by any group of individuals. These encroachments are began by white people living near the Indians, who covet the land possessed by them, and usually secured to them by pledges of the government's faith, and who endeavor to gain possession of it by lawful means: that is, by inducing the government to break that faith and violate those pledges.

Wherever its reservation may be, an Indian tribe is bitterly opposed by local popular feeling. Its people are hated because they are Indians, and envied because they hold lands that white men might own. In thought, if not in words, its white neighbors say of a tribe, "Cut it down; why cumbereth it the ground?" Local prejudice and local greed combine to force the Indians—who have no representative in Congress—from their homes, where perhaps they may have made some improvements, and to which often they are deeply attached. The people who wish them removed do not care where they are taken, if only it is away, somewhere else. Their object is to secure the land which they hope to have thrown open to settlement.

This is how the plan of expulsion is carried out. A treaty having been made with a tribe of Indians, a certain tract of country is assigned to them as a permanent home. After a time the land near them becomes settled, and the white people crowd about the reservation. The reservation may be good for something: it may be imagined to contain mines of coal or precious metals, or it may be a good cattle range, or the land may have valuable water on it. When this is the case, the people living in the neighborhood begin to urge upon their delegate, or their Congressman, or their Senator, the importance of moving the Indians, and throwing open their reservation to settlement. Both Senator and Congressman naturally wish to oblige their constituents, and forthwith a bill is introduced or a section is added to the Indian Appropriation Bill, providing for the desired removal. Most members of Congress, knowing nothing of the rights or wrongs of the measure, take it for granted that the local member must know what ought to be done, and are very likely to assent to it.

Less than ten years ago, I was present on a reservation in the Indian Territory when a commission was negotiating with the Indians to induce them to take their lands in severalty, and to sell the surplus. The commissioners made no secret of the fact that the administration had urged them to carry through the sale, because at the next election they wished to go before the people with the statement that they had thrown open to settlement by the public a certain number of acres of Indian reservations. This statement would influence many votes in the West; it would be a good political cry. The negotiations began, and by persuasion, promises, and at last by threats, about one third of the Indians were induced to sign the agreement. After that signatures came in very slowly. The commissioners hired their interpreters to assist them to obtain signers. The attorneys, who claimed that they had been retained by the Indians to defend their rights, worked hard to induce the people to sign. These attorneys were working on a contingent fee,—"the usual ten per cent for collection,"—and of course would receive nothing unless the treaty went through and the sale was made. Indians who were corrupt were hired, I was told, to vote more than once; signing first the name by which they went at the time, then the name which they had borne earlier in life, and later perhaps some still earlier name. The names of absent schoolboys were added to the list, on the mere statement by some Indian that they were in favor of the sale. So, by cajoling, promising, bribing, browbeating bullying, and using illegal votes, the sale, which was bitterly opposed by one half of the tribe, was at last carried through by a bare majority.

Even to-day the same thing is going on. Among the measures recently before Congress was one looking to the removal of the Northern Cheyennes from their present reservation in Montana to "some other place." The territory occupied by these people, although very small, is a fine stock range, which the neighboring cattlemen long to possess for their herds. Besides working with might and main on their representatives in Congress to secure the removal of these Indians to another reservation, these cattlemen endeavor to manufacture a public sentiment against the Indians by continually sending out press reports of the ill doings of the Northern Cheyennes, and two or three times a year Montana press dispatches to the newspapers tell of threatened outbreaks by these people. As a matter of fact, the Indians are entirely well disposed but they realize that an attempt is being made to take them away from their old country, and are uneasy and fearful lest it should succeed. Yet when these Indians surrendered, nearly twenty years ago, General Miles, representing the government, solemnly promised them that they should reside here on this piece of land so long as they should be friendly with the United States. This promise was subsequently repeated by high officials in Washington; yet to-day these Cheyennes fear that they will be moved, and are prevented from working on their homes by the apprehension that as soon as they accomplish anything these homes will be taken from them. Several years' work has been necessary to convince the authorities at Washington that the title of these Indians to their reservation should be confirmed, and that the white men settled on the reservation should be moved away.

There is now in contemplation a measure to take from the Metlakahtla Indians of Alaska—on the ground that there are mines on it—a large portion of the island allotted to them by the government more than ten years ago. This is a case of great hardship,—that of a tribe of Indians who with the help of one intelligent and devoted white friend, have become civilized and self-supporting by their own exertions. They moved from British to United States territory in search of freedom, and in their new home they have built a town, have a sawmill and a salmon cannery, and govern themselves. They ask nothing from anyone, save the poor privilege of living disturbed on the rock where they are settled. But now it is proposed to take a part of this away from them, so to deprive them of the water power which runs their sawmill and their cannery, of most of their timber land, of the stream which furnishes the salmon on which they subsist.

Last spring, on the day of my arrival at the Blackfoot agency I found there two strange Indians, who told me that they were Kutenais, living on the Flathead reservation; that their chief had heard that I was coming out to see the Blackfeet, and that I was the man who helped Indians, and therefore he had sent them as messengers, on foot, across the mountains, a distance of 150 miles, in order that they might tell me of the hard lot of the Kutenais, to see if I could not help them. They said that there were over eighty families of Kutenais living near Dayton Creek, on Lake MacDonald; that they received no rations from the government; that they had been told to take up farms on their reservation, and had done so; but that after they had built their houses, fenced in their land, and planted their little crops, the white people had come to them and told them to move away, that their homes were not on the reservation and did not belong to them. At first they had refused to move, but at last, when the whites had said that if they did not go the Great Father would send troops to move them, they gave up and went away. Now there is no place left on their reservation where they can farm, as all the country is rocky, timber-covered mountains. The faith that had led these men to take this long, toilsome journey to tell me their story was pathetic enough, and the sense of my utter inability to help them was humiliating, but there was nothing that I could do.

A search through the reports of the Indian commissioner shows that these Indians were recently ejected from lands which they had occupied since 1835, on account of a mistake made by a surveyor in locating the boundaries of the reservation. The farms that they had striven to cultivate proved to be without the erected boundary line, and as soon as this was discovered the neighboring whites insisted on the removal of the Indians. As the land did actually lie outside of the reservation, the Indians of course had no claim to it, and were forced to give it up, After this, in 1891, the agent for the Kutenais, acting under the Dawes Severalty Act, allotted to eighteen of the Indians claims off the reservation and upon the land from which they had been expelled. Of these claims, three were allowed, while fifteen have for seven years been suspended by the Land Office. White people have settled in the valley of Dayton Creek and built their fences about the plots held by the Indians, who have now no means of reaching their claims except by trespassing on the land occupied by the whites, which they are warned not to do. Within the white men's fences can be seen still standing the rotting rails and posts of the enclosures built years ago by the Indians when these claims were first allotted to them, and they strove to work as the white man works, and to improve their little farms as he does his. No wonder they are discouraged and hopeless at the result of their efforts, and it is hardly to be imagined that they will ever again make any real effort to become self-supporting so long as the memory of this wrong remains. Some method of repairing this injustice and of helping these Indians ought to be found.

No argument is needed to prove the discouraging effect on Indians—or indeed on men of any race or color—of such uncertainty about their location. If a white man were given the fairest tract of wild land on the continent, with the understanding that he might be ejected from his tenancy at any moment, he would have little motive to improve it, and would put on it just as little labor as he could get along with. Indians feel and act in precisely same way. Whether they are moved or not, the uncertainty under which they live takes away from them all motive for industry and self-help.

Indians are perfectly capable of making progress in the arts of civilization. This is shown by what has been accomplished during the last nine years by the Blackfoot Indians of northern Montana, with whose affairs I have long been closely familiar. A dozen years ago I won their confidence and regard and became deeply interested in them, and ever since I have acted as their counselor and next friend. To bring about the results obtained, it has been necessary to watch them carefully, to advise them against the commission of follies, to persuade them to industry, to reprove them for wrong-doing; in fact, to try to teach them to exercise what white man call ordinary common sense in the affairs of life, checking them or spurring them on as circumstances required. When I first knew the Blackfeet they were wild Indians, wearing blankets and robes, living for the most part in lodges and on a reservation remote from railroad or civilization. Except their ponies they had no property. They had no desire to work, nor any belief that it would be to their advantage to do so.

The country which they inhabit lies on the flanks of the Rocky Mountains, just south of the parallel of forty-nine degrees at an elevation of 3000 or 4000 feet, and is far too high, cold, and dry for the successful practice of agriculture. For years the Indian Bureau had been trying to induce them to farm, but nothing had ever been grown on the reservation except an occasional crop of oats and potatoes. The region however, is an excellent cattle range. In 1888 I determined that if these Indians were ever to become self-supporting it must be by cattle-raising, and a statement of the conditions convinced General [Thomas J.] Morgan, then Indian commissioner, that the experiment was worth trying. My visits of the next two years to the reservation were devoted to elaborate explanations to the Indians of the value to them of cattle; of the importance of never killing them for food, and of caring for them in winter, so that they should live, do well, and breed. It was explained that at the end of four yeas those who followed the advice given would have animals which they could sell, and that the money received for the beeves could be theirs to use as they might please. The idea of having cattle which they should own individually, and not as a tribe, was wholly new to them; when it was understood it was very welcome, and the prospect created quite an excitement in the community. A majority of the men cut hay for the stock that was to come, and built sheds and shelters to protect it from the winter's storms.

In 1890 about 1000 cattle were issued. Some families received only a single cow, others two, and others four or five. All went well with them. The succeeding winter was mild; no cattle died, and the calf crop was large. The people took great pride in their new possessions, and watched and tended them with much devotion. At intervals of a year or two more and more cattle were issued to them, until they had received about 10,000, and in the year 1897 it was estimated that, with the increase, the Blackfeet had between 20,000 and 22,000 head of cattle. Besides this, for three years past they have sold a great deal of beef; and their faith in the promises made to them, which led them for four years to refrain from eating their cattle and to take good care of them, has been abundantly justified. They have found a way by which money can be earned, and have come to understand that their future depends on their cattle and the care they take of them. It must not be supposed that all the men of the tribe have done equally well. While many have been unfailingly faithful, some have neglected their stock, or traded it off, or let it wander away. But, on the whole, they have done well, wonderfully well for Indians, and have been as steadfast and industrious as white men would have been.

The branding of the calves and the round-ups have been in charge of the agency employees, and this work has often been very much neglected. The Indians are not permitted to brand their calves, and they have suffered the losses by the failure of the government employees to brand those born in the fall of the year. These autumn calves, having been weaned and separated from the mothers, by spring become mavericks, animals whose ownership is not known, and so they are branded by anyone who may find them, chiefly by the half-breeds and white men living on the reservation, who are more familiar than are the Indians with the white cattleman's way of accumulating a herd.

The years during which the Blackfeet have had cattle have not been of ease and comfort. The people have had their troubles and perplexities, but the effort has been made to give them aid and direction by letters, by free visits, by consultations, by encouragement and advice, and by praise or severe reproof as either was needed. Often from old White Calf, long the chief of these people, a message is received something like this:—"I want you to come to us quickly. There are many things to be talked over. We are blind once more. We need you to open our eyes." Thus what the Blackfeet need, and all other Indians with them, is, not the good will to labor and to strive, but proper direction in order that they may labor and strive effectively. They lack that discretion and judgment in dealing with every-day matters which inheritance, training, and experience have brought to most middle aged business men, and these must be exercised for them. The power to look at things through the white man's eyes must be supplied to them. They must be made to share the wisdom of the white race. If the Indian Bureau at Washington can be induced to see that the

Blackfeet cattle are properly handled, the future is assured: but the Indian Bureau, being really a clerical office for the transaction of Indian business, often knows little about the actual condition of the people.

The wish to better their present condition is not peculiar to any particular tribe nor to any section of country. If they can be convinced that it will be for their advantage, all Indians are ready and willing to put forth effort; but where only failure rewards the work they perform, they become discouraged and think that they can never succeed. The Indian of today is living his life on the reservation, where he occupies a house and has acquired a certain degree of self-control. He is anxious to have a better living than he gets now, and is willing to work hard to secure it. He has given up many of his old wild ways and beliefs. He is a savage who has been more than half tamed. Civilization has brought to this Indian many hardships; it has abridged his liberty, has caused disease, has weakened or broken so many of the fine savage qualities that he once possessed, and has introduced him to liquor. As yet it has not brought him much that is good except humility and some self-control. His rights are little safeguarded, except so far as the Indian Rights Association can occasionally protect him. He has been taught but little of the individual's responsibilities. He is sometimes subjected to gross injustice.

His inability to speak our tongue or to think our thoughts must always be remembered in considering the Indian. He is voiceless; he is unable to claim any rights for himself or to tell his side of any story, for he has no method of communicating with civilized people except through an interpreter. He cannot speak for himself, and he has no one to speak for him, no one to advocate his cause. Even the young men who have been away to school and have learned how to speak good English speak it as a foreign tongue. They think in their own language, and translate their Indian thoughts into English, which is often not to be understood without further explanation. The Indian's psychological condition is bewildered and confused. Inheriting the beliefs of his people, developed through thousands of years, he is suddenly told that all these beliefs are false. His faith in his creed is destroyed; but while we have taken from him his old beliefs, we have not known enough to give him new ones which he can understand. Thus his mind is in a whirl, and he feels that there is nothing sure, nothing that he can depend on.

What the Indians require to-day is something more than mere food and clothing. They need to be directed with some intelligence and interest. The conditions of each tribe or each agency should be studied by a fairly intelligent and experienced person, and the particular method thus determined to be the one best suited to the needs of the people should be employed. Agents and agency employees who are careless or indifferent should not be retained in the Indian service, and it should be the business of the inspectors actually to learn how far the employees residing permanently on the reservation are sincerely interested in the Indians under their charge. It is gratifying to notice that the force of inspectors has recently been increased, and that a number of those holding the position feel a deep interest in their work, and are willing to follow up the agency employees so that they will be obliged to do their duty. The farmers employed on reservations where agriculture can be practiced should be real farmers. They should not pass their time in loafing about the agency. They should spend seedtime and harvest out among the camps and settlements, teaching the Indians how to perform the various operations of farming. The farmers on reservations where the Indians are stock-raisers should be practical cattlemen. They should understand their duties, and have something of the loyalty of the old-time cowboy. The cattle should be really cared for; stray cattle belonging to neighboring whites should be kept off the reservation, and the Indians cattle held on it. The Indians should be taught how to brand and care for their own stock. They should not be allowed to sell or kill it except by the agent's permission.

Liquor should be kept off the reservation, and those dealing in it or using it should be punished with extreme severity; in other words, the law should be enforced. The Department of the Interior and the Department of Justice must act together in this matter. In the past it has rather been the practice of each of these departments to throw the responsibility on the other.

We can do no more for the Indian than fit him to fight the battle of life, and we must begin by teaching him about its material things. He will readily learn industry and the white man's way, if he sees before him a reward for his work. The task of teaching him saving, thrift, is more difficult, since all his training leads him to share whatever he has with others. In order that he may compete with the white man, he must be taught to speak English and to read and write. This can be taught only to the children, but a part of whom at present attend school. There is the widest possible difference in the efficiency of the agency schools, and very great diversity of opinion exists as to the relative advantages of reservation and of Eastern boarding schools. The subject is a large one, and not now to be treated; but it is obvious that the Eastern schools cannot care for any great proportion of the children, and that good reservation schools are imperatively required.

We need not inquire here what is to be the ultimate fate of this race. Much more to the purpose is it to consider their present perplexities and immediate needs, and to endeavor as well as we may to help them along over the steep, rough trail by which they are climbing upward toward civilization and self-support. The obstacles which lie in the path are many, but they are not insuperable, and they may be greatly lessened by intelligent aid and encouragement. Interest in the Indian is steadily increasing. Many thoughtful people are coming to recognize that he possesses qualities that are worth studying. Writers take him for their theme, sculptors model him, and painters use for subjects scenes from his old wild life. Intelligent people who study him wish to know more about him, and soon learn his true character and give him his true place, demanding for the race the consideration which it ought to have.

The task of giving help to the Indian is one worthy of the best thought and effort of the country. The noblest work that any man can do is to make life easier for some of his fellows, and in the visible results which follow the stretching out of a hand in help and sympathy to an Indian tribe may be found rich reward and ample encouragement to renewed activity. I know of no field in which he who is really interested in his fellows may labor with a surer prospect of appreciation by those he is trying to help, or a more abundant certainty of answering effort by them. When once the Indian's confidence has been won, he strives earnestly to live up to the standard set before him by his white friend, and to repay by aspiration and endeavor all that has been done in behalf.

The Indians must still do battle, but in conflicts unlike those of the olden time. They may still win victories, but the victories will be of peace. The day has passed, too, when one may achieve glory by a campaign against hostile Indians, but worthier triumphs and more lasting rewards await him who shall fight by their side in this new and desperate struggle.

Source: George Bird Grinnell, "The Indian on the Reservation," *Atlantic Monthly* 83 (February 1899):255-67.

4-36. Agreement with the Yankton Sioux

October 2, 1899

On October 2, 1899, the United States, through Indian Inspector James McLaughlin, entered into an agreement with the Yankton Sioux Indians of South Dakota regarding the right and title to a parcel of land in Pipestone County, Minnesota, for a specified sum of money and other stipulations. This contractual accord represented a type of formal arrangement negotiated between the federal government and Native Americans during the Gilded Age, including certifications, signatures, and X marks, memoranda, and other considerations.

This agreement, made and entered into on the second day of October, eighteen hundred and ninety-nine, by and between United States Indian Inspector James McLaughlin, representing the United States, and the Yankton Sioux Indians, of the State of South Dakota, witnesseth:

ARTICLE I. The said Yankton Sioux Indians, for the consideration hereinafter named, do hereby cede, surrender, grant, and convey to the United States all the right, title, and interest which they have in and to a certain tract or parcel of land situated in the county of Pipestone, State of Minnesota, reserved for the use of said Indians by the provisions of Article VIII of the treaty entered into with that tribe on April nineteenth, eighteen hundred and fifty-eight, proclaimed by the President February twenty-sixth, eighteen hundred and fifty-nine, and mentioned in Article

XVI of the agreement I concluded with them December thirty-first, eighteen hundred and ninety-two, and ratified by Congress August fifteenth, eighteen hundred and ninety-four, said parcel of land being indicated on the township plats of the Government legal survey, approved August fifteenth, eighteen hundred and seventy-two, by the surveyor-general for the State of Minnesota as lying in sections 1 and 2 of township 106 north, range 46 west, and sections 35 and 36 of township 107 north, range 46 west of the 5th principal meridian, containing six hundred and forty-eight and two-tenths (648.2) acres, more or less, and embracing the red pipestone quarries, famous in Indian legend and in American literature and history.

ARTICLE II. It is hereby agreed, however, on the part of the United States that the Yankton Sioux Indians, and they alone, shall be permitted, as has been their custom for unnumbered generations, to go upon that portion of the tract of land hereby ceded, upon which the pipestone quarries are situated, under such regulations and conditions as may be prescribed by the Secretary of the Interior, for the purpose of procuring and removing pipestone for their use, at such times and in such quantities as they may desire. The tract to which this privilege applies shall not exceed forty (40) acres in area, and the limits thereof shall be indicated and suitably marked under the direction of the Secretary of the Interior; and it is further agreed that when the tract of land upon which the Yankton Indians may go to procure pipestone is indicated and marked as herein provided, a delegation of five (5) Yanktons, authorized by the tribe, are to be present and concur in the selection of the tract, and the designation of the tract is not to be confined to any one legal sub-division of forty acres, unless it be determined that the best quarry of pipestone is situated within the limits of such subdivision. The Yanktons are also to be permitted to camp and graze their teams upon the designated tract while visiting the quarry for the purpose of obtaining pipestone and while engaged in procuring and removing same.

ARTICLE III. In consideration for the tract of land ceded by the Yankton Indians, as provided in Article I of this agreement, the United States agrees to pay to and expend for said Indians the sum of one hundred thousand dollars ($100,000.00) as follows, to wit: Twenty-five thousand dollars ($25,000.00) shall be expended by the Secretary of the Interior in the purchase of stock cattle, viz: Twenty-five (25) head to be graded Durham or Hereford bulls, two (2) years old, and the remainder good two-year-old heifers of Durham and Hereford blood, to be distributed as equally as possible among the members of the Yankton tribe as soon as practicable after the ratification of this agreement. The balance of seventy-five thousand dollars ($75,000.00) shall be paid in cash pro rata, share and share alike, to each man, woman, and child belonging to said Yankton tribe, and under the jurisdiction of the Yankton Indian Agency, within ninety days from and after the date of the ratification of this agreement.

ARTICLE IV. It is understood and agreed that the United States will not sell or otherwise dispose of the lands hereby ceded by the Yankton Indians, but that the same shall be reserved and maintained as a national park or reservation, and that the superintendent or custodian of the reservation shall be required to protect the said pipestone quarry from vandalism, and prohibit all persons other than the Yankton Sioux Indians from procuring pipestone therefrom.

ARTICLE V. It is agreed by the parties hereto that seven (7) certain claims of said Yankton Indians, a memorandum of which of even date herewith has been handed by the Yankton committee to said James McLaughlin, U.S. Indian inspector, shall be transmitted with this agreement to the Secretary of the Interior for consideration and action by the Interior Department, that such Congressional legislation may be recommended in the premises as the Secretary of the Interior may deem just and equitable.

ARTICLE VI. This agreement shall take effect and be in force when signed by U.S. Indian Inspector James McLaughlin and by a majority of the male adult Indians, parties thereto, and when accepted and ratified by Congress. . . .

Memorandum of certain claims of the Yankton Sioux Indians prepared by their committee and handed by said committee to James McLaughlin, United States Indian inspector, for transmittal by him with his report to the Secretary of the Interior, in his negotiations with said Yanktons for cession to the United States of the pipestone quarry, in the State of Minnesota.

Claim I.—Under section 3, chapter 240 (26 Statutes, 764), the United States erected on the Pipestone Reservation, then the property of the Yankton Sioux tribe of Indians, certain buildings for school purposes, in opposition to the protests and contrary to the wishes of said Indians, which reservation the United States has unlawfully occupied ever since, and more especially since the conclusion of an agreement with the said tribe on the 31st day of December, 1892, and ratified by Congress August 15, 1894, in which agreement the said reservation is conceded to be and to have been the exclusive property in fee simple of said tribe. The said tribe, therefor, claim to have been damaged and aggrieved to the extent of twenty-five thousand dollars ($25,000).

Claim II.—Reimbursement under Article IV of the treaty proclaimed February 24, 1831, by and between the United States and the confederated tribes of Sacs and Foxes, Medawakanton, Wahpekute, Wahpeton and Sisseton bands or tribes of Sioux and others, fifteen hundred dollars ($1,500) with interest at the rate of 5 per cent per annum from said date, viz, February 24, 1831.

Claim III.—We ask for a full and thorough investigation of our claims against the hostile bands of Santees, Medawakanton, Wahpekute, Sisseton and Wahpeton for horses and cattle stolen and killed by said Santees, and for the destruction of other property during the Minnesota Indian War, and that we be indemnified for same.

Claim IV.—For ponies and horses taken from us by the military authorities in 1876, also, as provided in the provisions of Article V of a treaty proclaimed February 6, 1826, to be reimbursed by the Government of cattle and horses stolen from members of our tribe by citizens of the United States.

Claim V.—That the surviving members and their heirs, who received money, annuities, etc., under various treaties with the Minnesota Sioux prior to the Santee outbreak of 1862, and are now members of the Yankton tribe under existing treaties, receive their share of money from the bands to which they formerly belonged if such annuities, which were confiscated, should be restored.

Claim VI.—We respectfully pray that hereafter all money derived from leases that shall be made by the members of the Yankton Sioux tribe of Indians be paid to them annually in advance by the United States Indian agent upon his approval of the lease, instead of the agent being required to deposit the money in a United States depository and await Department approval of lease before we receive our lease money, as at present.

Claim VII.—We request that hereafter members of the Yankton Sioux tribe of Indians shall not be charged for material furnished or work done for them at the agency shops, maintenance of same having been guaranteed to us by the Government under our treaty of 1858. . . .

Source: 56th Cong., 1st sess., H. Doc. no. 535, serial 3995:26-30.

Chapter 5
Documents 1900-01

5-1. Impressions of an Indian Childhood

Zitkala-Sa

January 1900

A Sioux teacher, musician, author, lecturer, and lobbyist, Gertrude Simmons Bonnin (1876-1938) was born on the Yankton Sioux reservation in Dakota Territory. Also known as Zitkala-Sa or Red Bird, she attended White's Indiana Labor Institute, a boarding school for Native American children, and later Earlham College from 1895 to 1897. A violinist and traveler, she married Raymond Bonnin in 1902. She worked as an agent for the U.S. Bureau of Indian Affairs in Utah, unsuccessfully campaigned against the use of peyote, championed Native American rights, advocated Indian citizenship, and supported health care for her people, among other programs and reforms. In 1916, Bonnin relocated to Washington, D.C., where she died. Her remains were interred in the Arlington National Cemetery.

Recalling her school days as a youth, Bonnin reported that the transition from reservation life to the boarding school environment was one of shock. It was similar to the "iron routine" of a "civilizing machine." She added: "Like a slender tree, I had been uprooted from my mother, nature and God." Bonnin pointed out that she was "neither a wild Indian nor a tame one." According to Bonnin, "even nature seemed to have no place for me." Her essay, "Impressions of an Indian Childhood," debuted in the January, 1900, number of Atlantic Monthly. *In so many ways, Bonnin's experience on earth marvelously represented and epitomized the Native American virtues of life, love, awareness, acknowledgment, acceptance, forgiveness, understanding, faith, trust, worth, service, and peace.*

I. My Mother.

A wigwam of weather-stained canvas stood at the base of some irregularly ascending hills. A footpath wound its way gently down the sloping land till it reached the broad river bottom; creeping through the long swamp grasses that bent over it on either side, it came out on the edge of the Missouri.

Here, morning, noon, and evening, my mother came to draw water from the muddy stream for our household use. Always, when my mother started for the river, I stopped my play to run along with her. She was only of medium height. Often she was sad and silent, at which times her full arched lips were compressed into hard and bitter lines, and shadows fell under her black eyes. Then I clung to her hand and begged to know what made the tears fall.

"Hush; my little daughter must never talk about my tears;" and smiling through them, she patted my head and said, "Now let me see how fast you can run to-day." Whereupon I tore away at my highest possible speed, with my long black hair blowing in the breeze.

I was a wild little girl of seven. Loosely clad in a slip of brown buckskin, and light-footed with a pair of soft moccasins on my feet, I was as free as the wind that blew my hair, and no less spirited than a bounding deer. These were my mother's pride,—my wild freedom and overflowing spirits. She taught me no fear save that of intruding myself upon others.

Having gone many paces ahead I stopped, panting for breath, and laughing with glee as my mother watched my every movement. I was not wholly conscious of myself, but was more keenly alive to the fire within. It was as if I were the activity, and my hands and feet were only experiments for my spirit to work upon.

Returning from the river, I tugged beside my mother, with my hand upon the bucket I believed I was carrying. One time, on such a return, I remember a bit of conversation we had. My grown-up cousin, Warca-Ziwin (Sunflower), who was then seventeen, always went to the river alone for water for her mother. Their wigwam was not far from ours; and I saw her daily going to and from the river. I admired my cousin greatly. So I said: "Mother, when I am tall as my cousin Warca-Ziwin, you shall not have to come for water. I will do it for you."

With a strange tremor in her voice which I could not understand, she answered, "If the paleface does not take away from us the river we drink."

"Mother, who is this bad paleface? " I asked.

"My little daughter, he is a sham,—a sickly sham! The bronzed Dakota is the only real man."

I looked up into my mother's face while she spoke; and seeing her bite her lips, I knew she was unhappy. This aroused revenge in my small soul. Stamping my foot on the earth, I cried aloud, "I hate the paleface that makes my mother cry!"

Setting the pail of water on the ground, my mother stooped, and stretching her left hand out on the level with my eyes, she placed her other arm about me; she pointed to the hill where my uncle and my only sister lay buried. [She then said]:

> There is what the paleface has done! Since then your father too has been buried in a hill nearer the rising sun. We were once very happy. But the paleface has stolen our lands and driven us hither. Having defrauded us of our land, the paleface forced us away.
>
> Well, it happened on the day we moved camp that your sister and uncle were both very sick. Many others were ailing, but there seemed to be no help. We traveled many days and nights; not in the grand happy way that we moved camp when I was a little girl, but we were driven, my child, driven like a herd of buffalo. With every step, your sister, who was not as large as you are now, shrieked with the painful jar until she was hoarse with crying. She grew more and more feverish. Her little hands and cheeks were burning hot. Her little lips were parched and dry, but she would not drink the water I gave her. Then I discovered that her throat was swollen and red. My poor child, how I cried with her because the Great Spirit had forgotten us!
>
> At last, when we reached this western country, on the first weary night your sister died. And soon your uncle died also, leaving a widow and an orphan daughter, your cousin Warca-Ziwin. Both your sister and uncle might have been happy with us to-day, had it not been for the heartless paleface.

My mother was silent the rest of the way to our wigwam. . . . I saw no tears in her eyes[;] I knew that was because I was with her. She seldom wept before me.

II. The Legends.

During the summer days, my mother built her fire in the shadow of our wigwam.

In the early morning our simple breakfast was spread upon the grass west of our tepee. At the farthest point of the shade my mother sat beside her fire, toasting a savory piece of dried meat. Near her, I sat upon my feet, eating my dried meat with unleavened bread, and drinking strong black coffee.

The morning meal was our quiet hour, when we two were entirely alone. At noon, several who chanced to be passing by stopped to rest, and to share our luncheon with us, for they were sure of our hospitality.

My uncle, whose death my mother ever lamented, was one of our nation's bravest warriors. His name was on the lips of old men when talking of the proud feats of valor; and it was mentioned by younger men, too, in connection with deeds of gallantry. Old women praised him for his kindness toward them; young women held him up as an ideal to their sweethearts. Everyone loved him, and my mother worshiped his memory. Thus it happened that even strangers were sure of welcome in our lodge, if they but asked a favor in my uncle's name.

Though I heard many strange experiences related by these wayfarers, I loved best the evening meal, for that was the time old legends were told. I was always glad when the sun hung low in the west, for then my mother sent me to invite the neighboring old men and women to eat supper with us. Running all the way to the wigwams, I halted shyly at the entrances. Sometimes I stood long moments without saying a word. It was not any fear that made me so dumb when out upon such a happy errand; nor was it that I wished to withhold the invitation, for it was all I could do to observe this very proper silence. But it was a sensing of the atmosphere, to assure myself that I should not hinder other plans. My mother used to say to me, as I was almost bounding away for the old people: "Wait a moment before you invite any one. If other plans are being discussed, do not interfere, but go elsewhere."

The old folks knew the meaning of my pauses; and often they coaxed my confidence by asking, "What do you seek, little granddaughter?"

"My mother says you are to come to our tepee this evening," I instantly exploded, and breathed the freer afterwards.

"Yes, yes, gladly, gladly I shall come!" each replied. Rising at once and carrying their blankets across one shoulder, they flocked leisurely from their various wigwams toward our dwelling.

My mission done, I ran back, skipping and jumping with delight. All out of breath, I told my mother almost the exact words of the answers to my invitation. Frequently she asked, "What were they doing when you entered their tepee?" This taught me to remember all I saw at a single glance. Often I told my mother my impressions without being questioned.

While in the neighboring wigwams sometimes an old Indian woman asked me, "What is your mother doing?" Unless my mother had cautioned me not to tell, I generally answered her questions without reserve.

At the arrival of our guests I sat close to my mother, and did not leave her side without first asking her consent. I ate my supper in quiet, listening patiently to the talk of the old people, wishing all the time that they would begin the stories I loved best. At last, when I could not wait any longer, I whispered in my mother's ear, "Ask them to tell an Iktomi story, mother."

Soothing my impatience, my mother said aloud, "My little daughter is anxious to hear your legends." By this time all were through eating, and the evening was fast deepening into twilight.

As each in turn began to tell a legend, I pillowed my head in my mother's lap; and lying flat upon my back, I watched the stars as they peeped down upon me, one by one. The increasing interest of the tale aroused me, and I sat up eagerly listening for every word. The old women made funny remarks, and laughed so heartily that I could not help joining them.

The distant howling of a pack of wolves or the hooting of an owl in the river bottom frightened me, and I nestled into my mother's lap. She added some dry sticks to the open fire, and the bright flames leaped up into the faces of the old folks as they sat around in a great circle.

On such an evening, I remember the glare of the fire shone on a tattooed star upon the brow of the old warrior who was telling a story. I watched him curiously as he made his unconscious gestures. The blue star upon his bronzed forehead was a puzzle to me. Looking about, I saw two parallel lines on the chin of one of the old women. The rest had none. I examined my mother's face, but found no sign there.

After the warrior's story was finished, I asked the old woman the meaning of the blue lines on her chin, looking all the while out of the corners of my eyes at the warrior with the star on his forehead. I was a little afraid that he would rebuke me for my boldness.

Here the old woman began: "Why, my grandchild, they are signs,—secret signs I dare not tell you. I shall, however, tell you a wonderful story about a woman who had a cross tattooed upon each of her cheeks."

It was a long story of a woman whose magic power lay hidden behind the marks upon her face. I fell asleep before the story was completed.

Ever after that night I felt suspicious of tattooed people. Wherever I saw one sit I glanced furtively at the mark and round about it, wondering what terrible magic power was covered there.

It was rarely that such a fearful story as this one was told by the camp fire. Its impression was so acute that the picture still remains vividly clear and pronounced.

III. The Beadwork.

Soon after breakfast, mother sometimes began her beadwork. On a bright clear day, she pulled out the wooden pegs that pinned the skirt of our wigwam to the ground, and rolled the canvas part way up on its frame of slender poles. Then the cool morning breezes swept freely through our dwelling, now and then wafting the perfume of sweet grasses from newly burnt prairie.

Untying the long tasseled strings that bound a small brown buckskin bag, my mother spread upon a mat beside her bunches of colored beads, just as an artist arranges the paints upon his palette. On a lapboard she smoothed out a double sheet of soft white buckskin; and drawing from a beaded case that hung on the left of her wide belt a long, narrow blade, she trimmed the buckskin into shape. Often she worked upon small moccasins for her small daughter. Then I became intensely interested in her designing. With a proud, beaming face, I watched her work. In imagination, I saw myself walking in a new pair of snugly fitting moccasins. I felt the envious eyes of my playmates upon the pretty red beads decorating my feet.

Close beside my mother I sat on a rug, with a scrap of buckskin in one hand and an awl in the other. This was the beginning of my practical observation lessons in the art of beadwork. From a skein of finely twisted threads of silvery sinews my mother pulled out a single one. With an awl she pierced the buckskin, and skillfully threaded it with the white sinew. Picking up the tiny beads one by one, she strung them with the point of her thread, always twisting it carefully after every stitch.

It took many trials before I learned how to knot my sinew thread on the point of my finger, as I saw her do. Then the next difficulty was in keeping my thread stiffly twisted, so that I could easily string my beads upon it. My mother required of me original designs for my lessons in beading. At first I frequently ensnared many a sunny hour into working a long design, Soon I learned from self-inflicted punishment to refrain from drawing complex patterns, for I had to finish whatever I began.

After some experience I usually drew easy and simple crosses and squares. These were some of the set forms. My original designs were not always symmetrical nor sufficiently characteristic, two faults with which my mother had little patience. The quietness of her oversight made me feel strongly responsible and dependent upon my own judgment. She treated me as a dignified little individual as long as I was on my good behavior; and how humiliated I was when some boldness of mine drew forth a rebuke from her!

In the choice of colors she left me to my own taste. I was pleased with an outline of yellow upon a background of dark blue, or a combination of red and myrtle-green. There was another of red with a bluish gray that was more conventionally used. When I became a little familiar with designing and the various pleasing combinations of color, a harder lesson was given me. It was the sewing on, instead of beads, some tinted porcupine quills, moistened and flattened between the nail of the thumb and forefinger. My mother cut off the prickly ends and burned them at once in the centre fire. These sharp points were poisonous, and worked into the flesh wherever they lodged. For this reason, my mother said, I should not do much alone in quills until I was as tall as my cousin Warca-Ziwin.

Always after these confining lessons I was wild with surplus spirits, and found joyous relief in running loose in the open again. Many a summer afternoon, a party of four or five of my playmates roamed over the hills with me. We each carried a light sharpened rod about four feet long, with which we pried up certain sweet roots. When we had eaten all the choice roots we chanced upon, we shouldered our rods and strayed off into patches of a stalky plant under whose yellow blossoms we found little crystal drops of gum. Drop by drop we gathered this nature's rock-candy, until each of us could boast of a lump the size of a small bird's egg. Soon satiated with its woody flavor, we tossed away our gum, to return again to the sweet roots.

I remember well how we used to exchange our necklaces, beaded belts, and sometimes even our moccasins. We pretended to offer them as gifts to one another. We delighted in impersonating our own mothers. We talked of things we had heard them say in their conversations. We imitated their various manners, even to the inflection of their voices. In the lap of the prairie we seated ourselves upon our feet; and leaning our painted cheeks in the palms of our hands, we rested our elbows on our knees, and bent forward as old women were most accustomed to do.

While one was telling of some heroic deed recently done by a near relative, the rest of us listened attentively, and exclaimed in undertones, "Han! han!" (yes! yes!) whenever the speaker paused for breath, or sometimes for our sympathy. As the discourse became more thrilling, according to our ideas, we raised our voices in these interjections. In these impersonations our parents were led to say only those things that were in common favor.

No matter how exciting a tale we might be rehearsing, the mere shifting of a cloud shadow in the landscape near by was sufficient to change our impulses; and soon we were all chasing the great shadows that played among the hills. We shouted and whooped in the chase; laughing and calling to one another, we were like little sportive nymphs on that Dakota sea of rolling green.

On one occasion, I forgot the cloud shadow in a strange notion to catch up with my own shadow. Standing straight and still, I began to glide after it, putting out one foot cautiously. When, with the greatest care, I set my foot in advance of myself, my shadow crept onward too. Then again I tried it; this time with the other foot. Still again my shadow escaped me. I began to run; and away flew my shadow, always just a step beyond me. Faster and faster I ran, setting my teeth and clenching my fists, determined to overtake my own fleet shadow. But ever swifter it glided before me, while I was growing breathless and hot. Slackening my speed, I was greatly vexed that my shadow should check its pace also. Daring it to the utmost, as I thought, I sat down upon a rock imbedded in the hillside.

So! my shadow had the impudence to sit down beside me!

Now my comrades caught up with me, and began to ask why I was running away so fast.

"Oh, I was chasing my shadow! Didn't you ever do that?" I inquired, surprised that they should not understand.

They planted their moccasined feet firmly upon my shadow to stay it, and I arose. Again my shadow slipped away, and moved as often as I did. Then we gave up trying to catch my shadow.

Before this peculiar experience I have no distinct memory of having recognized any vital bond between myself and my own shadow. I never gave it an afterthought.

Returning our borrowed belts and trinkets, we rambled homeward. That evening, as on other evenings, I went to sleep over my legends.

IV. The Coffee-Making.

One summer afternoon, my mother left me alone in our wigwam, while she went across the way to my aunt's dwelling.

I did not much like to stay alone in our tepee, for I feared a tall, broad-shouldered crazy man, some forty years old, who walked loose among the hills. Wiyaka-Napbina (Wearer of a Feather Necklace) was harmless, and whenever he came into a wigwam he was driven there by extreme hunger. He went nude except for the half of a red blanket he girdled around his waist. In one tawny arm he used to carry a heavy bunch of wild sunflowers that he gathered in his aimless ramblings.

His black hair was matted by the winds, and scorched into a dry red by the constant summer sun. As he took great strides, placing one brown bare foot directly in front of the other, he swung his long lean arm to and fro.

Frequently he paused in his walk and gazed far backward, shading his eyes with his hand. He was under the belief that an evil spirit was haunting his steps. This was what my mother told me once, when I sneered at such a silly big man. I was brave when my mother was near by, and Wiyaka-Napbina walking farther and farther away.

"Pity the man, my child. I knew him when he was a brave and handsome youth. He was overtaken by a malicious spirit among the hills, one day, when he went hither and thither after his ponies. Since then he cannot stay away from the hills," she said.

I felt so sorry for the man in his misfortune that I prayed to the Great Spirit to restore him. But though I pitied him at a distance, I was still afraid of him when he appeared near our wigwam. Thus, when my mother left me by myself that afternoon, I sat in a fearful mood within our tepee. I recalled all I had ever heard about Wiyaka-Napbina; and I tried to assure myself that though he might pass near by, he would not come to our wigwam because there was no little girl around our grounds.

Just then, from without a hand lifted the canvas covering of the entrance; the shadow of a man fell within the wigwam, and a large roughly moccasined foot was planted inside.

For a moment I did not dare to breathe or stir, for I thought that could be no other than Wiyaka-Napbina. The next instant I sighed aloud in relief. It was an old grandfather who had often told me Iktomi legends.

"Where is your mother, my little grandchild?" were his first words.

"My mother is soon coming back from my aunt's tepee," I replied.

"Then I shall wait awhile for her return," he said, crossing his feet and seating himself upon a mat.

At once I began to play the part of a generous hostess. I turned to my mother's coffeepot.

Lifting the lid, I found nothing but coffee grounds in the bottom. I set the pot on a heap of cold ashes in the centre, and filled it half full of warm Missouri River water. During this performance I felt conscious of being watched. Then breaking off a small piece of our unleavened bread, I placed it in a bowl. Turning soon to the coffeepot, which would never have boiled on a dead fire had I waited forever, I poured out a cup of worse than muddy warm water. Carrying the bowl in one hand and cup in the other, I handed the light luncheon to the old warrior. I offered them to him with the air of bestowing generous hospitality.

"How! how!" he said, and placed the dishes on the ground in front of his crossed feet. He nibbled at the bread and sipped from the cup. I sat back against a pole watching him. I was proud to have succeeded so well in serving refreshments to a guest all by myself. Before the old warrior had finished eating, my mother entered. Immediately she wondered where I had found coffee, for she knew I had never made any, and that she had left the coffeepot empty. Answering the question in my mother's eyes, the warrior remarked, "My granddaughter made coffee on a heap of dead ashes, and served me the moment I came."

They both laughed, and mother said, "Wait a little longer, and I shall build a fire." She meant to make some real coffee. But neither she nor the warrior, whom the law of our custom had compelled to partake of my insipid hospitality, said anything to embarrass me. They treated my best judgment, poor as it was, with the utmost respect. It was not till long years afterward that I learned how ridiculous a thing I had done.

V. The Dead Man's Plum Bush.

One autumn afternoon, many people came streaming toward the dwelling of our near neighbor. With painted faces, and wearing broad white bosoms of elk's teeth, they hurried down the narrow footpath to Haraka Wambdi's wigwam. Young mothers held their children by the hand, and half pulled them along in their haste. They overtook and passed by the bent old grandmothers who were trudging along with crooked canes toward the centre of excitement. Most of the young braves galloped hither on their ponies. Toothless warriors, like the old women, came more slowly, though mounted on lively ponies. They sat proudly erect on their horses. They wore their eagle plumes, and waved their various trophies of former wars.

In front of the wigwam a great fire was built, and several large black kettles of venison were suspended over it. The crowd were seated about it on the grass in a great circle. Behind them some of the braves stood leaning against the necks of their ponies, their tall figures draped in loose robes which were well drawn over their eyes.

Young girls, with their faces glowing like bright red autumn leaves, their glossy braids falling over each ear, sat coquettishly beside their chaperons. It was a custom for young Indian women to invite some older relative to escort them to the public feasts. Though it was not an iron law, it was generally observed.

Haraka Wambdi was a strong young brave, who had just returned from his first battle, a warrior. His near relatives, to celebrate his new rank, were spreading a feast to which the whole of the Indian village was invited.

Holding my pretty striped blanket in readiness to throw over my shoulders, I grew more and more restless as I watched the gay throng assembling. My mother was busily broiling a wild duck that my aunt had that morning brought over.

"Mother, mother, why do you stop to cook a small meal when we are invited to a feast?" I asked, with a snarl in my voice.

"My child, learn to wait. On our way to the celebration we are going to stop at Chanyu's wigwam. His aged mother-in-law is lying very ill, and I think she would like a taste of this small game."

Having once seen the suffering on the thin, pinched features of this dying woman, I felt a momentary shame that I had not remembered her before.

On our way, I ran ahead of my mother, and was reaching out my hand to pick some purple plums that grew on a small bush, when I was checked by a low "Sh!" from my mother.

"Why, mother, I want to taste the plums!" I exclaimed, as I dropped my hand to my side in disappointment.

"Never pluck a single plum from this bush, my child, for its roots are wrapped around an Indian's skeleton. A brave is buried here. While he lived, he was so fond of playing the game of striped plum seeds that, at his death, his set of plum seeds were buried in his hands. From them sprang up this little bush"

Eyeing the forbidden fruit, I trod lightly on the sacred ground, and dared to speak only in whispers, until we had gone many paces from it. After that time, I halted in my ramblings whenever I came in sight of the plum bush. I grew sober with awe, and was alert to hear a-long-drawn-out whistle rise from the roots of it. Though I had never heard with my own ears this strange whistle of departed spirits, yet I had listened so frequently to hear the old folks describe it that I knew I should recognize it at once.

The lasting impression of that day, as I recall it now, is what my mother told me about the dead man's plum bush.

VI. The Ground Squirrel.

In the busy autumn days, my cousin Warca-Ziwin's mother came to our wigwam to help my mother preserve foods for our winter use. I was very fond of my aunt, because she was not so quiet as my mother. Though she was older, she was more jovial and less reserved. She was slender and remarkably erect. While my mother's hair was heavy and black, my aunt had unusually thin locks.

Ever since I knew her, she wore a string of large blue beads around her neck, —beads that were precious because my uncle had given them to her when she was a younger woman. She had a peculiar swing in her gait, caused by a long stride rarely natural to so slight a figure. It was during my aunt's visit with us that my mother forgot her accustomed quietness, often laughing heartily at some of my aunt's witty remarks.

I loved my aunt threefold: for her hearty laughter, for the cheerfulness she caused my mother, and most of all for the times she dried my tears and held me in her lap, when my mother had reproved me.

Early in the cool mornings, just as the yellow rim of the sun rose above the hills, we were up and eating our breakfast. We awoke so early that we saw the sacred hour when a misty smoke hung over a pit surrounded by an impassable sinking mire. This strange smoke appeared every morning, both winter and summer; but most visibly in midwinter it rose immediately above the marshy spot. By the time the full face of the sun appeared above the eastern horizon, the smoke vanished. Even very old men, who had known this country the longest, said that the smoke from this pit had never failed a single day to rise heavenward.

As I frolicked about our dwelling, I used to stop suddenly, and with a fearful awe watch the smoking of the unknown fires. While the vapor was visible, I was afraid to go very far from our wigwam unless I went with my mother.

From a field in the fertile river bottom my mother and aunt gathered an abundant supply of corn. Near our tepee, they spread a large canvas upon the grass, and dried their sweet corn in it. I was left to watch the corn, that nothing should disturb it. I played around it with dolls made of ears of corn. I braided their soft fine silk for hair, and gave them blankets as various as the scraps I found in my mother's workbag.

There was a little stranger with a black-and-yellow-striped coat that used to come to the drying corn. It was a little ground squirrel, who was so fearless of me that he came to one corner of the canvas and carried away as much of the sweet corn as he could hold. I wanted very much to catch him, and rub his pretty fur back, but my mother said he would be so frightened if I caught him that he would bite my fingers. So I was as content as he to keep the corn between us. Every morning he came for more corn. Some evenings I have seen him creeping about our grounds; and when I gave a sudden whoop of recognition, he ran quickly out of sight.

When mother had dried all the corn she wished, then she sliced great pumpkins into thin rings; and these she doubled and linked together into long chains. She hung them on a pole that stretched between two forked posts. The wind and sun soon thoroughly dried the chains of pumpkin. Then she packed them away in a case of thick and stiff buckskin.

In the sun and wind she also dried many wild fruits,—cherries, berries, and plums. But chiefest among my early recollections of autumn is that one of the corn drying and the ground squirrel.

I have few memories of winter days, at this period of my life, though many of the summer. There is one only which I can recall.

Some missionaries gave me a little bag of marbles. They were all sizes and colors. Among them were some of colored glass. Walking with my mother to the river, on a late winter day, we found great chunks of ice piled all along the bank. The ice on the river was floating in huge pieces. As I stood beside one large block, I noticed for the first time the colors of the rainbow in the crystal ice. Immediately I thought of my glass marbles at home. With my bare fingers I tried to pick out some of the colors, for they seemed so near the surface. But my fingers began to sting with the intense cold, and I had to bite them hard to keep from crying.

From that day on, for many a moon, I believed that glass marbles had river ice inside of them.

VII. The Big Red Apples.

The first turning away from the easy, natural flow of my life occurred in an early spring. It was in my eighth year; in the month of March, I afterward learned. At this age I knew but one language, and that was my mother's native tongue.

From some of my playmates I heard that two paleface missionaries were in our village. They were from that class of white men who wore big hats and carried large hearts, they said. Running direct to my mother, I began to question her why these two strangers were among us. She told me, after I had teased much, that they had come to take away Indian boys and girls to the East. My mother did not seem to want me to talk about them. But in a day or two, I gleaned many wonderful stories from my playfellows concerning the strangers.

"Mother, my friend Judewin is going home with the missionaries. She is going to a more beautiful country than ours; the palefaces told her so!" I said wistfully, wishing in my heart that I too might go.

Mother sat in a chair, and I was hanging on her knee. Within the last two seasons my big brother Dawee had returned from a three years' education in the East, and his coming back influenced my mother to take a farther step from her native way of living. First it was a change from the buffalo skin to the white man's canvas that covered our wigwam. Now she had given up her wigwam of slender poles, to live, a foreigner, in a home of clumsy logs.

"Yes, my child, several others besides Judewin are going away with the palefaces. Your brother said the missionaries had inquired about his little sister," she said, watching my face very closely.

My heart thumped so hard against my breast, I wondered if she could hear it.

"Did he tell them to take me, mother?" I asked, fearing lest Dawee had forbidden the palefaces to see me, and that my hope of going to the Wonderland would be entirely blighted.

With a sad, slow smile, she answered: "There! I knew you were wishing to go, because Judewin has filled your ears with the white men's lies. Don't believe a word they say! Their words are sweet, but, my child, their deeds are bitter. You will cry for me, but they will not even soothe you. Stay with me, my little one! Your brother Dawee says that going East, away from your mother, is too hard an experience for his baby sister."

Thus my mother discouraged my curiosity about the lands beyond our eastern horizon; for it was not yet an ambition for Letters that was stirring me. But on the following day the missionaries did come to our very house. I spied them coming up the footpath leading to our cottage. A third man was with them, but he was not my brother Dawee. It was another, a young interpreter, a paleface who had a smattering of the Indian language. I was ready to run out to meet them, but I did not dare to displease my mother. With great glee, I jumped up and down on our ground floor. I begged my mother to open the door, that they would be sure to come to us. Alas! They came, they saw, and they conquered!

Judewin had told me of the great tree where grew red, red apples; and how we could reach out our hands and pick all the red apples we could eat. I had never seen apple trees. I had never tasted more than a dozen red apples in my life; and when I heard of the orchards of the East, I was eager to roam among them. The missionaries smiled into my eyes, and patted my head. I wondered how mother could say such hard words against them.

"Mother, ask them if little girls may have all the red apples they want, when they go East," I whispered aloud, in my excitement.

The interpreter heard me, and answered: "Yes, little girl, the nice red apples are for those who pick them; and you will have a ride on the iron horse if you go with these good people."

I had never seen a train, and he knew it.

"Mother, I'm going East! I like big red apples, and I want to ride on the iron horse! Mother, say yes! " I pleaded.

My mother said nothing. The missionaries waited in silence; and my eyes began to blur with tears, though I struggled to choke them back. The corners of my mouth twitched, and my mother saw me.

"I am not ready to give you any word," she said to them. "To-morrow I shall send you my answer by my son."

With this they left us. Alone with my mother, I yielded to my tears, and cried aloud, shaking my head so as not to hear what she was saying to me. This was the first time I had ever been so unwilling to give up my own desire that I refused to hearken to my mother's voice.

There was a solemn silence in our home that night. Before I went to bed I begged the Great Spirit to make my mother willing I should go with the missionaries.

The next morning came, and my mother called me to her side. "My daughter, do you still persist in wishing to leave your mother?" she asked.

"Oh, mother, it is not that I wish to leave you, but I want to see the wonderful Eastern land," I answered.

My dear old aunt came to our house that morning, and I heard her say, "Let her try it."

I hoped that, as usual, my aunt was pleading on my side. My brother Dawee came for mother's decision. I dropped my play, and crept close to my aunt.

"Yes, Dawee, my daughter, though she does not understand what it all means, is anxious to go. She will need an education when she is grown, for then there will be fewer real Dakotas, and many more palefaces. This tearing her away, so young, from her mother is necessary, if I would have her an educated woman. The palefaces, who owe us a large debt for stolen lands, have begun to pay a tardy justice in offering some education to our children. But I know my daughter must suffer keenly in this experiment. For her sake, I dread to tell you my reply to the missionaries. Go, tell them that they may take my little daughter, and that the Great Spirit shall not fail to reward them according to their hearts."

Wrapped in my heavy blanket, I walked with my mother to the carriage that was soon to take us to the iron horse. I was happy. I met my playmates, who were also wearing their best thick blankets. We showed one another our new beaded moccasins, and the width of the belts that girdled our new dresses. Soon we were being drawn rapidly away by the white man's horses. When I saw the lonely figure of my mother vanish in the distance, a sense of regret settled heavily upon me. I felt suddenly weak, as if I might fall limp to the ground. I was in the hands of strangers whom my mother did not fully trust. I no longer felt free to be myself, or to voice my own feelings. The tears trickled down my cheeks, and I buried my face in the folds of my blanket. Now the first step, parting me from my mother, was taken, and all my belated tears availed nothing.

Having driven thirty miles to the ferryboat, we crossed the Missouri in the evening. Then riding again a few miles eastward, we stopped before a massive brick building. I looked at it in amazement, and with a vague misgiving, for in our village I had never seen so large a house. Trembling with fear and distrust of the palefaces, my teeth chattering from the chilly ride, I crept noiselessly in my soft moccasins along the narrow hall, keeping very close to the bare wall. I was as frightened and bewildered as the captured young of a wild creature.

Source: Zitkala-Sa, "Impressions of an Indian Childhood," *Atlantic Monthly* 85 (January 1900):27-47.

➳ ● ➳

5-2. The Zuni Indians

Matilda Coxe Stevenson

1901

A noted anthropologist and reformer, Matilda Coxe Stevenson (ca. 1850-1915), a native Texan, studied the women, men, language, and religion of the Zuni, culminating in the publication of The Zuni Indians *(1904). She also researched the Hopi and Pueblo Indians. Stevenson joined the staff of the Smithsonian Institution's Bureau of Ethnology, and in that capacity undertook several investigatory expeditions to the American Southwest, beginning in 1879 to New Mexico, where she became fascinated with Zuni culture. One of Stevenson's published works, "The Zuni Indians: Their Mythology, Esoteric Societies, and Ceremonies," appeared in the twenty-third annual report of the U.S. Bureau of American Ethnology for 1901-1902. Based on fieldwork dating to 1896 and 1897, Stevenson discussed male transvestitism, societal roles, and tribal relationships. In another passage, reprinted below, Stevenson described the death of a friend, We'wha, a Zuni male transvestite, who successfully camouflaged and concealed his biological gender not only from Stevenson but also from President Grover Cleveland and Democratic Congressman John G. Carlisle, both of whom believed We'wha to be a woman, as did other political figures. We'wha had visited Washington, D.C. for six months when Carlisle, a Kentucky lawyer/editor and future senator and secretary of the treasury, was speaker of the U.S. House of Representatives (1883-1889). Carlisle and his wife later sent We'wha a sack of seed to help with "her" crops and agricultural pursuits.*

The custom of youths donning female attire at puberty, which exists to some extent among the pueblos of New Mexico and Arizona, has given rise to conflicting statements. An assertion made, not only by the writer after her first visit to Zuni, but also by others, was that these persons were hermaphrodites. One is led into this error by the Indians, who, when referring to men dressed as women, say, "She is a man," which is certainly misleading to one not familiar with Indian thought. . . . After more intimate acquaintance with the pueblos the writer is able to give the facts as they are. Men who adopt female attire do so of their own volition, having from childhood hung about the house and usually preferring to do the work of women. On reaching puberty their decision is final. If they are to continue woman's work they must adopt woman's dress; and though the women of the family joke the fellow, they are inclined to look upon him with favor, since it means that he will remain a member of the household and do almost double the work of a woman, who necessarily ceases at times from her labors at the mill and other duties to bear children and to look after the little ones; but the ko'thlama (a man who has permanently adopted female attire) is ever ready for service, and is expected to perform the hardest labors of the female department. The men of the family, however, not only discourage men from unsexing themselves in this way, but ridicule them. There have been but five such persons in Zuni since the writer's acquaintance with these people; and until about ten years ago there had been but two, these being the finest potters and weavers in the tribe. One was the most intelligent person in the pueblo, especially versed in their ancient lore. He was conspicuous in ceremonials, always taking the part of the captive Kor'-kokshi in the dramatization of the Kia'nakwe. His strong character made his word law among both the men and the women with whom he associated. Though his wrath was dreaded by men as well as by women, he was beloved by all the children, to whom he was ever kind. Losing his parents in infancy, he was adopted by an aunt on his father's side, and the loving gratitude he exhibited for his aunt and her grief at his death afforded a lesson that might well be learned by the more enlightened. Such was his better side. He was said to be the father of several children, but the writer knew of but one child of whom he was regarded as certainly being the father. The other ko'thlama, who was one of the richest men in the village, allied himself to a man during one of the visits of the writer to Zuni, and to the time of her departure from Zuni in 1897 this couple were living together, and they were two of the hardest workers in the pueblo and among the most prosperous. The third and fourth assumed woman's attire during the absence of the writer. The fifth, a grandson on the maternal side of Nai'uchi, elder brother Bow priest, donned the dress during the visit of the writer to Zuni in 1896. The mother and grandmother were quite willing that the boy should continue in the work in which he seemed interested, but the grandfather, who was much disgusted, endeavored to shame him out of his determination to follow woman's work. He did not, however, attempt any authority in the matters, and on the boy's reaching manhood the trousers were replaced by woman's attire. There is a side to the lives of these men which must remain untold. They never marry women, and it is understood that they seldom have any relations with them. . . .

A death which caused universal regret and distress in Zuni was that of We'wha, undoubtedly the most remarkable member of the tribe. This person was a man wearing woman's dress, and so carefully was his sex concealed that for years the writer believed him to be a woman. Some declared him to be an hermaphrodite, but the writer gave no credence to the story, and continued to regard We'wha as a woman; and as he was always referred to by the tribe as "she"—it being their custom to speak of men who don woman's dress as if they were women—and as the writer could never think of her faithful and devoted friend in any other light, she will continue to use the feminine gender when referring to We'wha. She was perhaps the tallest person in Zuni: certainly the strongest, both mentally and physically. Her skin was much like that of the Chinese in color, many of the Zunis having this complexion. During six months' stay in Washington she became several shades lighter. She had a good memory, not only for the lore of her people, but for all that she heard of the outside world. She spoke only a few words of English before coming to Washington, but acquired the language with remarkable rapidity, and was soon able to join in conversation. She possessed an indomitable will and an insatiable thirst for knowledge. Her likes and dislikes were intense. She would risk anything to serve those she loved, but toward those who crossed her path she was vindictive. Though severe she was considered just. At an early age she lost her parents and was adopted by a sister of her father. She belonged to the Badger clan, her foster mother belonging to the Dogwood clan. Owing to her bright mind and excellent memory, she was called upon by her own clan and also by the clans of her foster mother and father when a long prayer had to be repeated or a grace was to be offered over a feast. In fact she was the chief personage on many occasions. On account of her physical strength all the household work requiring great exertion was left for her, and while she most willingly took the harder work from others of the family, she would not permit idleness; all had to labor or receive an upbraiding from We'wha, and nothing was more dreaded than a scolding from her.

In the fall of 1896 a Sha'lăko god was entertained at her home. Although at this time We'wha was suffering from valvular heart disease, she did most of the work, including the laying of a stone floor in the large room where the ceremonial was to occur. She labored early and late so hard that when the time came for holding the ceremony she was unable to be present. From this time she was listless and remained alone as much as possible, though she made no complaint of illness. When a week or more had passed after the close of the great autumn ceremonial of the Sha'lăko, and the many guests had departed, the writer dropped in at sunset to the spacious room in the house of We'wha's foster father, the late José Palle. We'wha was found crouching on the ledge by the fireplace. That a great change had come over her was at once apparent. Death evidently was rapidly approaching. She had done her last work. Only a few days before this strong-minded, generous-hearted creature had labored to make ready for the reception of her gods; now she was preparing to go to her beloved Ko'thluwala'wa. When the writer asked, "Why do you not lie down?" We'wha replied: "I can not breathe if I lie down: I think my heart break." The writer at once sent to her camp for a comfortable chair, and fixed it at a suitable angle for the invalid, who was most grateful for the attention. There was little to be done for the sufferer. She knew that she was soon to die and begged the writer not to leave her.

From the moment her family realized that We'wha was in serious condition they remained with her, ever ready to be of assistance. The family consisted of the aged foster mother, a foster brother, two foster sisters with their husbands and children, and an own bother with his wife and children. The writer never before observed such attention as every member of the family showed her. The little children ceased their play and stood in silence close to their mothers, occasionally toddling across the floor to beg We'wha to speak. She smiled upon them and whispered. "I can not talk." The foster brother was as devoted as the one related by blood.

During two days the family hoped against hope. Nai'uchi, the great theurgist, came three times and pretended to draw from the region of the heart bits of mutton, declared to have been "shot" there by a witch who was angry with We'wha for not giving her a quarter of mutton when she asked for it. We'wha appeared relieved when the theurgist left. She knew that she was dying and appeared to desire quiet. After Nai'uchi's last visit, the foster brother, with streaming eyes prepared te'likinawe (prayer plumes) for the dying, the theurgist having said that her moments on earth were few. We'wha asked the writer to come close and in a feeble voice she said, in English: "Mother, I am going to the other world. I will tell the gods of you and Captain [James] Stevenson. I will tell them of Captain [John G.] Carlisle, the great seed priest, and his wife, whom I love. They are my friends. Tell them good-by. Tell all my friends in Washington good-by. Tell President [Grover] Cleveland, my friend, good-by. Mother, love all my people; protect them; they are your children; you are their mother." These sentences were spoken with many breaks. The family seemed somewhat grieved that We'wha's last words should be given to the writer, but she understood that the thoughts of the dying were with and for her own people. A good-by was said to the others, and she asked for more light.

It is the custom for a member of the family to hold the prayer plumes near the mouth of the dying and repeat the prayer, but this practice was not observed in We'wha's case. She requested the writer to raise the back of the chair, and when this was done she asked if her prayer plumes had been made. Her foster brother answered "Yes," whereupon she requested him to bring them. The family suppressed their sobs that the dying might not be made sad. The brother offered to hold the plumes and say the prayers, but We'wha feebly extended her hand for them, and clasping the prayer plumes between her hands made a great effort to speak. She said but a few words and then sank back in her chair. Again the brother offered to hold the plumes and pray, but once more she refused. Her face was radiant in the belief that she was going to her gods. She leaned forward with the plumes tightly clasped, and as the setting sun lighted up the western windows, darkness and desolation entered the hearts of the mourners, for We'wha was dead.

Blankets were spread upon the floor and the brothers gently laid the lifeless form upon them. After the body was bathed and rubbed with meal, a pair of white cotton trousers were drawn over the legs, the first male attire she had worn since she had adopted woman's dress years ago. The rest of her dress was female. The body was dressed in the finest clothing; six shawls of foreign manufacture, gifts from Washington friends, besides her native blanket wraps, and a white Hope blanket bordered in red and blue, were wrapped around her. The hair was done up with the greatest care. Three silver necklaces, with turquoise earrings attached and numerous bangles, constituted the jewels.

We'wha's death was regarded as a calamity, and the remains lay in state for an hour or more, during which time not only members of the clans to which she was allied, but the rain priests and theurgists and many others, including children, viewed them. When the blanket was finally closed, a fresh outburst of grief was heard, and then all endeavored to suppress their sobs, for the aged foster mother had fallen unconscious to the floor. The two brothers carried the remains unattended to the grave. The sisters made food offerings to the fire. The foster brother on his return prepared prayer plumes for each member of the immediate family, and also the writer. The little procession, including the foster mother, who had recovered sufficiently to accompany the others, then made its way to the west of the village and on the river bank deposited the clothing, mask, and prayer plumes in the manner heretofore described. Upon the return to the house the foster mother had the rest of We'wha's possessions brought together that they might be destroyed. All her cherished gifts from Washington friends, including many photographs, were brought out; all must be destroyed. This work was performed by the mother, who wept continually. All was sacrificed but pictures of Mr. and Mrs. Carlisle, Mr. Stevenson, and the writer. These were left in their frames on the wall. With another outburst of grief the old woman declared they must remain, saying: "We'wha will have so much with her. I can not part with these. I must keep the faces of those who loved We'wha and whom she loved best. I must keep them to look upon."

Source: Matilda Coxe Stevenson, "The Zuni Indians: Their Mythology, Esoteric Societies, and Ceremonies," *Twenty-third Annual Report of the U.S. Bureau of American Ethnology, 1901-1902* (Washington, D.C.: Smithsonian Institution and Government Printing Office, 1904):37-38, 150, 310-13, 374.

Appendices

Table 1. Presidents of the United States

Andrew Johnson	1865-1869
Ulysses S. Grant	1869-1877
Rutherford B. Hayes	1877-1881
James A. Garfield	1881-1881
Chester A. Arthur	1881-1885
Grover Cleveland	1885-1889
Benjamin Harrison	1889-1893
Grover Cleveland	1893-1897
William McKinley	1897-1901
Theodore Roosevelt	1901-1909

Table 2. Commissioners of Indian Affairs

Nathaniel Green Taylor	1867-1869
Ely Samuel Parker	1869-1871
Francis A. Walker	1871-1873
Edward Parmelee Smith	1873-1875
John A. Smith	1875-1877
Ezra A. Hayt	1877-1880
Roland E. Trowbridge	1880-1881
Hiram Price	1881-1885
John D. C. Atkins	1885-1888
John H. Oberly	1888-1889
Thomas Jefferson Morgan	1889-1893
Daniel M. Browning	1893-1897
William A. Jones	1897-1904

Table 3. Secretaries of War

John A. Rawlins	1869-1969
William T. Sherman	1869-1869
William W. Belknap	1869-1876
Alphonso Taft	1876-1876
James D. Cameron	1876-1877
George W. McCrary	1877-1879
Alexander Ramsey	1879-1881
Robert Todd Lincoln	1881-1885
William C. Endicott	1885-1889
Redfield Proctor	1889-1891
Stephen B. Elkins	1891-1893
Daniel S. Lamont	1893-1897
Russell A. Alger	1897-1899
Elihu Root	1899-1904

Table 4. Secretaries of the Interior

Jacob D. Cox	1869-1870
Columbus Delano	1870-1875
Zachariah Chandler	1875-1877
Carl Schurz	1877-1881
Samuel J. Kirkwood	1881-1882
Henry M. Teller	1882-1885
Lucius Q. C. Lamar	1885-1888
William F. Vilas	1888-1889
John W. Noble	1889-1893
Hoke Smith	1893-1896
David R. Francis	1896-1897
Cornelius N. Bliss	1897-1898
Ethan A. Hitchcock	1898-1907

Table 5. Government Appropriations for Indian Education

Year	*Appropriation*	*Year*	*Appropriation*
1877	$ 20,000	1890	$1,364,568
1878	30,000	1891	1,842,770
1879	30,000	1892	2,291,650
1880	75,000	1893	2,315,612
1881	75,000	1894	2,243,497
1882	135,000	1895	2,060,695
1883	487,000	1896	2,056,515
1884	675,000	1897	2,517,265
1885	992,800	1898	2,631,771
1886	1,110,065	1899	2,638,390
1887	1,211,415	1900	2,936,080
1888	1,179,916	1901	2,080,367
1889	1,348,015		

Source: U.S. Department of the Interior, *Report of the Commissioner of Indian Affairs*, 1920.

Chronology

1867

Military campaign led by General Winfield Scott Hancock against the Cheyennes and Arapahos on the central plains.

Kidder Massacre occurred when Cheyenne and Sioux Indians ambushed and killed a Second U.S. Cavalry detachment of eleven men and an Indian guide near Beaver Creek, Sherman County, Kansas.

After successful negotiations by Secretary of State William Henry Seward, the United States purchased Alaska from Russia, thereby adding the Eskimos and Aleuts to its own Native population.

The largest treaty-making gathering in U.S. history took place at Medicine Lodge Creek in Kansas, culminating in the landmark Treaty of Medicine Lodge.

Congress passed the Peace Commission Act.

Meeting of the Grand Council of 6,000 Indians at Bear Butte, the sacred mountain of the Cheyennes, attended by Crazy Horse, Red Cloud, Sitting Bull, and other Native American leaders.

Treaties with the Sauk and Foxes, the Sioux (Sisseton and Wahpeton bands), the Senecas, Mixed Senecas, and Shawnees, the Quapaws, the Potawatomis and the Chippewa of the Mississippi.

Cherokee National Council passed a law requiring cattlemen to pay ten cents per head for cattle passing through Cherokee land, a fee permitted by an act of 1834. In an attempt to overcome unregulated grazing of outside cattle and to avoid barren ground, other tribes soon followed suit.

Birth of Navajo singer, medicine man, and artist Hosteen Klah, an important innovator in Navajo weaving.

Peace Commission conducted a survey of Native American affairs and recommended that the current treaty process be abandoned.

Creek Nation adopted a constitutional government and held first elections.

1868

Treaty of Fort Laramie.

Navajo leaders Manuelito, Barboncito, and others traveled to Washington, D.C., to plead for the release of their people imprisoned at Bosque Redondo. Navajos were freed and allowed to return home.

Navajo Indian Reservation created by Treaty of Bosque Redondo.

While signing the treaty establishing the Navajo Reservation, Barboncito said: "We do not want to go to the right or left, but straight back to our country."

Statement of Barboncito, Navajo Head Chief: "After we get back to our country it will brighten up again, the Navajo will be as happy as the land, black clouds will rise and there will be plenty of rain. Corn will grow in abundance and everything will look happy."

Founding of Peter Cooper's U.S. Indian Commission.

Cherokee writer John Rollin Ridge published *Poems*, the first volume of poetry penned by a Native American.

The camp of Cheyenne peace chief Black Kettle on the Washita River in western Indian Territory (Oklahoma) was attacked, while people were asleep, by the Seventh U.S. Cavalry led by George Armstrong Custer.

Death of Black Kettle.

Treaty of Fort Sumner.

Death of Roman Nose, a Southern Cheyenne.

Dog Soldiers (Cheyenne) under Tall Bull battled soldiers in western Kansas.

Death of Jesse Chisholm, mixed-blood Cherokee frontiersman, interpreter, and trader.

Ishi, the "last wild Indian in the United States," and other Yahi escaped into the wilderness in California.

Publication of *An Appeal for the Indians* by Lydia Maria Child, writer and reformer.

Publication of John C. Cremony's *Life Among the Apaches*.

Resolution of the Indian Peace Commission.

Death of Charlie Bent, participant in the Plains Indian wars, son of Indian agent William Bent, nephew of New Mexico Territorial Governor Charles Bent, and brother of warrior, writer, and interpreter George Bent.

Edwin L. Godkin, editor of the *Nation*, offered a perceptive piece on "The Indian Difficulty" for that periodical.

Publication of Edward D. Neill's *Effort and Failure to Civilize the Aborigine: Letter to Hon. N. G Taylor, Commissioner of Indian Affairs*.

Nez Perce Treaty, last Indian treaty ratified by the U.S. government.

1869

Congress formed the Board of Indian Commissioners, a nonpartisan advisory task force.

Secretary of the Interior Jacob Dolson Cox, a former Ohio governor and future congressman and law school dean, reported: "A new policy is not so much needed as an enlarged and more enlightened application of the general principles of the old one. We are now in contact with all the aboriginal tribes within our borders, and can no longer assume that we may, even for a time, leave a large part of them out of the operation of our system."

Secretary of the Interior Jacob Dolson Cox, explaining the purpose of the Board of Indian Commissioners, wrote: "The design of those who suggested the commission was that something like a Christian Commission should be established, having in view the civilization of the Indians, and laboring to stimulate public interest in this work while cooperating with the Department."

William Welsh, a reformer and philanthropist, appointed first chairman of the Board of Indian Commissioners by President Ulysses S. Grant but resigned soon thereafter.

First report of the Board of Indian Commissioners expounded:

> While it cannot be denied that the government of the United States, in the general terms and temper of its legislation, has evinced a desire to deal generously with the Indians, it must be admitted that the actual treatment they have received has been *unjust and iniquitous beyond the power of words to express*. Taught by the government that they had rights entitled to respect, when these rights have been assailed by the rapacity of the white man the arm which should have been raised to protect them has been ever ready to sustain the aggressor. The history of the government connections with the Indians is *a shameful record of broken treaties and unfulfilled promises*.

Ely S. Parker, a Seneca and personal friend to President Ulysses S. Grant, appointed commissioner of Indian affairs.

General Edward O. C. Ord confessed that he "encouraged the troops to capture and root out the Apaches by every means and to hunt them as they would wild animals."

Lawrie Tatum, a portly Quaker, appointed Indian agent for the Kiowa and Comanche tribes.

U.S. marshals seized the Watie and Boudinot Tobacco Company, created by Elias C. Boudinot and his uncle, Stand Watie, for nonpayment of taxes, even though Article 10 of an 1866 treaty with the Cherokees promised immunity from agricultural taxes.

New England reformer and writer Wendell Phillips called for a federal constitutional amendment extending citizenship to all Native Americans.

1870

Sojourn of Red Cloud and twenty-two Sioux leaders including Spotted Tail to Washington, D.C., where they dined at the White House and talked with President Ulysses S. Grant.

After Congress prohibited army officers from holding the post of Indian agent, President Ulysses S. Grant inaugurated Peace Policy by giving control of Indian agencies to various Christian denominations. This new federal policy would be based on acculturation and eventual U.S. citizenship for Native Americans.

Cherokee Tobacco Case (78 U.S. 616).

First session of the General Council in Indian Territory (Oklahoma) held at Okmulgee, Creek Nation.

Major Eugene M. Baker slaughtered Heavy Runner and the Blackfeet in Montana.

Congress appropriated $100,000 for Native American education.

Red Cloud, a Sioux leader, addressed a white audience at Cooper Institute in New York, noting that the Great Spirit had made them both. His speaking tour became known as Red Cloud's Peace Crusade.

The second federal decennial census to enumerate Native Americans as a separate race counted only those living with the general population.

Death of Ethan Allen Hitchcock.

Apaches captured Herman and Willie Lehmann, two young brothers.

Ghost Dance of 1870.

U.S. Indian Commission issued *A Specific Plan for the Treatment of the Indian Question.*

William Welsh's open letter of December 7 to the secretary of the interior charged that fraudulent purchases of goods for Native Americans existed within the Indian Bureau.

Apaches in Arizona blindfolded Dr. Abraham Thorne, an army doctor who befriended Indians, and led him to a canyon on Superstition Mountain, where he saw piles of pure gold nuggets.

Death of Delgadito, artist, medicine man, spiritual leader, Navajo chief, and first Navajo metalsmith who introduced silversmithing as a beautiful work and source of income for his people.

1871

Rider attached to Indian Appropriations Act stated that Congress would no longer negotiate treaties with Indian nations, that future agreements would be by congressional acts and executive orders, and that Native Americans were to be subject to U.S. law, not to be treated as foreign nations.

McKay v. Campbell (2 Sawyer 118).

U.S. Senator Eugene Casserly, a California Democrat and journalist, correctly observed that the major misfortune of Native Americans had been that they held great bodies of rich lands, geographically promising and highly coveted.

Death of Barboncito at Canyon de Chelly.

Apache leader Eskiminzin and his people lived in peace at Camp Grant until a group of Tucson citizens, aided by Papago Indians, stormed the place, killing, mutilating, raping, and kidnapping Apaches, an action known as Camp Grant Massacre.

The weekly newspaper *Arizona Miner* called the infamous Camp Grant Massacre "a lucky day for Americans" because of the deaths of more than one hundred Native Americans labeled "villainous wretches."

Buffalo robes became fashionable in the East.

Death of Old Joseph, Nez Perce leader.

Little Raven, a Southern Arapaho leader, spoke to white audiences in Washington, D.C., about injustices.

Salt Creek Massacre led by Kiowas under Satanta, known as "orator of the plains."

Death of Satank, Kiowa leader.

Death of John Otherday, a Wahpeton Sioux and son of Zitkaduta, a Christian convert and army scout.

Death of Numaga (Young Winnemucca), leader in the Paiute War.

President Ulysses S. Grant informed Secretary of War William W. Belknap that a report to the Indian Bureau held out promise of "bringing in the wild indians of New Mexico and Arizona by giving them proper assurances of protection."

An Indian appropriations act signed by President Ulysses S. Grant required the Board of Indian Commissioners to approve all payments for supplies purchased by the Indian Bureau.

Charles Lowe commented on "The President's New Indian Policy" for the third volume of *Old and New*.

Birth of William Jones, an anthropologist who gained distinction as the first Native American (Fox) to earn a Ph.D.

Resignation of Ely S. Parker as commissioner of Indian affairs.

Francis A. Walker appointed commissioner of Indian affairs.

Publication of *Belden the White Chief*, edited by James S. Brisbin.

H. R. Clum served temporarily as acting commissioner of Indian affairs.

President Ulysses S. Grant sent Vincent Colyer, a reformer, Indian commissioner, and painter, to Arizona to work for peace among the Chiricahua Apaches and to help establish a reservation system.

Arizona citizens petitioned President Ulysses S. Grant to support a vigorous war policy toward Native Americans instead of the idealistic program of the Board of Indian Commissioners.

General William T. Sherman wrote to Major General John M. Schofield: "The Pinals and Tonto Apaches have been at war ever since the time we acquired that miserable land from Mexico. They have no reservations, and wander from New Mexico to Arizona, killing and stealing."

1872

Santee Sioux embraced the new Drum Cult religion (Dream Dance), an originator of which was Tallfeather Woman, a Sioux.

The Comanche chief Ten Bears died following an exhausting trip to Washington, D.C., to discuss peace agreements.

Commissioner of Indian Affairs Francis A. Walker affirmed that he would prefer to see Native Americans exterminated altogether rather than permit them to intermarry with whites. He believed that there was no question of national dignity "involved in the treatment of savages by a civilized power," adding that he would rejoice heartily when Indians ceased to be in a position to dictate to the government and had been "reduced to the condition of suppliants for charity."

Elias Cornelius Boudinot, a Cherokee lawyer, businessman, journalist, and assimilationist, spoke before the U.S. House of Representatives Committee on Territories on February 7 and March 5 in behalf of a territorial government for the Indian Territory (Oklahoma).

Publication of Mrs. Fanny Kelly's *Narrative of My Captivity Among the Sioux Indians*.

In a letter to George H. Stuart, a commissioner with the Indian Rights Association, President Ulysses S. Grant stated, "If any change is made [in the present policy toward the Indian] it must be on the side of Civilization & Christianization. . . . I do not believe our Creator ever placed different races of men on this earth with the view of having the stronger exert all his energies in exterminating the weaker."

1873

U.S. government banned the practice of Native American ceremonial sweating (Sweat Lodge).

Modoc War.

General Edward Canby's declination to heed the warning of Modoc woman Toby Riddle led to his death, the execution of Toby's peace-loving uncle Kintpuash, and the exile of her people.

Death of Captain Jack, a Modoc.

Winema, an interpreter, acted as peacemaker in the Modoc War.

Edward P. Smith became commissioner of Indian affairs.

Battle of Massacre Canyon and death of Sky Chief, Pawnee leader and supporter of the U.S. military.

General William T. Sherman stated: "I believe that Satanta has some fifty murders. . . . I know the man well. With irons on his hand he is humble and harmless enough, but on a horse he is the devil incarnate."

Spotted Tail (Sioux) visited the Black Hills mining camps following the discovery of gold to ascertain the value of the precious mineral.

1874

Beginning of the Red River or Buffalo Wars.

Death of Apache leader Cochise.

San Carlos Reservation established in Arizona.

Publication of *The Indian Question* by Francis A. Walker.

Death of Yellow Thunder, a Winnebago, peace advocate, and Catholic convert.

Publication of *Indian Office: Wrongs Doing and Reforms Needed* by William Welsh.

Francis A. Walker's essay, "Indian Citizenship," published in *International Review*.

Death of Henry H. Spalding, educator and missionary.

Death near La Paz in Arizona Territory of Irataba, influential chief and strong leader of Mohave Indians, peacemaker, guide for various expeditions, and traveler.

1875

Death of Kiowa leader Kicking Bird.

Thomas Keam established Keam's Canyon Trading Post east of First Mesa in Arizona.

Surrender of Quanah Parker, last chief of the Comanches, at Fort Sill in Oklahoma.

George Bird Grinnell served as a naturalist in Colonel William Ludlow's expedition to Yellowstone Park.

William Henry Holmes studied remains of Anasazi civilization in the Southwest.

Publication of *A Quaker Among the Indians* by Thomas C. Battey, Indian agent and teacher.

Death of Henry Budd, a Canadian Native Anglican minister.

Publication of *Wigwam and Warpath* by Alfred B. Meacham, reformer and historian.

John Q. Smith selected as commissioner of Indian affairs.

Delegation of Sioux Indians to Washington, D.C., included Red Cloud, Lone Horn, Swan, Rattling Ribs, Spotted Tail, Mandan, Black Bear, and Little Wound.

On October 30, the *Wyoming Weekly Leader* reported conditions among the Sioux people on their reservation in this manner: "The latest reliable news from the Indian agencies is . . . that Red Cloud, Red Dog and other noted red men are suffering from dyspepsia and other digestive disasters induced by want of exercise and 'slathers' of Kansas City bacon. Three cheers for that bacon!"

General George Crook conceded that "the hardest thing is to go and fight those [Native Americans] whom you know are in the right."

A commission from Washington dispatched to treat with the Sioux Indians "for the relinquishment of the Black Hills."

Stating that he would not sell any land to whites, "not even a pinch of dust," Sitting Bull declared: "We want no white men here. The Black Hills belong to me. If the whites try to take them, I will fight."

Removal of the Gordon party from the Black Hills area.

Commissioner of Indian Affairs Edward Parmelee Smith remarked: "Whatever you do for an Indian which he can do for himself . . . is a damage to him and a wrong to the government. . . . No other blessing can come to an Indian as great as that of industry."

Red Cloud Commission issued its report.

1876

Birth of Gertrude Simmons Bonnin (Zitkala-Sa), Sioux author and activist.

Great Sioux War began.

Sioux and Cheyenne warriors surprise and annihilate the army of General George A. Custer at the Battle of Little Bighorn (Custer's Last Stand).

Buffalo Calf Road, a Northern Cheyenne, gained prominence as a female fighter during the battle of the Rosebud.

Apache agent John Clum and his Native American police force crossed into New Mexico Territory to capture Geronimo and Victorio.

Death of Victorio, Apache war leader.

Sitting Bull's statement after the Custer massacre: "If the Great Spirit had desired me to be a white man he would have made me so in the first place. It is not necessary for eagles to be crows."

Death of Yellow Hair, a Sioux, killed by William "Buffalo Bill" Cody.

Death of American Horse (Iron Shield), leader in the Sioux Wars.

Dissolution of the Chiricahua Reservation in Arizona.

In his annual report, Commissioner of Indian Affairs John Q. Smith recorded statistically: (1) 367 school buildings upon reservations; (2) 437 teachers; (3) 11,328 pupils; (4) $362,496 expended for education, an average of thirty-two dollars per pupil; (5) 25,622 literate Native Americans; and (6) 177 church buildings on reservations.

Commissioner of Indian Affairs John Q. Smith professed: "The traditionary belief which largely prevails that the Indian Service throughout its whole history has been tainted with fraud, arises not only from the fact that frauds have been committed, but also because, from the nature of the service itself, peculiar opportunities for fraud may be found."

Little Wolf, a Northern Cheyenne, was shot seven times but survived.

President Ulysses S. Grant appointed W. V. Rinehart agent for the Malheur Reservation in Oregon, the last Indian agent at Malheur.

Nat Love, a former Tennessee slave and an African-American cowboy who worked on an Arizona cattle ranch, captured near the Gila River by Yellow Dog and a group of Pima Indians, who treated his wounds with medicinal herbs, adopted him under the tribal name Buffalo Papoose, and expected him to marry Yellow Dog's daughter. Love stole a horse and escaped within a month of his captivity, riding to west Texas and freedom.

By terms of the Indian Appropriations Act, Congress designated one million dollars for the subsistence of the Sioux Indians and for purposes of their civilization.

Natchez (Naiche), son of Cochise, guided his people through their transition and surrender to General Oliver O. Howard.

Felix R. Brunot, president of the first Board of Indian Commissioners, wrote a lengthy letter to his friend and colleague William E. Dodge, in which he denounced the proposed transfer of American Indian affairs from the Interior to the War Department: "Under [military rule], force will be brought to bear upon the Indians; this will beget resistance and end in war; and war will, of course, though white men are slain, destroy the Indian. . . . I am fully convinced that the transfer would not be in the interest, either of justice, economy, humanity, civilisation, Christianity, or even honesty of administration."

1877

The Nez Perce War

Zuni land grant recognized.

Death of Crazy Horse.

Flight of Chief Joseph.

Death of Blackfoot.

Chief Joseph's statement of surrender.

Death of Lame Deer, a leader in the Sioux wars.

Death of Kamiakin, Yakima chief.

Little Hawk, a Sioux leader, condemned General George Crook's duplicity.

Battle of White Bird Canyon.

John V. Farwell of Chicago, a member of the Board of Indian Commissioners, declared: "If the reservation was a plantation, the Indians were the most degraded of slaves."

The Sioux Commission reported to Congress:

> A great crisis has arisen in Indian affairs. The wrongs of the Indians are admitted by all. Thousands of the best men in the land feel keenly the nation's shame. They look to Congress for redress. Unless immediate and appropriate legislation is made for the protection and government of the Indians, they must perish, and our country bear forever the disgrace, and suffer the retribution of its wrong-doing. Our children's children will tell the sad story in hushed tones, and wonder how their fathers dared to trample on justice and trifle with God.

Catholic World bemoaned: "The abandonment of the picturesque blanket for the civilizing coat, the embroidered buckskin leggings for the plain pantaloons, and the gay plume of gorgeous feathers for the hideous hat is certainly a mark of progress."

Two Moons, a Northern Cheyenne leader in the War for the Black Hills and an army scout, surrendered to Colonel Nelson A. Miles at Fort Keogh, Montana.

E. Butler, a Catholic writer, affirmed:

> An Indian agency is not usually a school of morality. . . . Agency life has no tendency to elevate the Indian. . . . His initiation to the order of warriors is a terrible ordeal of physical suffering, which must be borne without flinching or murmuring. . . . Why is it that the Indians who give us so much trouble become peaceable when they settle on the Canadian side of the border? . . . It is not the interest of the Indian Ring to have the Indian question settled. . . . The usual cause of Indian wars is want of good faith in carrying out the obligations of treaties. . . . The remedy of remedies is common honesty in our dealings with the Indian. . . . But too many are interested in keeping up the present system to warrant even the slenderest hope of any radical change.

P. Girard commented on "Our New Indian Policy and Religious Liberty" for *Catholic World.*

Bates v. Clark (85 U.S. 234).

E. Butler took "A Glance at the Indian Question" in a piece for *Catholic World.*

Spotted Tail questioned Captain George M. Randall about contradictions in Christianity.

Ezra A. Hayt assumed office as commissioner of Indian affairs.

Death of Looking Glass, Nez Perce warrior.

Death of the Nez Perce shaman Toohoolhoolzote.

Death of Ollikut, a Nez Perce leader, in the Bear Paw Mountains.

1878

Bannock War.

Red Cloud's people moved to Pine Ridge Agency on the White Clay River.

Death of Satanta, Kiowa leader.

John Lorenzo Hubbell purchased a trading post on the Navajo Reservation in Arizona Territory.

General George Crook declared that America's treatment of the Indian was an outrage.

Death of Buffalo Horn, a leader in the Bannock War.

Dull Knife, a Northern Cheyenne, fled northward from the Indian Territory (Oklahoma).

Alfred B. Meacham and Thomas A. Bland established *Council Fire*, a journal dealing with Native American issues.

Department of War sought administrative control over Native American affairs from the Department of the Interior.

Formation of the Ladies' National League to Protect the Indians.

Editor M. P. Roberts contributed an editorial to the Creek Nation *Indian Journal* on April 10, in which he contrasted redeeming features of sample individuals among the tribes of the Indian Territory to those of certain members of the "civilized" dominant white race. He wisely observed, "From all races and classes the good can be found if sought."

On May 24, General John Pope delivered an address, "The Indian Question," before the Social Science Association at Cincinnati, Ohio.

Publication of *The Indian Question* by Lieutenant Colonel Elwell S. Otis, presenting an army point of view.

J. W. Douglas, Yankton Agency, Dakota Territory, said: "Contrary to the popular impression, I believe that the Indian will work patiently and continuously, if the fruits of his labor are secured to him."

John C. Pyle, Indian agent for the Navajo in Arizona, queried:

> Cannot our Government afford to be a little magnanimous, and give to a peaceable and industrious tribe of Indians a few more square miles of barren sands? But I suppose it would be worse than folly to ask more territory for any tribe, however deserving, from a Government that does not secure to the Indian the peaceable possession of lands already guaranteed to him by solemn treaty stipulation.

On a reservation near Fort Totten, Mrs. Standing Elk, an inauspicious middle-aged Sioux woman who felt ill and heard ghosts calling, put her house in order and then moved outside into a tepee to await her fate and death. Wanting a suitable coffin to fit her properly, she exclaimed: "It is not well that a woman should lie in a coffin made for a man." She was measured; a nearby carpenter built the casket; and the prospective widower took it home for her approval. His impatient wife, ready to pass away, disliked having to be delayed on her final journey because of her husband's procrastination. With face painted for death and relatives grouped about her, the incensed woman berated her distraught husband upon his return. After scolding him for bringing a coffin too large for her body, the irate lady, without assistance, carried the wood coffin on her shoulders into her house. Apparently the entire episode cured her bodily ailments. Several years later, the coffin, fitted with shelves, was being used as a cupboard by the extremely healthy wife of Standing Elk.

Making Medicine (O-kuh-ha-tuh), a Cheyenne warrior who had been imprisoned at Fort Marion, Florida, was baptized into the Episcopal Church, taking the name David Pendleton Oakerhater.

1879

Ute War.

Sheepeater War.

Birth of Cherokee entertainer and humorist William Penn Adair Rogers (Will Rogers) in the Cherokee Nation (Oklahoma).

Richard Henry Pratt founded Carlisle Indian School at Carlisle, Pennsylvania, to "civilize" Native American children and erase tribal culture.

Founding of the Woman's National Indian Association.

United States v. Crook (5 Dillon 453-69). Judge Elmer S. Dundy's decision held that Native Americans were "persons" under the law and entitled to habeas corpus, a catalyst for reform.

Chief Joseph said: "An Indian respects a brave man, but he despises a coward. He loves a straight tongue, but he hates a forked tongue."

Luther Standing Bear, author and later a film actor, began classes at the Carlisle Indian School in Pennsylvania.

Helen Hunt Jackson sent a letter to *New York Tribune* editor Whitelaw Reid in which she pledged persistent and wholehearted endeavors to help Native Americans.

General Nelson A. Miles contributed "The Indian Problem" to the March volume of *North American Review*, in which he noted that four hundred years of conflict between settlers and native had produced no resolution to the perennial problem of accommodation and wondered when a practical and judicious system would be placed in operation to advance native civilization and terminate wars.

Death of Kiowa chief Lone Wolf.

Chief Joseph and Yellow Bull sojourned to Washington, D.C., to plead for better treatment for their people to audiences among whom were cabinet officials and congressmen.

Creation of the Bureau of American Ethnology as a branch of the Smithsonian Institution.

Valentine T. O. McGillycuddy became an agent for the Pine Ridge Sioux reservation in South Dakota.

Boston Indian Citizenship Association organized.

In a letter published October 16 in the *New York Tribune*, General George Crook lamented:

> When the Indian's horses and cattle are big enough to be of service, they are driven off in herds by white renegades; when his wheat and corn and vegetables are almost ready for the market, his reservation is changed; and sometimes, as in the case of the Poncas, he is compelled to abandon everything. Were we to treat some of our foreign immigrants in such a matter, it would not take long to turn them into prowling vagabonds, living by robbery and assassination.

Winnemucca, Northern Paiute and father of Sarah Winnemucca, said: "Look at us. Do we appear like wild animals? My people are as capable of learning as the other races. . . . We are tired of promises."

Natchez, brother of Sarah Winnemucca, stated: "We are all human beings. Have the whites no hearts? . . . We want our liberty to go when we feel like it on the same terms as white men."

Albert K. Smiley, a Quaker educator, secured appointment to the Board of Indian Commissioners.

Chief Joseph remarked: "The earth is the mother of all people. . . . There need be no trouble. . . . Let me be a free man. . . . Treat all men alike."

Quinkent and Ute warriors killed Nathan Cook Meeker, an Indian agent and journalist, who sought to apply cooperative farm management to Native Americans.

J. D. Cox wrote an article for *International Review* entitled "The Indian Question."

1880

Sun Dance banned.

Susette La Flesche published *The Ponca Chiefs: An Indian's Attempt to Appeal from the Tomahawk to the Courts.*

Birth of Laura Minnie Cornelius Kellogg, Oneida activist and writer, in Wisconsin.

United States v. Osborne (6 Sawyer 406).

Attempt to enumerate non-taxed Indians living on reservations used only for a few located near military installations.

Death of Ouray, Ute-Apache.

Publication of *Our Indian Wards* by George W. Manypenny, peace commissioner and reformer.

Lecture tour of eastern cities by Ponca leader Standing Bear, brother of Big Snake.

Little Wolf killed another Cheyenne named Starving Elk and went into voluntary exile.

Pioneer ethnologist Frank Hamilton Cushing (1857-1900) began living with the Zuni Pueblo in New Mexico, observing and sketching them, thereby making him one of the most important white observers of Native American culture in the nineteenth century.

Roland E. Trowbridge took office as commissioner of Indian affairs.

Publication of *The Ponca Chiefs* by Thomas Henry Tibbles under the pseudonym Zylyff.

Introduction to the Study of Mortuary Customs among the North American Indians published in Washington by H. C. Yarrow.

J. M. Linn sought to answer and define "The Relation of the Church to the Indian Question" in the October number of *Presbyterian Review*.

E. M. Marble served briefly as acting commissioner of Indian affairs.

George W. Manypenny wrote: "That a better and brighter day may speedily come to the despised Indian should be the aspiration and prayer of every man and woman in our broad land."

Ute Treaty went into effect.

Quinkent, an imprisoned Ute leader, declared insane at Fort Leavenworth, Kansas.

The Woman's National Indian Association presented President Rutherford B. Hayes and Congress with a petition urging the government to recognize the importance of respecting treaties between the United States and Native Americans.

On January 4, Brave Bull, living at the Rosebud Agency, sent this affectionate letter, translated from the Sioux, to his daughter, a pupil at the Carlisle Indian School:

> My Dear Daughter,—Ever since you left me I have worked hard, and put up a good house, and am trying to be civilized like the whites, so you will never hear anything bad from me. When Captain Pratt was here he came to my house, and asked me to let you go to school. I want you to be a good girl and study. I have dropped all the Indian ways, and am getting like a white man, and don't do anything but what the agent tells me. I listen to him. I have always loved you, and it makes me very happy to know that you are learning. I get my friend Big Star to write. If you could read and write, I should be very happy. Your father, Brave Bull. Why do you ask for moccasins? I sent you there to be like a white girl, and wear shoes.

On April 15, from the Pine Ridge Agency, Cloud Shield wrote to his son, a student at the Carlisle Indian School:

> My Dear Son,—I send my picture with this. You see that I had my War Jacket on when taken, but I wear white man's clothes, and am trying to live and act like white men. Be a good boy. We are proud of you, and will be more so when you come back. All our people are building houses and opening up little farms all over the reservation. You may expect to see a big change when you get back. Your mother and all send love. Your affectionate father, Cloud Shield.

President Rutherford Hayes, on a nationwide tour during his last year in office, stopped at Maricopa in Arizona Territory to confer with Native American leaders.

George H. Morgan, a lieutenant in the Third U.S. Cavalry, recorded his thoughts and observations dealing with army life at Fort Washakie, Wyoming, in "Army Life on an Indian Reservation in the '80s."

1881

Death of Spotted Tail (Sinte Gleska).

United States v. McBratney (104 U.S. 621).

Helen Hunt Jackson wrote *A Century of Dishonor*.

Nampeyo, a gifted Tewa Hopi potter and ceramic artist, married Lesso.

Omaha activist and speaker Susette La Flesche, known as Bright Eyes, wrote *Nedawi*, possibly the first non-legend short story written by a Native American.

Surrender of Sitting Bull at Fort Buford, North Dakota.

Publication of *Houses and House Life of the American Aborigine* by Lewis Henry Morgan.

Hiram Price appointed commissioner of Indian affairs.

Commissioner of Indian Affairs Hiram Price observed that if white men were treated in the same way that the federal government treated Native Americans the result would be a race of worthless vagabonds. Claiming that labor was an essential element in producing civilization, he suggested that government teach Native Americans to labor for their own support, thereby developing their true manhood and making them self-supporting.

President Chester A. Arthur proposed a policy of Native American reform for congressional action which consisted of making the laws of the various states and territories applicable to the Indian reservations within their borders, allowing natives to receive the protection of the law, permitting the allotment in severalty of a reasonable quantity of land secured to them by patent, and providing liberal appropriations for the support of Native American schools.

Death of Lewis Henry Morgan.

Zotom, Kiowa artist, ordained a deacon in the Episcopal ministry and sent to the Indian Territory (Oklahoma) to work among his people.

The former Cheyenne warrior David Pendleton Oakerhater (Making Medicine) was ordained into the diaconate of the Episcopal Church, returning to Indian Territory to minister to his fellow tribesmen for the next fifty years; the Episcopal Church canonized Oakerhater in 1986.

John Wesley Powell, linguist and explorer, became director of the U.S. Geological Survey.

Hollow Horn Bear arrested Crow Dog for the murder of Spotted Tail.

George F. Canfield analyzed "The Legal Position of the Indian" for the January issue of *American Law Review*.

Susette La Flesche addressed the Association for the Advancement of Women, speaking on "The Position, Occupation, and Culture of Indian Women."

Publication of *The Hidden Power* by Thomas H. Tibbles, referring to how helpless Native Americans lost their self-respect as wards of Indian agents at the same time that contractors on reservations grew wealthy.

James McLaughlin (White Hair), fluent in the Siouan language, appointed Indian agent to the Sioux of the Standing Rock Reservation.

Wa-ha-sha-ga (James Springer) affirmed: "I want title to my land, so that no one can take from my children the land on which I have worked."

An article, "Indian Education at Hampton and Carlisle," garnered attention for the April issue of *Harper's New Monthly Magazine* and for the author, Helen W. Ludlow, who urged missionaries to work with and not against nature and who reminded readers that whites were "but the saved remnant of a race."

Death of Nakaidoklini, Coyotero Apache medicine man, shaman, and prophet during the Apache Wars, who preached a new religion centered around a sacred pollen dance.

Phoenix (Arizona Territory) city ordinance made it illegal for Native Americans to appear on city streets without sufficient clothing to cover their bodies.

Carl Schurz provided a summation of Native America in "Present Aspects of the Indian Problem" for the July issue of *North American Review*.

One month before he left office, President Rutherford B. Hayes submitted an eloquent and empathetic written message to Congress on the forced relocation of the Ponca Indians to the Indian Territory. It was his desire to give to "these injured people that measure of redress which is required alike by justice and by humanity."

1882

Indian Rights Association established in Philadelphia.

Congress passed legislation to "civilize" the Pueblos.

Establishment of Papago (Tohono O'Odham) Reservation in Arizona.

Hopi Reservation set aside in Arizona by executive order.

Herbert Welsh, reformer and philanthropist, became executive secretary of the Indian Rights Association.

Thomas Henry Tibbles, reformer and journalist, married Susette La Flesche.

First Indian Service hospital established at Carlisle, Pennsylvania.

After conferring with a defeated Sitting Bull, General William T. Sherman testified:

> If the lands of the white man are taken, civilization justifies him in resisting the invader. Civilization does more than this: it brands him as a coward and a slave if he submits to the wrong. If the savage resists, civilization, with the Ten Commandments in one hand and the sword in the other, demands his immediate extermination. . . . Among civilized men, war usually springs from a sense of injustice. The best possible way, then, to avoid war is to do no act of injustice. When we learn that the same rule holds good with Indians, the chief difficulty is removed. But it is said our wars with them have been almost constant. Have we been uniformly unjust? We answer, unhesitatingly, yes.

Congress formally authorized the Carlisle Indian School in Pennsylvania and appropriated funds for its operation.

William Justin Harsha, a minister associated with the Reformed Church in America, contributed a perceptive piece, "Law for the Indians," to the February number of *North American Review.*

William Justin Harsha concluded that "there is no conflict between the white men and the Onondagas in New York State simply because the Indians have the protection of the State laws. . . . [In Canada] he [Native American] is regarded as a person before the law. If he commits a crime he is held individually responsible for it, and [in the United States] the entire tribe is made chargeable for the misdeeds of its members."

Publication of *The Red Man and the White Man in North America from Its Discovery to the Present Time* by George E. Ellis.

A report, "Catholic Grievances in Relation to the Administration of Indian Affairs," presented to the annual convention of the Catholic Young Men's National Union, held in Boston on May 10 and 11.

Prominent neurologist William A. Hammond examined and measured anthropometrically the physiques and genitals of bote (women-men) among the Crow Indians in order to determine physiological or neurological causes of women-men's effeminization.

Death of Alfred B. Meacham, superintendent of Indian affairs for Oregon, historian, lecturer, and reformer.

Probable death of White Bird, a Nez Perce shaman.

Publication of *Our Wild Indians* by Colonel Richard Irving Dodge, who wrote: "The actual number of murders and outrages committed by Indians on citizens is so small as would scarcely be thought of if perpetrated by whites. . . . The newspapers of the land are much to blame for the exaggerated feeling against Indians."

1883

Ex Parte Crow Dog (109 U.S. 556).

Courts for Indian offenses on reservations established.

Sarah Winnemucca Hopkins published *Life Among the Paiutes: Their Wrongs and Claims*, edited by Mary Tyler Mann.

Hualapai Reservation in Arizona established by executive order.

Shaker, a native religion, founded by John Slocum.

Death of Governor Joe, Osage leader.

Death of Dull Knife, Northern Cheyenne leader.

Death of Peter Cooper, philanthropist and reformer.

Sitting Bull settled on Standing Rock Reservation in North Dakota.

Mary Mann, widow of the educator-reformer Horace Mann, from Massachusetts and Ohio, confessed: "I was always considered fanatical about Indians, but I have a wholly new conception of them now, and we civilized people may well stand abashed before their purity of life and their truthfulness."

Boston Evening Transcript on May 3 quoted Sarah Winnemucca as having said: "I have asked the agents why they did these wrong things. They have told me it is necessary for them to do so in order to get money enough to send to the great white Father at Washington to keep their position. I assure you that there is an Indian ring; that it is a corrupt ring and that it has its head and shoulders in the treasury at Washington."

Albert K. Smiley, a Quaker humanitarian, reformer, and member of the Board of Indian Commissioners, began hosting conferences for Friends of the Indian at scenic Lake Mohonk, located in the mountains near New Paltz, New York, where differences of opinion could be resolved "so that all should act together and be in harmony, and so that the prominent persons connected with Indian affairs should act as one body and create a public sentiment in favor of the Indians."

Publication of *The Indian Question* by General Samuel Chapman Armstrong.

Sarah Winnemucca remarked that "everyone knows what a woman must suffer who undertakes to act against bad men."

1884

John Elk v. Charles Wilkins (112 U.S. 94).

Pueblo Industrial School established in New Mexico.

Northern Cheyenne Reserve set apart in Montana (Tongue River).

Establishment by executive order of the Fort Yuma Reservation, straddling the Arizona and California border.

Congress appropriated funds for Alaskan Indian education.

Chilocco Industrial School established in the Cherokee Outlet in Indian Territory (Oklahoma).

Haskell Institute opened in Kansas.

Indian Homestead Act.

Lake Mohonk Conference resolved that all adult male Native Americans should be admitted to the full privileges of citizenship by a process analogous to naturalization.

Act of July 4 required agents or superintendents in charge of Indian reservations to submit Indian census rolls each year.

Death of Wendell Phillips, reformer and writer, who urged a cabinet-level position to guarantee Indian rights and favored the adoption of a constitutional amendment for Native American citizenship.

Possible death of Sacajawea, a Shoshone guide, at age 100, according to theory of Dr. Grace R. Hebard and some historians.

Frederic Remington sold his first drawings in Kansas City.

Birth of John Collier, commissioner of Indian affairs from 1933 to 1945.

Birth of Eleanor Roosevelt, first First Lady to champion cause of Native Americans and other oppressed groups.

Publication of *Ramona*, a novel by Helen Hunt Jackson.

Alice Cunningham Fletcher remarked: “Were the Indians as keen for crime as many believe them to be, not a human being could be safe in their midst during the present hiatus between the old tribal law and our failure to give the protection of the courts.”

Amelia Stone Quinton, general secretary of the Woman’s National Indian Association, addressed 102 meetings in various states.

Sarah Winnemucca wrote: “I have not contended for Democratic, Republican, Protestant, or Baptist for an agent. I have worked for freedom.”

Flint Knife, a Blackfoot, admitted prior to his death: “I wish that white people had never come into my country.”

Born in Arizona, Carlos Montezuma, a Native American activist, earned a degree in chemistry from the University of Illinois.

A missionary department was added to the Woman’s National Indian Association.

1885

Death of Helen Hunt Jackson, writer and reformer.

Congress passed the Major Crimes Act, making Native Americans subject to territorial or state laws in which they committed serious offenses. The act listed seven serious crimes and authorized U.S. officials to arrest Native Americans, subject to the laws of the territory, on their reservations where the crime occurred. The seven crimes were murder, manslaughter, rape, assault with intent to kill, arson, burglary, and larceny.

Henry Chee Dodge appointed Navajo head chief by the Bureau of Indian Affairs.

John D. C. Atkins became commissioner of Indian affairs.

Publication of *Boots and Saddles* by Elizabeth Bacon Custer.

General George Crook's letter on giving the ballot to Native Americans published by the Indian Rights Association.

Death of Stone Calf, a Southern Cheyenne champion of peace.

William Strong, associate justice of the U.S. Supreme Court from 1870 to 1880, stated:

> The immediate admission of the Indians to all the rights of citizenship, including suffrage, I cannot agree to that. I am in favor of their being admitted to citizenship as rapidly as there is any degree of fitness for it. I believe all those Indians, who have lands in severalty, ought to be admitted to citizenship; but whether to admit them to the suffrage is another question. I am greatly in favor of education. Suffrage is not an indispensable requisite of citizenship.

Formation of the National Indian Defense Association.

Elizabeth P. Peabody, active in behalf of several good causes, raised $1,200 for a school (Peabody Institute) for Sarah Winnemucca to operate.

1886

United States v. Kagama (118 U.S. 375).

Geronimo surrendered to Lieutenant Charles Gatewood.

Noted warrior women Lozen and Dahteste surrendered with Geronimo.

Geronimo told General George Crook that his reputation as a troublemaker stemmed largely from reprehensible actions of whites, including Indian agents, newspapermen, and interpreters who told lies about him.

Birth of Maria Montoya Martinez, Native American artist, in San Ildefonso Pueblo, New Mexico.

Federal Indian agents began requesting prohibition of peyote.

Publication of Elizabeth P. Peabody's *Sarah Winnemucca's Practical Solution to the Indian Problem.*

Three years before his death, Jefferson Davis contributed an article, "The Indian Policy of the United States," for the November issue of *North American Review*.

1887

The Native American estate in the United States amounted to 136,394,985 acres.

Congress passed General Allotment Act (Dawes Act).

Charles A. Eastman, Native American (Sioux) reformer and writer, graduated from Dart-mouth College and three years later earned a medical degree from Boston University.

Commissioner of Indian Affairs John D. C. Atkins emphasized in his annual report that barbarous dialects should be blotted out because English was sufficiently good enough for a white man, a black man, and a red man and that native tongues created numerous detriments and impracticabilities toward civilization.

Howling Wolf, Cheyenne artist and son of Minimic, lobbied against Dawes Act.

Charles C. Painter, Indian Rights Association lobbyist, wrote *The Dawes Land in Severalty Bill and Indian Emancipation.*

Elizabeth P. Peabody published *The Paiutes: The Second Report of the Model School of Sarah Winnemucca.*

U.S. Senator Henry L. Dawes of Massachusetts said at the Lake Mohonk Conference: "The greed and hunger and thirst of the white man for the Indian's land are almost equal to his hunger and thirst for righteousness."

Report of the business committee of the fifth annual meeting of the Lake Mohonk Conference stressed the importance of instruction in English at Native American schools but warned that "no policy can be endured which forbids Christian men and women to teach Christian truth, or to prepare instruction in it in any part of this Commonwealth that is consistent with that civil and religious liberty which is unhampered in every other part of our land, and must hereafter be unhampered within all Indian reservations."

Publication in *Overland Monthly* and *Out West Magazine* of "Indian War Papers" by General Oliver O. Howard.

1888

Birth of star athlete James Francis Thorpe in Indian Territory (Oklahoma).

White Men and Indian Women Marriage Act.

U.S. Office of Education issued a special report entitled *Indian Education and Civilization*, published by the Government Printing Office.

Equal Rights Party nominated as its candidate for vice president the Quaker pacifist and social reformer Alfred Henry Love, who had petitioned the U.S. Senate for the adoption of a constitutional amendment to make Native Americans citizens.

Death of Joseph La Flesche.

Wovoka, a prophet and founder of the Ghost Dance religion, turned ill with a fever, which heralded his visions for the future.

John H. Oberly became commissioner of Indian affairs.

Special Report to the Bureau of Education on Indian Education and Civilization by Alice Cunningham Fletcher published as a Senate Document.

The appropriation bill for the Indian Service enacted by Congress contained a provision authorizing the use of the Bible in the vernacular by church schools.

Austin Abbott's article, "Indians and the Law," appeared in the November number of *Harvard Law Review*.

White Bread, chief of Caddos, wrote to President Grover Cleveland: "The story of our wrongs and sufferings is too long to be told you now."

Publication by anthropologist James Owen Dorsey of *Osage Traditions*.

Herbert Welsh discussed "Indian Affairs under the Present Administration" in the August number of *Civil-Service Reformer*.

Lyman Abbott presented a paper, "Education for the Indian," at the Sixth Annual Meeting of the Lake Mohonk Conference of the Friends of the Indian, reprinted in the *Conference Proceedings*.

1889

U.S. officials persuaded the Sioux to relinquish eleven million acres of land to settlers (Sioux Act).

Crook Commission investigated hardship on Sioux reservation and recommended major reforms to Congress.

Origin in Nevada of the Ghost Dance by Paiute shaman Wovoka.

Opening of the Unassigned Lands in the Indian Territory (Oklahoma) to non-Indian settlement, by land run.

Susan La Flesche, first female Native American (Omaha) physician, graduated from the Woman's Medical College of Pennsylvania, located in Philadelphia.

Commissioner of Indian Affairs Thomas J. Morgan advocated the elimination of all Native American reservations and tribes.

Birth of Yankton Sioux anthropologist Ella Cara Deloria.

Congress passed an act to establish a U.S. court within Indian Territory (Oklahoma).

Death of Little Raven, Southern Arapaho chief and peace advocate.

In his annual report to Secretary of the Interior John W. Noble, Commissioner of Indian Affairs Thomas J. Morgan detailed a plan for a national system of Native American schools, modeled on the public school system of the states, and included two appendices dealing with the general policy of the government concerning Native Americans and a formal line of divisional responsibility for the administration of Indian affairs.

Commissioner of Indian Affairs Thomas J. Morgan contended: "The Indians must conform to the white man's ways, peaceably if they will, forcibly if they must."

After traveling through eastern states and western Europe as a performer in William "Buffalo Bill" Cody's Wild West Show, Black Elk, Lakota holy man, returned home.

Death of James Bouchard, first Native American (Delaware) in the United States to be ordained a Catholic priest.

Right Reverend Martin Marty, O.S.B., posed the matter of "The Indian Problem and the Catholic Church" in *Catholic World* for February.

Sitting Bull, at a meeting of the Silent Eaters Society of the Hunkpapa Sioux, denounced the government's Indian commissioners for betraying promises.

Creation of the Jerome Commission.

A. B. Holder published "The Bote: Description of a Peculiar Sexual Perversion Found Among the North American Indians," in *The New York Medical Journal*.

Death of John Beeson, author and reformer who once envisioned a free and separate Native American nation, which he later amended to a Native American territory that sent elected delegates to Congress.

Carlos Montezuma completed work for the medical degree at the Chicago Medical College.

Writing from Idaho, Alice Cunningham Fletcher chastised the "greed" of the whites.

Frederic Remington described an 1885 Native American episode in the Territory of Arizona in "On the Indian Reservation" in *The Century* in July.

1890

Rufus F. Zogbaum published "Life at an Indian Agency" in the January 4 number of *Harper's Weekly.*

James Mooney contributed an article on "Cherokee Theory and Practice of Medicine" for the January issue of *Journal of American Folklore.*

George Truman Kercheval contributed "The Wrongs of the Ute Indians" to the January issue of *Forum.*

Many plains tribes embraced Ghost Dance religion which promoted visions of a future free of U.S. dominance over Native American lands.

Kicking Bear and Short Bull introduced the Ghost Dance religion to the Sioux Indians at Pine Ridge Reservation in South Dakota.

Kicking Bear said:

> I bring to you the promise of a day in which there will be no white man to lay his hand on the bridle of the Indian's horse; when the red man of the prairie will rule the world and not be turned from the hunting grounds by any man. I bring you word from your fathers the ghosts, that they are now marching to join you, led by the Messiah who came once to live on earth with the white men, but was cast out and killed by them.

Blowing on an eagle-borne whistle, Yellow Bird, a Sioux medicine man, advocated resis-tance to U.S. soldiers demanding that Indian firearms be relinquished at Wounded Knee.

Three hundred Sioux were massacred by the U.S. Army at Wounded Knee on Pine Ridge Reservation in South Dakota.

Surveying the grotesque agonies of death and frozen corpses at Wounded Knee, Black Elk (Sioux) calculated that a people's beautiful dream had died there in the bloody mud and that a nation's hoop had been broken and scattered.

Death of Sioux chief Big Foot at Wounded Knee.

James McLaughlin, Indian agent, called for the arrest of Sitting Bull by means of Indian police rather than federal troops.

Bishop Henry Benjamin Whipple produced a descriptive, accurate, and revealing portrait in "My Life Among the Indians" for the April number of *North American Review*.

Writing from Standing Rock Agency on October 17, James McLaughlin sent a lengthy letter to Commissioner of Indian Affairs Thomas J. Morgan pertaining to Sitting Bull, the Ghost Dance craze, and the "Indian Millennium."

Indian agent and reformer James McLaughlin telegraphed Commissioner of Indian Affairs Thomas J. Morgan: "A few Indians still dancing but does not mean mischief at present. I have matters well in hand and when proper time arrives can arrest Sitting Bull by Indian police without bloodshed."

Death of Sitting Bull.

U.S. government redistributed seventeen million acres of Native American lands to settlers and corporations.

Statement by Crowfoot, a Blackfoot: "What is life? It is the flash of a firefly in the night. It is the breath of a buffalo in the wintertime. It is the little shadow which runs across the grass and loses itself in the sunset."

Death of Crowfoot.

Archaeologist Adolph F. A. Bandelier published *Final Report of Investigations Among the Indians of the Southwestern United States, 1880-1885*.

Death of Elias Cornelius Boudinot, Cherokee lawyer, businessman, and assimilationist.

Population of Indian Territory and Native American reservations totaled 325,464.

U.S. government paid out $642,000 that year for Native American labor, including school employees, farmers, interpreters, police personnel, judges of Indian courts, log cutters, supply haulers, and others, confirming the fact that Native Americans did work and could be self-supporting.

Winema granted a pension by the federal government.

Death of General George Crook.

Frank D. Baldwin and John F. Kent appointed to help supervise army's investigation of Wounded Knee.

Death of Eskiminzin, Apache chief.

Herbert Welsh published "The Indian Question Past and Present" in the October, 1890, copy of *New England Magazine*.

Death of Lozen, the great woman warrior and Mimbreno Apache.

Alice Cunningham Fletcher believed that "honor and justice" demanded that she complete her assignment in Idaho.

In May, Quanah Parker gave his blessing on the new little town of Quanah, named in his honor, that had been established in Hardeman County in northwestern Texas in 1884:

> It is well, you have done a good thing in honor of a man who has tried to do right both to the people of his tribe and to his pale faced friends. May the God of the white man bless the town of Quanah. May the sun shine and the rain fall upon the fields and the granaries be filled. May the lightning and the tempest shun the homes of her people, and may they increase and dwell forever. God bless Quanah. I have spoken.

Commissioner of Indian Affairs Thomas J. Morgan discussed "Education of the Indians" during a session at the annual conference of the National Education Association, remarks later published in the association's *Proceedings*.

1891

General Nelson A. Miles published "The Future of the Indian Question" in the January number of *North American Review*, in which he blamed both whites and Indians for the condition of affairs.

Indian Depredations Act.

Creek novelist Sophia Alice Callahan published *Wynema: A Child of the Forest*, the first novel by a Native American woman.

Death of Sarah Winnemucca Hopkins, educator, lecturer, and writer.

Sioux Indian Act.

Indian Schools Act.

Land Allotment Act.

Hiram Price discussed Christian civilization, education, cultural differences, livelihoods, and intoxicating liquor, among other issues, in "The Government and the Indians," published in the February number of *Forum*.

Fort Berthold Reservation established in North Dakota.

Birth of Napoleon B. Johnson, first president of the National Congress of American Indians.

Congress enacted legislation for the relief of mission Native Americans.

Death of Confederate Indian commissioner Albert Pike.

Letter of Mrs. J. Bellangee Cox, founder and first director of the Lincoln Institution and Educational Home to educate Native American children, to Postmaster General John Wanamaker, pointing out that she had predicted trouble on the Pine Ridge Reservation, urging natives to live in cities, and commenting that Indians wanted work: "No people can be restful without it. So long as they are herded together in idleness we will be subject to these dreadful outbreaks. Idleness has been the cause of all this trouble."

Plenty Horses, a Sioux, shot and killed Lieutenant Edward W. Casey.

John Gregory Bourke published *On the Border with Crook.*

John Gregory Bourke in March contributed "General Crook in the Indian Country" to *Century Magazine*.

President Benjamin Harrison in his third written State of the Union message to Congress outlined matters pertaining to the "Indian question," noting that Sioux tribes were "naturally warlike and turbulent" with warriors excited over the coming of a messiah but that General Nelson A. Miles had protected settlers and brought "the hostiles into subjection with the least possible loss of life."

Publication of *The American Race* by anthropologist Daniel G. Brinton.

John Gregory Bourke contended that:

> much of our trouble with these tribes could have been averted had we shown what would appear to them as a spirit of justice and fair dealing in this negotiation. It is hard to make the average savage comprehend why it is that as soon as his reservation is found to amount to anything he must leave and give up to the white man. Why should not Indians be permitted to hold mining or any other kind of land? The policy of the American people has been to vagabondize the Indian, and throttle every ambition he may have for his own elevation.

The American Bar Association unanimously declared: "It is the opinion of this association that the United States should provide, at the earliest possible moment, courts and a system of law for the Indian reservations."

U.S. Senator Henry L. Dawes, a Massachusetts Republican, observed: "I never knew a white man to get his foot on an Indian's land who ever took it off."

Thomas A. Bland wrote *A Brief History of the Late Military Invasion of the Home of the Sioux*.

William Wirt Hastings, an 1889 graduate of Vanderbilt University's law department, became attorney general for the Cherokee Nation; he served as a congressman from Oklahoma in the U.S. House of Representatives from 1915 to 1921 and 1923 to 1935.

Amelia S. Quinton's contribution, "Care of the Indian," published in *Woman's Work in America*, edited by Annie Nathan Meyer.

The Indian Rights Association published *A Crisis in Indian Affairs*.

On April 13 Secretary of the Interior John W. Noble issued certain civil service classifications pertaining to the Indian Service.

Application of civil service rules to the Indian Service began with classification of four groups of employees: (1) physicians; (2) school superintendents and assistant superintendents; (3) school teachers; and (4) matrons.

In an article, "The Meaning of the Dakota Outbreak," for the April issue of *Scribner's Magazine*, Herbert Welsh discussed the Wounded Knee episode.

William B. Hornblower's piece, "The Legal Status of the Indian," appeared in the *Report of the Annual Meeting of the American Bar Association*.

Thomas Henry Tibbles published *New Government for Indians*.

Publication in *Science* of "African and American: The Contact of Negro and Indian" by anthropologist Alexander F. Chamberlain of Clark University, who in 1892 was awarded the first Ph.D. in anthropology in the United States.

G. W. Baird described "General Miles's Indian Campaigns" in the July number of *Century Magazine*.

Congress enacted legislation providing for Native Americans to lease tribal lands to outsiders.

Secretary of the Interior John W. Noble asserted:

> It should be understood once for all by the Chickasaw Nation and all similarly situated that the dominion within the boundaries of the Untied States rests solely with the Government of the United States and its laws approved by the Chief Executive of the United States, in all matters pertaining to the Indian people, and particularly to the five civilized tribes who have been given a form of government for local purposes; and it must be understood, that so far from being authorized to condemn any one for becoming a citizen of the United States, it is expected that this great privilege shall be honored by them, and that they shall make its attainment the chief object of their elevation and progress. It is that allegiance which they must ultimately bear to the United States of America for its long continued care of them. Loyalty to the Government must be the counterpart of its powerful protection.

Phoenix Indian School, a coeducational boarding institution for Native American primary and secondary students, established in Arizona, as Commissioner of Indian Affairs Thomas J. Morgan convinced citizens of Phoenix that in the long run it was "cheaper to educate Indians than to kill them."

Opening of surplus lands of the Pottawatomie, Shawnee, Iowa, and Sac and Fox reservations in Indian Territory (Oklahoma) to non-Indian settlement, by land run.

Thomas J. Morgan devoted a significant segment to the Sioux outbreak and the tragedy at Wounded Knee in his December, 1890, annual report.

1892

Indian Appropriations Act directed use of army officers as Indian agents.

Intoxication in Indian Country Act.

Jerome Agreement.

Future vice president Charles Curtis elected to the U.S. House of Representatives from Kansas.

Importation of reindeer into Alaska from Siberia by white bureaucrats to improve Native American economic conditions.

Commissioner of Indian Affairs Thomas J. Morgan commented on the curious influx of former army officers into the Bureau of Indian Affairs who had become Indian agents empowered to transact native business and maintain among them an absolute military despotism.

Death of Spokan Garry (Spokane).

George Bird Grinnell published an article on the last of the buffalo for the September number of *Scribner's Magazine*.

Philip Joseph Deloria, a Sioux, ordained a minister in the Episcopal Church.

Death of Kowee, chief of the Auk Tlingit.

Skolaskin, a Sanpoil medicine man and prophet, released from Alcatraz.

Death of George W. Manypenny, reformer and former commissioner.

Opening of surplus lands of the Cheyenne and Arapaho reservations in Indian Territory (Oklahoma) to non-Indian settlement, by land run.

R. W. Shufeldt published "A Comparative Study of Some Indian Homes" in the October issue of *Popular Science Monthly*.

1893

Alice Cunningham Fletcher contributed "Personal Studies of Indian Life: Politics and 'Pipe-Dancing'," to the January number of *The Century Illustrated Monthly Magazine*.

Publication of *Experiences of a Special Indian Agent* by Eugene Elliot White.

Indian Appropriations Act contained provision to eliminate the position of Indian agent.

The Quechan (Yuma) people lost much ancestral land when white officials bullied Native leaders into signing unwanted agreements and forging signatures to others.

Death of historian Francis Parkman.

Frederick Jackson Turner's work on "The Significance of the Frontier in American History."

Thomas Wildcat Alford became chairman of the Business Committee of the Absentee Shawnees in Indian Territory (Oklahoma) to correct injustices of allotment.

Death of Ganado Mucho, Navajo cattleman and peace advocate.

Daniel M. Browning appointed commissioner of Indian affairs.

George Bird Grinnell advocated the enforcement of liquor laws as a necessary protection to Native Americans.

John Wesley Powell, anthropologist and explorer, posed the question "Are Our Indians Becoming Extinct?" for the May, 1893, issue of *Forum*.

Frederic Ward Putnam, museum curator and anthropologist, organized exhibits of Native American life at World's Columbian Exposition in Chicago.

Death of Edward Fitzgerald Beale, western explorer, surveyor, road builder, and Indian superintendent.

The Boston Indian Citizenship Committee forwarded a letter to president-elect Grover Cleveland urging him to treat Native Americans fairly and responsibly during his administration.

Herbert Welsh, corresponding secretary of the Indian Rights Association, suggested to president-elect Grover Cleveland the appointment of James McLaughlin to the Indian Commission.

Members of several Democratic clubs in the Indian Territory (Oklahoma) petitioned President Grover Cleveland to adhere to home rule principles by appointing "competent and trustworthy" residents of that territory to fill federal offices rather than choosing individuals from the outside who were "unacquainted and unidentified" with the people and conditions of the Indian Territory.

Secretary of the Interior Hoke Smith, a Georgia Democrat, declared in his first annual report that Native Americans were being "advanced to a condition suited for citizenship" and emphasized that reservation schools should hasten the development of children "mentally and morally as rapidly as possible."

Robert L. Owen, chairman of a Native American advisory delegation, forwarded a letter to the chiefs of the Cherokee, Muskogee (Creek), Seminole, Choctaw, and Chickasaw tribes warning them of bills in the U.S. Congress that might threaten Native American political and property rights.

Secretary of the Interior Hoke Smith toured several Native American reservations and agencies in the West.

Mary L. Bonney said: "How great a debt to the Indian has our nation contracted by all these crimes against his natural rights, his manhood, his humanity! And many of these wrongs still exist."

Opening of surplus lands of the Cherokee Outlet in Indian Territory (Oklahoma) to non-Indian settlement, by land run.

Manuelito said: "My grandchild, education is the ladder. Tell our people to take it."

1894

Publication of *The Life and Adventures of Frank Grouard* (Chief of Scouts).

First known motion picture recording of Native Americans in *The Sioux Ghost Dance*, a Thomas A. Edison film.

Death of Hunkpapa Sioux leader Gall.

Death of Keokuk (Sac and Fox).

Publication of *Woman's Share in Primitive Culture* by Otis Tufton Mason, anthropologist and museum curator.

Publication of *The Sia* by Matilda Coxe Stevenson.

Death of Omaha tribal leader Two Crows.

Death of S. Alice Callahan.

Charles F. Lummis founded and served as editor of the magazine *Out West*.

Death of Charles Journeycake, trapper, guide, preacher, and Lenni Lenape (Delaware) tribal leader.

Report of the Dawes Commission.

Death of Alexander M. Stephen, anthropologist and observer of Hopi culture.

From 1894 to 1897, Charles Alexander Eastman, physician, writer, and great-grandson of Cloudman (Sioux), established thirty-two Native American YMCA groups.

Death of Manuelito, Navajo leader.

Death of Elizabeth Palmer Peabody, a Boston bookshop owner, author, reformer, lecturer, and educator who advocated the study of history in public schools and promoted education for Native Americans.

Susan La Flesche (Omaha) married Henri Picotte and shortly thereafter started a medical practice for Native Americans and others in Bancroft, Nebraska.

James Henderson Kyle prepared "How Shall the Indians Be Educated?" for the October number of *North American Review*.

1895

Death of Ely S. Parker.

Ethnologist J. Walter Fewkes excavated ruins of Sikyatki, shedding new light on Hopi culture and ceremonies.

Mountain Chief (Blackfoot) signed treaty ceding Glacier National Park.

Death of Richard I. Dodge, army officer and historian.

Death of Nana, war chief in the Apache Wars.

John Wesley Powell published an essay, "Proper Training and the Future of the Indians," in the January issue of *Forum*.

President Grover Cleveland appointed former congressman William M. Springer, an Illinois Democrat and lawyer, U.S. judge for the Northern District of Indian Territory and later chief justice of the U.S. Court of Appeals for Indian Territory, in which capacities he served from 1895 to 1900.

Orville H. Platt penned "Problems in the Indian Territory" for the February number of *North American Review*.

Francis E. Leupp, a future commissioner of Indian affairs, published a book, *Civil Service Reform Essential to a Successful Indian Administration*, and an article, "The Spoils System and the Indian Service," which appeared in the May 23 issue of *Public Opinion.*

Choctaw General Council rejected Dawes Commission Land Plans.

Secretary of the Interior Hoke Smith dispatched Francis E. Leupp, a journalist and reformer, to the Southern Ute area as a confidential agent in preparation for negotiating a treaty pertaining to their land.

O. B. Super showcased "Indian Education at Carlisle," in the April, 1895, issue of *New England Magazine*, in which he described Native American education at the Indian Industrial School at Carlisle, Pennsylvania.

On May 4, 1895, President Grover Cleveland wrote a letter to Interior Secretary Hoke Smith regarding Native American matters. Believing in ultimate U.S. citizenship for Indians, Cleveland reminded Smith that positive results achieved slowly were better than swift outcomes gained by "broken pledges and false promises."

First appearance on May 9 of *City and State*, a weekly newspaper for which Herbert Welsh served as publisher and managing editor.

Secretary of the Interior Hoke Smith professed that the agent constituted "the most important instrumentality for the development of the Indian" and hoped that the missionary spirit would encapsulate the hearts of all employees at Native American schools and reservations."

President Grover Cleveland pledged to Attorney General Judson Harmon that he wanted "to do something solving the Indian problem in a sensible, decent, and Christian way."

Secretary of the Interior Hoke Smith expressed in his annual report his desire to have the federal government act as a "faithful trustee" in the disposition of Native American lands, instructing his agents not to act as "representatives of white men who desire possession of these lands."

The Boston *Congregationalist* described Secretary of the Interior Hoke Smith as a person who took "a Christian view of the Indian problem."

Dennis T. Flynn, a Republican delegate to the U.S. House of Representatives from the Territory of Oklahoma, vehemently condemned Secretary of the Interior Hoke Smith for his failure to open the Wichita Indian Reservation for white settlement.

James McLaughlin declined an appointment as assistant commissioner of Indian affairs because (1) he preferred service in the field and direct contact with Native Americans; (2) he had certain ideas on how Indians should be treated and did not want to apply those concepts and possibly be overruled by administrative superiors; and (3) he recognized that the exigencies of politics and changes of administrations could force people out of governmental service.

Opening of surplus lands of the Kickapoo Reservation in Indian Territory (Oklahoma) to non-Indian settlement, by land run.

George Bird Grinnell published *The Story of the Indian.*

1896

Talton v. Mayes (163 U.S. 376).

Lucas v. United States (163 U.S. 612).

Ward v. Race Horse (162 U.S. 504).

Death of John Slocum, Coast Salish spiritual leader.

After graduating from the University of Illinois and later the Chicago Medical College, Carlos Montezuma (Wasajah), physician, editor, and reformer, opened a private practice in Chicago specializing in stomach and intestinal diseases.

Death of John Gregory Bourke, author, reformer, and anthropologist.

Death of Lewis Bennett, Seneca athlete.

Extension of civil service rules covering most employees of the Indian Service.

Benjamin Orange Flower discussed Potawatomi leader Simon Pokagon's remarks at the 1893 World's Columbian Exposition in a piece, "An Interesting Representative of a Vanishing Race," in the July issue of *The Arena*.

Death of Valentine Trant O'Connell McGillycuddy, Indian agent.

"Indian Medicine Men," an article by L. G. Yates, appeared in the August copy of *Overland.*

Ruth Shaffner's essay, "Civilizing the American Indian," was printed in *The Chautauquan* in June.

James Mooney wrote "The Mescal Plant and Ceremony" for *Therapeutic Gazette*.

An early study of the value of peyote, "Therapeutic Uses of Mescal Buttons," written by Drs. D. W. Prentiss and Francis P. Morgan, appeared in *Therapeutic Gazette*.

D. A. Richardson reported on mescal buttons (peyote) usage for the *New York Medical Journal*.

George Bird Grinnell contended that Secretary of the Interior Hoke Smith, the Indian Bureau, and their respective offices seemed to have made "an honest effort toward a better treatment of the Indians and a more businesslike conduct of Indian affairs."

1897

Education Appropriation Act.

Indian Liquor Act.

Anthropologist and reformer James Mooney published *The Ghost Dance Religion and the Sioux Outbreak of 1890.*

John G. Brady appointed territorial governor of the District of Alaska.

Chief Joseph (Nez Perce) visited President William McKinley in Washington.

William Arthur Jones became commissioner of Indian affairs.

William A. Jones, commissioner of Indian affairs from 1897 to 1904 under Presidents William McKinley and Theodore Roosevelt, and a former banker, teacher, Wisconsin state legislator, and businessman, claimed that education was the greatest factor in solving the future status of Native Americans.

Publication by J. D. McGuire of *Pipes and Smoking Customs of the American Aborigines*.

Hugh Lenox Scott began studying Native American sign languages at the Bureau of American Ethnology of the Smithsonian Institution in Washington.

Louis Francis Sockalexis became the first Native American (Penobscot) initiated into professional baseball.

Simon Pokagon, a Potawatomi leader, published "The Future of the Red Man" in the August volume of *Forum*.

Simon Pokagon bemoaned the ravages of alcoholic beverages, referring to the "intoxicating cup" as "a traitor within our camp," cunning as the fox: "It embraces and kisses but to poison like the snake—without the warning rattle. . . . Were it an open enemy outside our lines, we might meet it with success."

Simon Pokagon predicted the passing away of Indian reservations by the mid-twentieth century, the scattering of Indians, and a general mixing up of the races: "Through intermarriage the blood of our people, like the waters that flow into the great ocean, will be forever lost in the dominant race; and generations yet unborn will read in history of the red men of the forest, and inquire, 'Where are they?'"

1898

Curtis Act.

Klondike Gold Rush.

Death of Matilda J. Gage.

Potawatomi leader Simon Pokagon discussed "Indian Superstitions and Legends" in the July issue of *Forum*.

Indian Medical Association formed.

Hamlin Garland's article, "General Custer's Last Fight as Seen by Two Moons," appeared in the September issue of *McClure's Magazine*. A research informant and Northern Cheyenne, Two Moons was used as a model for the buffalo or Indian head nickel designed by James Fraser and released in 1913.

Publication by Francis E. Leupp, commissioner of Indian affairs from 1905 to 1909, of "Protest of the Pillager Indians" in the December number of *Forum*.

John Wesley Powell's perceptive piece on the origin of the Amerind, "Whence Came the American Indians?" appeared in the February issue of *Forum*.

Death of Felix Reville Brunot.

Publication by James Mooney of *Calendar History of the Kiowa*.

Stuart Culin described "American Indian Games" in the October-December number of *Journal of American Folk-Lore*.

Alice Cunningham Fletcher's article, "The Import of the Totem," appeared in *Science*.

In remarks published in the *Boston Evening Transcript*, on November 19, 1898, Theodore Roosevelt defended America's overall treatment of the Indians:

> Let us remember that it was absolutely impossible in the past to do such justice to the Indians as we expect to be done today. This continent had to be won. We need not waste our time in dealing with

> any sentimentalist who believes that, on account of any abstract principle, it would have been right to leave this continent to the domain, the hunting ground of squalid savages. It had to be taken by the white race. Our Government has tried to be just—it has been more than just—it has been generous. . . . No other nation—not the English in South Africa or Australia, not the French in Africa, not the Russian in Siberia—has ever purchased land with the attempt at entire fair play to the aboriginal owners that we have shown.

1899

Hamlin Garland published "Rising Wolf–Ghost Dancer" in the January volume of *McClure's Magazine*.

Publication in the February copy of *Atlantic Monthly* of George Bird Grinnell's essay, "The Indian on the Reservation."

Jones v. Meehan (175 U.S. 1).

Publication of *Queen of the Woods* by Simon Pokagon.

Death of Simon Pokagon.

Stephens v. Cherokee Nation (174 U.S. 445).

Death of army officer Henry Ware Lawton.

Quanah Parker, a progressive and son of white captive Cynthia Ann Parker, named Comanche principal chief.

Publication of *Our Red Brothers and the Peace Policy of President Ulysses S. Grant* by Lawrie Tatum.

George A. Dorsey published "The Hopi Indians of Arizona" in the October, 1899, issue *Popular Science Monthly.*

1900

U.S. federal census reported 237,196 Native Americans. Approximately one thousand Native Americans were reported to live in cities. Indian tribes held some eighty million acres of land across the United States. Since 1800 they had lost more than 95 percent of their lands to non-Indians.

Office of Indian Affairs had a budget of $7.75 million, employed 4,259 people (more than half in education), and reported that 10,000 Native American children attended 25 off-reservation boarding schools. Others were enrolled in the 81 reservation boarding schools, 147 day schools, and 32 contract schools.

Three hundred Oneida Indians voted in the New York State elections.

Death of Young-Man-Afraid-of-His-Horses (Sioux).

Death of Washakie, Northern Shoshone.

Alice Cunningham Fletcher published *Indian Story and Song from North America.*

Publication of *The Middle Five: Indian Schoolboys of the Omaha Tribe* by Francis La Flesche.

Death of Frank Hamilton Cushing, anthropologist and archaeologist who discovered remnants of the Hohokam culture in Arizona.

Publication of *Lights and Shadows of a Long Episcopate* by Henry B. Whipple.

Herbert Welsh wrote *The Other Man's Country: An Appeal to Conscience.*

Calling for the need of better government in the Indian Territory (Oklahoma), David W. Yancey observed that the Territory of Alaska was governed better than Indian Territory, which had a larger population.

The Carlisle Indian Industrial School's football team defeated Phoenix Industrial School in Arizona by the score of 83 to 6.

Death of Mary Lucinda Bonney, an educator and reformer who sought U.S. citizenship and equal protection for Native Americans under U.S. law.

Publication in *American Catholic Quarterly Review* of "Government Secularization of the Education of Catholic Indian Youth" by Detroit writer Richard R. Elliott.

1901

Chitto Harjo (Crazy Snake) organized a faction of fullblood Creek Indians in Indian Territory (Oklahoma) in a movement known as the Crazy Snake rebellion to resist allotment and dissolution of tribal government.

Congress amended the Dawes Act to provide citizenship for the Five Civilized Tribes and other Native peoples in Indian Territory (Oklahoma).

Ainsworth Rand Spofford, former librarian of Congress, read a paper, "Rare Books Relating to the American Indians," before the Anthropological Society of Washington, which was later published in *American Anthropologist.*

Gertrude Simmons Bonnin (Zitkala-Sa), a social reformer, wrote *Old Indian Legends.*

Sequoyah League, a philanthropic group working for welfare of California Indians, founded, primarily through the efforts of writer/reformer Charles Lummis.

Death of reformer and missionary Henry Benjamin Whipple (Straight Tongue), first Episcopal bishop of Minnesota, who had urged the creation of a cabinet-level post exclusively for the management of Native American policy.

In his annual report, Commissioner of Indian Affairs William A. Jones expressed interest in moving Native Americans toward self-support.

Death of John Wilson (Caddo-Delaware), who originated the Big Moon peyote ceremony.

Opening of the surplus lands of the Kiowa-Comanche and the Wichita-Caddo Reservations in Indian Territory (Oklahoma) to non-Indian settlement, by lottery.

Gilded Age ended as Progressive Era and twentieth century began.

Source Notes

The sources listed for each document in the text have been reproduced in this section for the reader's convenience and further study. The source(s) follow the document number, title, and the page numbers on which the document is printed.

Chapter 1 Documents 1867-69

1-1. Treaty of Medicine Lodge Creek (pp. 11-30)
Charles J. Kappler, ed., *Indian Affairs: Laws and Treaties*, Vol. 2, *Treaties* (Washington, D.C.: Government Printing Office, 1904), 2:977-89.

1-2. Nathaniel G. Taylor to Andrew Johnson (pp. 30-32)
Andrew Johnson Papers, Manuscripts Division, Library of Congress, Washington, D.C.

1-3. Report of the Indian Peace Commission (pp. 32-69)
N. G. Taylor et al., *Annual Report of the Commissioner of Indian Affairs for the Year 1868* (Washington, D.C.: Government Printing Office, 1868), 26-50. See also H. Ex. Doc., no. 97, 40th Cong., 2d sess.

1-4. Treaty of Fort Laramie (pp. 69-78)
Charles J. Kappler, ed., *Indian Affairs: Laws and Treaties* (Washington: Government Printing Office, 1904), 2:998-1003. See also Francis Paul Prucha, ed., *Documents of United States Indian Policy*, 3d ed. (Lincoln: University of Nebraska Press, 2000), 1-9, 13.

1-5. Treaty of Bosque Redondo (pp. 78-85)
Treaty Between the United States of America and the Navajo Tribe of Indians Concluded June 1, 1868; Ratification advised July 25, 1868; Proclaimed August 12, 1868. (15 Stat. 667).

1-6. Speech in the House of Representatives (pp. 85-87)
Congressional Globe, 40th Cong., 3d sess., February 27, 1869, 1704-5.

1-7. Instructions to the Board of Indian Commissioners (pp. 87-91)
Ely S. Parker to Commissioners, May 29, 1869, *Annual Report of the Board of Indian Commissioners, 1869*, 3-5. See also Ulysses S. Grant to Commissioners, June 3, 1869, Ulysses S. Grant Papers, Manuscripts Division, Library of Congress, Washington, D.C., and Ely S. Parker Papers, American Philosophical Society Library, Philadelphia, Pennsylvania.

Chapter 2 Documents 1870-79

2-1. Editorial (pp. 93-95)
Cheyenne (Wyoming) *Daily Leader*, March 9, 1870.

2-2. Declaration and Appeal to the President . . . (pp. 95-98)
Ulysses S. Grant Papers, Manuscripts Division, Library of Congress, Washington, D.C.

2-3. Speech at Cooper Union (pp. 98-100)
New York Times, July 17, 1870.

2-4. Annual Message to Congress (pp. 101-2)
James D. Richardson, comp., *A Compilation of the Messages and Papers of the Presidents, 1789-1897*, 10 vols. (Washington, D.C.: Government Printing Office, 1898), 7:109-10.

2-5. Ely S. Parker to Columbus Delano (pp. 103-6)
Office of Indian Affairs, *Annual Report of the Commissioner of Indian Affairs to the Secretary for the Year 1871* (Washington, D.C.: Government Printing Office, 1872), 29-30.

2-6. Christianization of Native Americans (p. 106)
Arizona Citizen, April 22, 1871.

2-7. The Peace Policy (pp. 107-8)
New York Herald, June 8, 1871.

2-8. Report of a Visit to Red Cloud (pp. 108-24)
Office of Indian Affairs, *Annual Report of the Commissioner of Indian Affairs to the Secretary for the Year 1871* (Washington, D.C.: Government Printing Office, 1872), 22-29, NADP Document RA1871A.

2-9. Letter of Resignation (pp. 124-25)
Ely S. Parker to Ulysses S. Grant, June 29, 1871, Presidents Collection, Rutherford B. Hayes Presidential Center, Fremont, Ohio.

2-10. Ulysses S. Grant to Ely S. Parker (p. 125)
Ulysses S. Grant Papers, Manuscripts Division, Library of Congress, Washington, D.C.; *New York Herald*, July 18, 1871; Ely S. Parker Papers, American Philosophical Society Library, Philadelphia, Pennsylvania.

2-11. Ulysses S. Grant to Red Cloud et al. (pp. 125-27)
Washington Evening Star, May 28, 1872.

2-12. Response to President Grant's Speech (pp. 127-28)
Washington Evening Star, May 28, 1872.

2-13. Annual Report of the Commissioner of Indian Affairs (pp. 128-37)
Extract from *Annual Report of the Commissioner of Indian Affairs*, November 1, 1872, in H. Ex. Doc., no. 1, 42d Cong., 3d sess., serial 1560, 391-99.

2-14. Testimony of Blackfoot (pp. 137-41)
H. Ex. Doc., no. 89, 43d Cong., 1st sess., 28-42.

2-15. Henry B. Whipple to Ulysses S. Grant (pp. 141-43)
Ulysses S. Grant Papers, Manuscript Division, Library of Congress, Washington, D.C. See also *New York Tribune*, April 1, 1876.

2-16. Senate Speech (pp. 143-47)
George Francis Dawson, *Life and Services of General John A. Logan as Soldier and Statesman* (Chicago: Belford, Clarke, and Company, 1887), 224-27. See also *Congressional Record*, 44th Cong., 1st sess., June 20, 1876.

2-17. E. W. Smith to George A. Custer (pp. 147-49)
Paul Andrew Hutton, ed., *The Custer Reader* (Lincoln: University of Nebraska Press, 1992), 273-75.

2-18. Petition to President Ulysses S. Grant (pp. 149-51)
Ulysses S. Grant Papers, Manuscript Division, Library of Congress, Washington, D.C.

2-19. Report on the Battle of Little Bighorn (pp. 151-54)
Alfred H. Terry to Adjutant General, July 8, 1876, National Archives, Washington, D.C.

2-20. An Account of George A. Custer's Defeat at the Little Bighorn (pp. 155-58)
John S. Poland, United States Military Station, Standing Rock Indian Agency, Dakota Territory, to Assistant Adjutant General, Department of Dakota, July 24, 1876, National Archives, Washington, D.C.

2-21. Native American Friendship and Heroism (pp. 158-59)
Henry Clay Trumbull, *Friendship the Master Passion, Or, The Nature and History of Friendship, and Its Place as a Force in the World* (Philadelphia: John D. Wattles, 1894), 71-72, 165-66.

2-22. Approval of an Agreement with the Sioux Nation and Others (pp. 159-64)
Charles J. Kappler, ed., *Indian Affairs: Laws and Treaties*, vol. 1, *Laws* (Washington: Government Printing Office, 1904), 168-71.

2-23. Speech of Crazy Horse (pp. 164-65)
Annette Rosenstiel, *Red and White: Indian Views of the White Man, 1492-1982* (New York: Universe Books, 1983), 141-42.

2-24. The Last Day: The Surrender (pp. 165-70)
Lucullus Virgil McWhorter, *Yellow Wolf: His Own Story* (Caldwell, Idaho: Caxton Printers, Ltd., 1986), 220-26.

2-25. Surrender Speech (pp. 170-71)
New York Times, October 11, 1877.

2-26. Remarks of Spotted Tail (pp. 171-73)
Annette Rosenstiel, *Red and White: Indian View of the White Man, 1492-1982* (New York: Universe Books, 1983), 139; W. D. Vanderwerth, ed., *Indian Oratory: Famous Speeches by Noted Indian Chieftains* (Norman: University of Oklahoma Press, 1971), 220-21.

2-27. Hegira of Dull Knife (pp. 173-74)
(Dodge City, Kansas) *Ford County Globe*, October 29, 1878.

2-28. Speech of Chief Joseph (pp. 174-76)
Annette Rosenstiel, *Red and White: Indian Views of the White Man, 1492-1982* (New York: Universe Books, 1983), 142-45.

2-29. An Indian's View of Indian Affairs (pp. 177-200)
Young Joseph and Right Rev. W. H. Hare, "An Indian's Views of Indian Affairs," *North American Review* 128 (April 1879): 412-34.

2-30. Speech of Susette La Flesche (pp. 200-5)
Boston Daily Advertiser, November 26, 1879.

2-31. Annual Message to Congress (pp. 205-9)
James D. Richardson, comp., *A Compilation of the Messages and Papers of the Presidents, 1789-1897*, 10 vols. (Washington, D.C.: Government Printing Office, 1898), 7:575-78. See also Rutherford B. Hayes Papers, Rutherford B. Hayes Presidential Center, Fremont Ohio.

2-32. Speeches of Sarah Winnemucca (pp. 209-210)
Daily Alta California, December 4, 24, 1879.

2-33. First Days at the Carlisle Indian School (pp. 210-25)
E. A. Brininstool, ed., *My People the Sioux* (Boston: Houghton Mifflin Company, 1928), 133-50. See also Luther Standing Bear, *Land of the Spotted Eagle* (Lincoln: University of Nebraska Press, 1978), 230-37.

2-34. *United States v. Crook* (pp. 226-41)
U.S. v. Crook, (5 Dillon, 453-69).

Chapter 3 Documents 1880-89

3-1. Carl Schurz to Helen Hunt Jackson (pp. 243-46)
Frederic Bancroft, ed., *Speeches, Correspondence and Political Papers of Carl Schurz*, 6 vols. (New York: G. P. Putnam's Sons, 1913), 3:496-499.

3-2. Helen Hunt Jackson to Carl Schurz (pp. 246-47)
Frederic Bancroft, ed., *Speeches, Correspondence and Political Papers of Carl Schurz*, 6 vols. (New York: G. P. Putnam's Sons, 1913), 3:499-500.

3-3. Annual Report to the Secretary of the Interior (pp. 247-51)
H. Ex. Doc., no. 1, 46th Cong., 3d sess., serial 1959, 3-4, 11-13.

3-4. Sarah Winnemucca to Samuel Jordan Kirkwood (pp. 251-52)
Sarah Winnemucca Hopkins, *Life Among the Piutes: Their Wrongs and Claims* (1883; reprint, Las Vegas: University of Nevada Press, 1994), 244-45.

3-5. Annual Report of the Commissioner of Indian Affairs (pp. 252-56)
H. Ex. Doc., no. 1, 47th Cong., 1st sess., 1-3.

3-6. First Message to Congress (pp. 256-59)
James D. Richardson, comp., *A Compilation of the Messages and Papers of the Presidents, 1789-1897*, 10 vols. (Washington, D.C.: Government Printing Office, 1898), 8:54-57.

3-7. Sitting Bull to William Selwyn and the President (pp. 259-61)
W. Fletcher Johnson, *The Red Record of the Sioux: Life of Sitting Bull and History of the Indian War of 1890-91* (Philadelphia: Edgewood Publishing Company, 1891), 162-67.

3-8. Senate Speech (pp. 262-71)
Congressional Record, 11, pt. 1, 46th Cong., 3d sess., 780-81, 783, 934-35.

3-9. A Century of Dishonor (pp. 271-76)
Helen Hunt Jackson, *A Century of Dishonor* (New York: Harper and Brothers, 1881), 334-42.

3-10. *Ex Parte Crow Dog* (pp. 277-79)
Ex Parte Crow Dog, 109 U.S. 556; 109 *U.S. Reports*, 557, 571-572. See Sidney L. Harring, *Crow Dog's Case: American Indian Sovereignty, Tribal*

Law, and United States Law in the Nineteenth Century (New York: Cambridge University Press, 1994).

3-11. Life Among the Paiutes (p. 280)
Sarah Winnemucca Hopkins, *Life Among the Paiutes: Their Wrongs and Claims*, ed. Mary Tyler Mann (Boston and New York: Privately Printed, 1883), 258-59.

3-12. *John Elk v. Charles Wilkins* (pp. 281-307)
John Elk, Plaintiff in Error v. Charles Wilkins, 112 U.S. 94 (See S.C. Reporter's ed., 94-123).

3-13. *United States v. Kagama* (pp. 307-13)
United States v. Kagama, 118 U.S. 375 (1886)

3-14. Sarah Winnemucca to *Silver State* (p. 313)
(Winnemucca, Nevada) *Silver State*, July 9, 1886.

3-15. Surrender of Geronimo (pp. 313-16)
S. M. Barrett, ed., *Geronimo's Story of His Life* (1907; reprint, Alexander, North Carolina: Alexander Books, 1998), 118-21.

3-16. Indian Citizenship (pp. 316-25)
Philip C. Garrett, "Indian Citizenship," *Proceedings of the Fourth Annual Lake Mohonk Conference* (1886), 8-11.

3-17. General Allotment Act (Dawes Severalty Act) (pp. 325-32)
U.S. Statutes at Large, 49th Cong., 2d sess., 24, Ch. 119: 388-91.

3-18. The English Language and Native American Schools (pp. 332-36)
John D. C. Atkins, *Annual Report of the Commissioner of Indian Affairs*, September 21, 1887, H. Ex. Doc., no. 1, 50th Cong., 1st sess., 19-21.

3-19. Marriage between White Men and Native American Women (pp. 336-37)
U.S. Statutes at Large, 25:392.

3-20. Annual Message to Congress (pp. 337-38)
James D. Richardson, comp., *A Compilation of the Messages and Papers of the Presidents, 1789-1897*, 10 vols. (Washington, D.C.: Government Printing Office, 1898), 10:789-90.

3-21. Preston B. Plumb to John W. Noble (pp. 339-41)
Benjamin Harrison Papers, Manuscripts Division, Library of Congress, Washington, D.C.

3-22. Alice C. Fletcher to Frederic W. Putnam (pp. 341-44)
Frederic Ward Putnam Papers, Peabody Museum Archives, Pusey Library, Harvard University, Cambridge, Massachusetts.

3-23. The Bote and Sexuality (pp. 344-47)
A. B. Holder, "The Bote: Description of a Peculiar Sexual Perversion Found Among North American Indians," *New York Medical Journal* 50 (December 7, 1889):623-25.

3-24. Directive to Indian Agents and Superintendents . . . (pp. 347-48)
Report of the Secretary of the Interior, H. Ex. Doc., 51st Cong., 2d sess., vol. 2, 1890, 167.

3-25. Herbert Welsh to Benjamin Harrison (pp. 348-49)
Benjamin Harrison Papers, Manuscripts Division, Library of Congress, Washington, D.C.

3-26. Sitting Bull to Members of Silent Eaters Society (pp. 349-51)
Annette Rosenstiel, *Red and White: Indian Views of the White Man, 1492-1982* (New York: Universe Books, 1983), 148-49.

Chapter 4 Documents 1890-99

4-1. Thomas J. Morgan to Henry L. Dawes (pp. 353-60)
Benjamin Harrison Papers, Manuscripts Division, Library of Congress, Washington, D.C.

4-2. Preston B. Plumb to Herbert Welsh (pp. 360-63)
Benjamin Harrison Papers, Manuscripts Division, Library of Congress, Washington, D.C.

4-3. Sermon to Ghost Dancers (pp. 363-64)
Thomas E. Sanders and Walter W. Peek, eds., *Literature of the American Indian* (Beverly Hills, Calif.: Glencoe Press, 1973), 343.

4-4. The Messiah Letter (pp. 364-65)
Thomas E. Sanders and Walter W. Peek, eds., *Literature of the American Indian* (Beverly Hills, Calif.: Glencoe Press, 1973), 337.

4-5. Letter to Editor of *Chicago Tribune* (pp. 365-66)
Thomas E. Sanders and Walter W. Peek, eds., *Literature of the American Indian* (Beverly Hills, Calif.: Glencoe Press, 1973), 357-58.

4-6. The Butchering at Wounded Knee (pp. 366-71)
Black Elk, *Black Elk Speaks: Being the Life Story of a Holy Man of the Oglala Sioux* (New York: William Morrow Company, 1932), 255-62.

4-7. Dissemination of Tales among the Natives of North America (pp. 371-81)
Franz Boas, "Dissemination of Tales among the Natives of North America," *Journal of American Folk-lore* 4 (January 1891):13-20.

4-8. Thomas J. Morgan to John W. Noble (pp. 381-91)
Benjamin Harrison Papers, Manuscripts Division, Library of Congress, Washington, D.C.

4-9. Account of the Death of Sitting Bull . . . (pp. 392-98)
James McLaughlin, "Account of the Death of Sitting Bull and the Circumstances Attending It," (Philadelphia: Indian Rights Association, 1891).

4-10. Amendment to the Dawes Act (pp. 399-401)
U.S. Statutes at Large, 26:794-96.

4-11. Thomas J. Morgan to Benjamin Harrison (pp. 401-4)
Benjamin Harrison Papers, Manuscripts Division, Library of Congress, Washington, D.C.

4-12. A People Without Law (pp. 404-440)
James Bradley Thayer, "A People Without Law," *Atlantic Monthly* 68 (October 1891):540-51, and (November 1891):676-87.

4-13. Annual Message to Congress (pp. 440-44)
James D. Richardson, comp., *A Compilation of the Message and Papers of the Presidents 1789-1897*, 10 vols. (Washington, D.C.: Government Printing Office, 1898), 10:201-3.

4-14. The Ghost Dance and Pine Ridge (pp. 44-51)
"Dr. V. T. McGillycuddy on the Ghost Dance," in Stanley Vestal, *New Sources of Indian History, 1850-1891: The Ghost Dance, The Prairie Sioux, A Miscellany* (Norman: University of Oklahoma Press, 1934), 81-90.

4-15. Address to the People of the United States (pp. 452-59)
Henry Davenport Northrop, *Indian Horrors* (Chicago: L. P. Miller and Company, 1891), 590-600.

4-16. Wynema (pp. 459-61)
S. Alice Callahan, *Wynema: A Child of the Forest* (Philadelphia: H. J. Smith and Company, 1891), 46, 73, 95.

4-17. How to Bring the Indian to Citizenship . . . (pp. 462-75)
Herbert Welsh, "How to Bring the Indian to Citizenship, and Citizenship to the Indian," *Boston Commonwealth*, April 9, 1892, 1-14.

4-18. Henry B. Whipple to Benjamin Harrison (pp. 475-76)
Benjamin Harrison Papers, Manuscripts Division, Library of Congress, Washington, D.C.

4-19. Fighting, Feeding, or Educating Native Americans (pp. 476-80)
Thomas J. Morgan, "Compulsory Education," in *Proceedings of the Tenth Annual Meeting of the Lake Mohonk Conference of Friends of the Indian*, 1892, 51-54.

4-20. Jerome Commission Report (pp. 480-86)
Charles J. Kappler, ed., *Indian Affairs: Laws and Treaties*, vol. 1 (Washington, D. C.: Government Printing Office, 1904); S. Ex. Doc., no. 17, 52d Cong., 2d sess., vol. 1, January 4, 1893, serial set 3055.

4-21. Speech to Woman's National Indian Association (pp. 486-87)
Grover Cleveland Papers, Manuscripts Division, Library of Congress, Washington, D.C.

4-22. The Shawnee Prophet and the Peyote Cult (pp. 487-94)
"What the Shawnee Prophet Told the Winnebago," and "John Rave's Account of the Peyote Cult and of His Conversion," in Paul Radin, *The Winnebago Tribe* (Washington, D.C.: U.S. Bureau of American Ethnology, 1923), 389-94, 69-74; Paul Radin, "The Religious Experience of an American Indian" (1950):249-90, in Paul Radin Papers, Department of Special Collections and University Archives, Marquette University Libraries, Milwaukee, Wisconsin.

4-23. Report of the Dawes Commission (pp. 495-504)
S. Misc. Doc., no. 24, 53d Cong., 3d sess., serial 3281, 8-12.

4-24. The Woman's National Indian Association (pp. 504-9)
The Congress of Women: Held in the Woman's Building, World's Columbian Exposition, Chicago, U.S.A. 1893 (Chicago: Monarch Book Company, 1894), 71-73. See also Indian Rights Association Papers, Historical Society

of Pennsylvania, Philadelphia; Amelia Stone Quinton Papers, Huntington Library, San Marino, California.

4-25. Assessment of the Cherokee Nation (pp. 509-14)
S. H. Mayes, and others, to the Senate and House of Representatives of the United States Congress, 1895, Cherokee Nation Papers, Oklahoma Historical Society, Oklahoma City.

4-26. Modern Treaty Making with Native Americans (pp. 514-17)
James McLaughlin, *My Friend the Indian* (Boston: Houghton Mifflin Company, 1910), 291-95. See also James McLaughlin Papers, Archives of Assumption Abbey, Richardton, North Dakota, and Louis L. Pfaller, *James McLaughlin: The Man with an Indian Heart* (New York: Vantage Press, 1978).

4-27. Songs of the Ghost Dance (pp. 518-24)
American Poetry: The Nineteenth Century (New York: The Library of America, 1993), 2:727-35; Thomas E. Sanders and Walter W. Peek, eds., *Literature of the American Indian* (Beverly Hills, Calif.: Glencoe Press, 1976), 186-87; James Mooney, "The Ghost-Dance Religion and the Sioux Outbreak of 1890," *Fourteenth Annual Report of the Bureau of American Ethnology*, 1896.

4-28. Home Life Among the Indians (pp. 524-41)
Alice Cunningham Fletcher, "Home Life Among the Indians: Records of Personal Experience," *Century Magazine* 54, n.s., 32 (June 1897):252-63.

4-29. The Future of the Red Man (pp. 541-53)
Simon Pokagon, "The Future of the Red Man," *Forum* 23 (1897):698-708.

4-30. Assessment of the Dawes Commission (pp. 553-54)
John D. Benedict, *History of Muskogee and Northeastern Oklahoma*, 3 vols. (Chicago: S. J. Clarke Publishing Company, 1922), 1:142.

4-31. Curtis Act (pp. 554-57)
U.S. Statutes at Large, 30:497-98, 502, 504-5. See also William E. Unrau, *Mixed Bloods and Tribal Dissolution: Charles Curtis and the Quest for Indian Identity* (Lawrence: University Press of Kansas, 1989); Leonard Schlup, "Charles Curtis: The Vice President from Kansas," *Manuscripts* 35 (Summer 1983):183-201; Charles Curtis Papers, Kansas State Historical Society Library, Topeka.

4-32. General Custer's Last Fight as Seen by Two Moons (pp. 557-62)
Hamlin Garland, "General Custer's Last Fight as Seen by Two Moons," *McClure's Magazine* 11 (September 1898):443-48.

4-33. Our Indian Problem (pp. 563-73)
Lyman Abbot, "Our Indian Problem," *North American Review* 167 (December 1898):719-28.

4-34. Rising Wolf: Ghost Dancer (pp. 573-76)
Hamlin Garland, "Rising Wolf: Ghost Dancer," *McClure's Magazine* 12 (January 1899):241-48.

4-35. The Indian on the Reservation (pp. 576-97)
George Bird Grinnell, "The Indian on the Reservation," *Atlantic Monthly* 83 (February 1899):255-67.

4-36. Agreement with the Yankton Sioux (pp. 597-601)
56th Cong., 1st sess., H. Doc. no. 535, serial 3995:26-30.

Chapter 5 Documents 1900-01

5-1. Impressions of an Indian Childhood (pp. 603-21)
Zitkala-Sa, "Impressions of an Indian Childhood," *Atlantic Monthly* 85 (January 1900):27-47.

5-2. The Zuni Indians (pp. 621-27)
Matilda Coxe Stevenson, "The Zuni Indians: Their Mythology, Esoteric Societies, and Ceremonies," *Twenty-third Annual Report of the U.S. Bureau of American Ethnology, 1901-1902* (Washington, D.C.: Smithsonian Institution and Government Printing Office, 1904):37-38, 150, 310-13, 374.

Further Readings

Armstrong, William H. *Warrior in Two Camps: Ely S. Parker, Union General and Seneca Chief.* Syracuse, N.Y.: Syracuse University Press, 1978.

Berthrong, Donald J. *The Cheyenne and Arapaho Ordeal: Reservation and Agency Life in the Indian Territory, 1875-1907.* Norman: University of Oklahoma Press, 1976.

Carlson, Leonard A. *Indians, Bureaucrats, and Land: The Dawes Act and the Decline of Indian Farming.* Westport, Conn.: Greenwood Press, 1981.

Champagne, Duane, ed. *Chronology of Native North American History: From Pre-Columbian Times to the Present.* Detroit: Gale Research, Inc., 1994.

Cozzens, Peter, ed. *Eyewitnesses to the Indian Wars, 1865-1890.* 5 vols. Mechanicsburg, Pa.: Stackpole Books, 2001-2005.

Driver, Harold E. *Indians of North America.* Chicago: University of Chicago Press, 1962.

Fritz, Henry E. *The Movement for Indian Assimilation, 1860-1890.* Philadelphia: University of Pennsylvania Press, 1963.

Hagan, William T. *The Indian Rights Association: The Herbert Welsh Years, 1882-1904.* Tucson: University of Arizona Press, 1985.

______. *Taking Indians Lands: The Cherokee (Jerome) Commission, 1889-1893.* Norman: University of Oklahoma Press, 2003.

Hoxie, Frederick E. "The End of the Savage: Indian Policy in the United States Senate, 1880-1900," *The Chronicles of Oklahoma* 45 (Summer 1977): 157-179.

Keller, Robert H., Jr. *American Protestantism and United States Indian Policy, 1869-1882.* Lincoln: University of Nebraska Press, 1983.

Kvasnicka, Robert M., and Herman J. Viola, eds. *The Commissioners of Indian Affairs, 1824-1977.* Lincoln: University of Nebraska Press, 1979.

Littlefield, Daniel F., Jr., and James W. Parins. *A Biobibliography of Native American Writers, 1772-1924.* Metuchen, N.J.: Scarecrow Press, 1981.

Mardock, Robert W. *The Reformers and the American Indian.* Columbia: University of Missouri Press, 1971.

McDonnell, Janet A. *The Dispossession of the American Indian, 1887-1934.* Bloomington: Indiana University Press, 1991.

Milner, Clyde A., II, and Floyd A. O'Neil. *Churchmen and the Western Indians, 1829-1920.* Norman: University of Oklahoma Press, 1985.

Priest, B. Loring. *Uncle Sam's Stepchildren: The Reformation of the United States Indian Policy, 1865-1887.* New Brunswick, N.J.: Rutgers University Press, 1942.

Prucha, Francis Paul. *American Indian Policy in Crisis: Reformers and the Indian, 1865-1900*. Norman: University of Oklahoma Press, 1976.

______. *The Churches and the Indian Schools, 1888-1912*. Lincoln: University of Nebraska Press, 1979.

______. *Documents of United States Indian Policy, Second Edition, Expanded.* Lincoln: University of Nebraska Press, 1975, 1990.

Robertson, Lindsay G. *Conquest by Law: How the Discovery of America Dispossessed Indigenous Peoples of Their Lands*. New York: Cambridge University Press, 2005.

Schmeckebier, Laurence. *The Office of Indian Affairs: Its History, Activities and Organization*. Baltimore: Johns Hopkins University Press, 1927.

Utley, Robert M. *The Indian Frontier, 1846-1890*. Rev. ed. Albuquerque: University of New Mexico Press, 1984.

Waldman, Carl. *Atlas of the North American Indian*. New York: Facts On File Publications, 1985.

______. *Biographical Dictionary of American Indian History to 1900*. Rev. ed. New York: Checkmark Books/Facts On File, 2001.

White, Phillip M. *American Indian Chronology: Chronologies of the American Mosaic*. Westport, Conn: Greenwood Press, 2006.

Index